I0793338

IMAGES
of America

St. Francisville and West Feliciana Parish

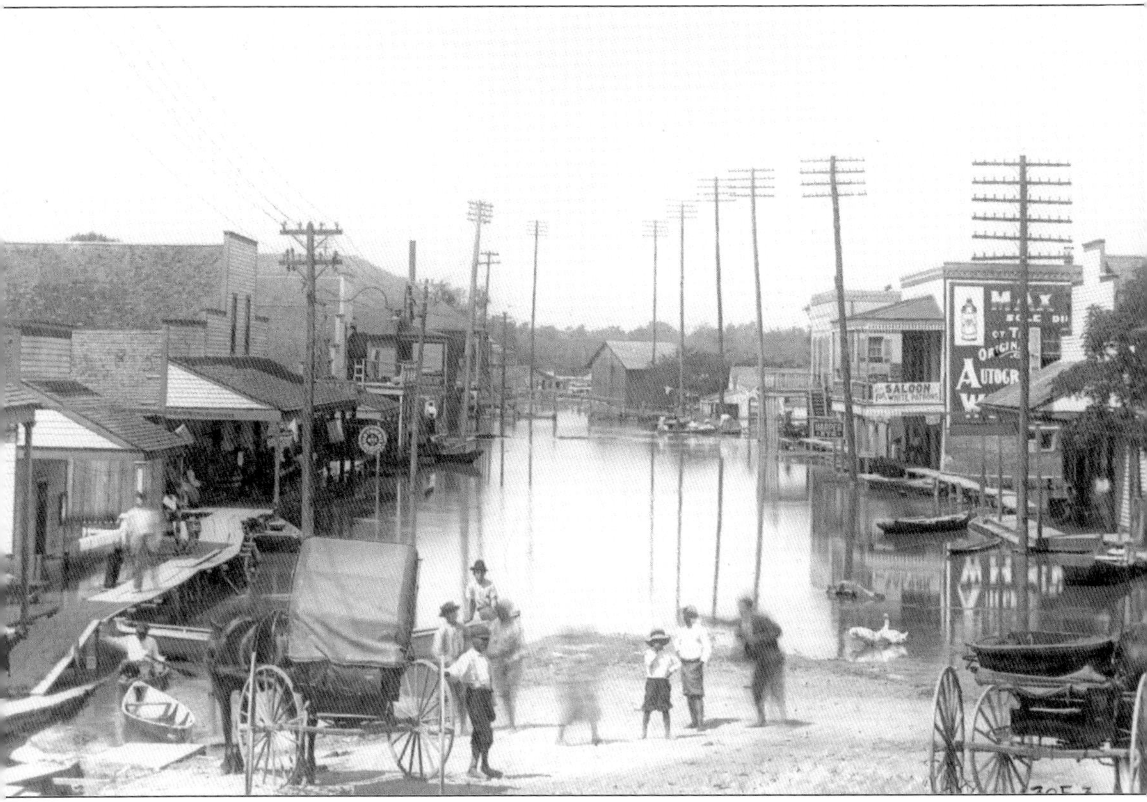

Founded in the closing years of the 18th century, right on the banks of the Mississippi River below St. Francisville, the port city of Bayou Sara was often inundated by floodwaters rushing through crevasses or breaks in the inadequate levee system. The water filled streets and flooded businesses and residences. (Courtesy of West Feliciana Historical Society.)

On the Cover: Charles Weydert, shown with his daughters Augusta (left) and Gretchen, owned hardware stores and blacksmith shops in Bayou Sara. He later moved his businesses up the hill, safe from Mississippi River floods. His 1896 hardware store in St. Francisville is now the headquarters and museum of the West Feliciana Historical Society. (Courtesy of Weydert family.)

IMAGES
of America

St. Francisville and West Feliciana Parish

Anne Butler and Norman C. Ferachi

ARCADIA
PUBLISHING

ISBN 978-1-4671-1302-1

Published by Arcadia Publishing
Charleston, South Carolina

Printed in the United States of America

Library of Congress Control Number: 2014940303

For all general information, please contact Arcadia Publishing:
Telephone 843-853-2070
Fax 843-853-0044
E-mail sales@arcadiapublishing.com
For customer service and orders:
Toll-Free 1-888-313-2665

Visit us on the Internet at www.arcadiapublishing.com

To all those historians and preservationists whose efforts and accomplishments give us our unique sense of place and our hope that preservation really can move into the future hand in hand with progress.

Contents

Acknowledgments

What a debt we owe to those who have come before, and to those who continue the task of preserving and appreciating our history as a basis for a hopeful future: Libby Dart, longtime head of the West Feliciana Historical Society, and her stalwart lieutenants, Nancy Vinci and Ann Bennett; Lucille Leake, who came up with the inspired idea of a spring pilgrimage through historic homes, and Ed Daniel, whose Rural Homestead provides a balance by demonstrating the daily skills of simpler country folk; Hannah Rosenthal Wood, whose never-ending efforts maintained the lovely little Hebrew Rest cemetery; Billie Magee, whose dreams of a cultural center saved the first public school building, and Nancy Vinci, who has taken up that torch and run with it; longtime St. Francisville mayor Billy D'Aquilla and the preservation committees who, with few exceptions, have protected significant structures throughout town; Violet Pate, dedicated historian of our oldest black Baptist church; photographers and artists who have found inspiration in our landscapes and architecture, like Anne Plettinger and genealogist Ann Weller; owners of historic structures who froze in winter, baked in summer, put pots beneath the leaks, dodged falling plaster, and held on over all those years of tight money, failed crops, wars, and other pestilences; the Underwoods and Trimbles, rescuers of great old gardens; and all the others with the awareness and great good sense to appreciate what a fragile treasure we have.

It is gratifying to see second-, third-, even fourth-generation descendants of those early preservationists continuing their efforts and enjoying the fruits of their struggles. Yes, St. Francisville and West Feliciana Parish have an enduring sense of place. We thank the community members who shared their photographs and family stories. We are especially grateful to museum director Helen Williams and the West Feliciana Historical Society board of directors for recognizing the importance of preserving their collections, now being digitally archived. Many of the images in this book appear courtesy of the West Feliciana Historical Society (WFHS). We have done our best in regards to accuracy; please remember, this volume is not intended to be all-inclusive.

INTRODUCTION

The earliest inhabitants of West Feliciana were Native Americans of the Houma and Tunica tribes, who had a thriving trade with European explorers traversing the Mississippi River. The first formal settlement, Sainte Reyne aux Tonicas, was a short-lived, small fort established in 1729 by the French. For the remainder of the 18th century, the area was dominated by England and then Spain. Both governments encouraged settlement by offering large land grants, and the earliest settlers were predominantly Anglo planters with the means to establish immense plantations growing indigo, cotton, and sugarcane on the rich, well-watered Feliciana soils.

Laid out in 1807 high upon a narrow loessial finger ridge overlooking the Mississippi River, St. Francisville served as the cultural and commercial center for the surrounding plantation country, as well as the seat of parish government after 1824. The little town actually began as a cemetery when Capuchin monks from across the river ferried their dead to St. Francisville's high bluffs for burial, safe from floodwaters. The monks gave the settlement the name of their patron saint.

Below the hill, on flatlands along the river, the town of Bayou Sara developed in the late 1790s, and it would become the most important antebellum port on the Mississippi River between New Orleans and Natchez. A mile of dockside warehouses stored cotton collected from outlying plantations by one of the country's earliest standard-gauge railroads for shipment on riverboats to markets around the world; there were also extensive commercial and residential districts. Bayou Sara was damaged by shelling during the Civil War, devastated by raging fires that wiped out 50 or more structures at a time, and inundated by floodwaters over and over until widespread floods in 1912 and in the 1920s completely obliterated it.

Atop the bluff, St. Francisville thrived. Its early roads were muddy quagmires traversed by herds of cattle and horse-drawn wagons bound for the river port at Bayou Sara under the hill. Yet, town developer John H. Johnson optimistically gave the streets names like Prospect and Prosperity, and progress was swift. By 1809, a hotel had been erected. A Masonic lodge was chartered in 1817. In 1819, the state's second library was begun, and an open-air brick market was built with arches through which produce wagons could be driven. By 1828, the state's first Episcopal congregation outside New Orleans had joined in worship. The local newspaper sent its editor to cover the War of 1812 as one of the earliest war correspondents.

St. Francisville is described, with little exaggeration, as a town two miles long and two yards wide, for the land falls off steeply into deep hollows on either side of the inhabited ridge. The two main streets are Ferdinand and Royal, tributes to the Spanish monarch who continued to claim Louisiana's east side of the Mississippi River as part of Spanish West Florida even after the Louisiana Purchase of 1803. The strong-willed Anglo-Saxon settlers of the area chafed under inept Spanish rule and twice revolted.

The 1804 Kemper Brothers Rebellion was more colorful than successful, its plotters turned over to authorities but subsequently rescued. The plotters repaid one erstwhile captor by cutting off his ears and displaying them, pickled in wine, in the family tavern, if stories can be believed. A second rebellion, in 1810, was carefully organized and well planned. The successful coup resulted in the capture of the Spanish fort in Baton Rouge and the establishment of the Republic of West Florida. Its capital was established in St. Francisville, its constitution was well conceived, and its proud blue flag was centered by a single white star. The republic's glory days numbered only 74 before the territory joined the rest of Louisiana to become a state in 1812.

That flag still flies in St. Francisville today, where moss-draped live oaks overhang roadways and many of the early buildings have been restored in a downtown district that is listed in its entirety in the National Register of Historic Places. The West Feliciana Historical Society for decades has instilled an appreciation for history and spearheaded preservation efforts, and a separate foundation works to restore the beautiful brick Julius Freyhan school building and adjacent Temple Sinai as community cultural centers in tribute to the early Jewish immigrants whose mercantile and financial acumen proved vital in this agrarian society's postwar economic recovery.

This is also a Main Street community participating in the National Trust program designed to encourage and support the preservation of significant commercial centers that were once the hearts and souls of early communities and the repositories of residents' collective memories. St. Francisville's downtown remains the viable center of life today, its mixture of commercial and residential structures giving it a 24-hour presence, with shops and art galleries, restaurants, town and parish government offices, a museum and tourist information center, bed-and-breakfasts, and beautiful old churches. These establishments stand side by side with beloved historic townhouses and little Victorian cottages dripping with gingerbread trim, surrounded by well-tended gardens full of blossoming azaleas and camellias. While other strictly commercial downtown districts fold up the sidewalks once the businesses close for the day, here, as dusk falls, downtown is alive with dog-walkers and joggers and strollers conversing with neighbors across picket fences.

No wonder St. Francisville has become a year-round tourist destination. In the surrounding countryside, there are a number of antebellum plantation homes and 19th-century gardens open for tours. The Tunica Hills offer unmatched recreational opportunities, including hiking, bicycling, hunting, and nature studies. The Louisiana Office of State Parks has exciting plans for treetop interpretive centers and river bluff outlooks, maximizing environmentally safe enjoyment of this incredible area. The rugged terrain of the Tunica Hills is unique in the state, with steep ravines left from the Ice Age harboring flora and fauna found nowhere else in Louisiana. Also unique is the cyclical flooding along this, the only un-leveed stretch of the lower Mississippi River, where Cat Island National Wildlife Refuge preserves the country's largest bald cypress tree and harbors large seasonal populations of migratory waterfowl. Both migratory and resident birdlife remain as plentiful as in the 1820s, when the artist John James Audubon was spellbound by the richness of the natural bounties; he painted dozens of his famous bird studies while tutoring the daughter of Oakley Plantation, one of several significant properties in the parish now preserved as state historic sites.

In the 1970s, the West Feliciana Historical Society began the Audubon Pilgrimage, a spring tour of historic homes and gardens with docents in authentic, award-winning 1820s costumes. This proved not only a means of sharing important treasures with visitors while raising funds for preservation projects, but also a way of instilling pride and an enduring sense of community in local residents. Other special events throughout the year include festivals paying tribute to birds and glorious gardens, prison rodeos and craft shows, gatherings of regional artists and writers, and even a Civil War reenactment celebrating the universality of Masonic brotherhood and a moment of civility in the midst of a bloody conflict.

So, yes, Virginia, there is life in Louisiana outside of New Orleans and Cajun Country. Here in English Plantation Country, and in St. Francisville, where the population is still just under 2,000, residents revel in their uniqueness and welcome visitors to share an appreciation of it.

One

Early History

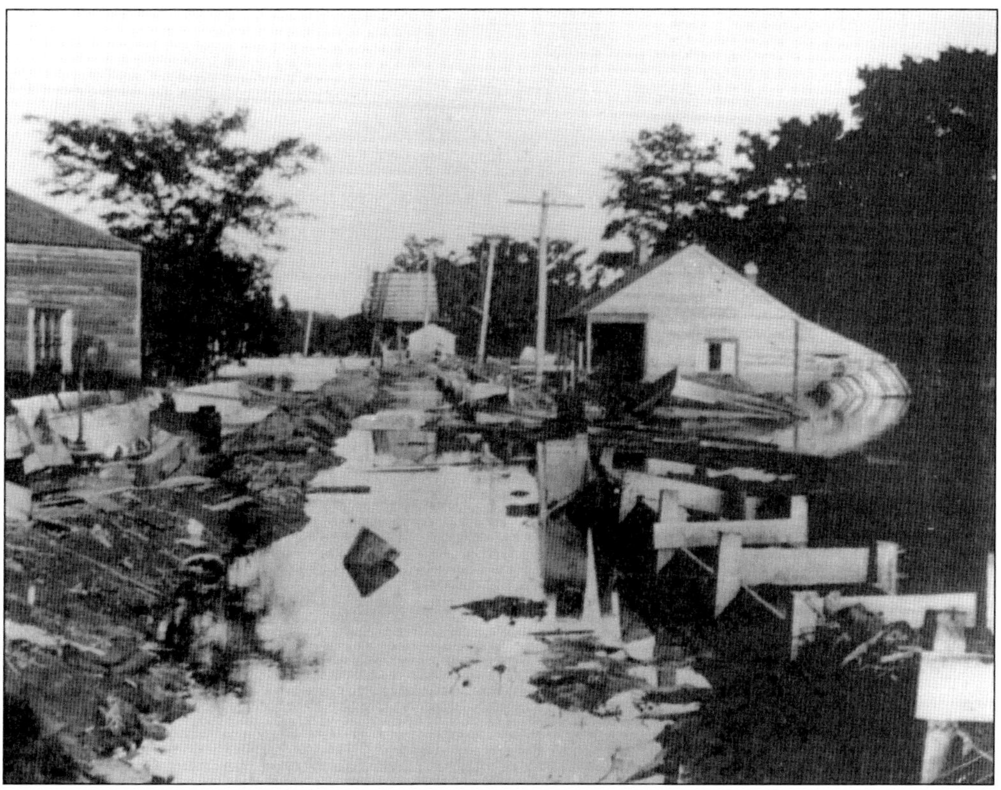

Testament to the power of the Mississippi River's strong currents, the devastation caused by the rampaging floodwaters is evident on the streets of Bayou Sara. The port city's residents and business owners proved just as powerful and resilient, cleaning up and starting over nearly every spring until the 1920s. (WFHS.)

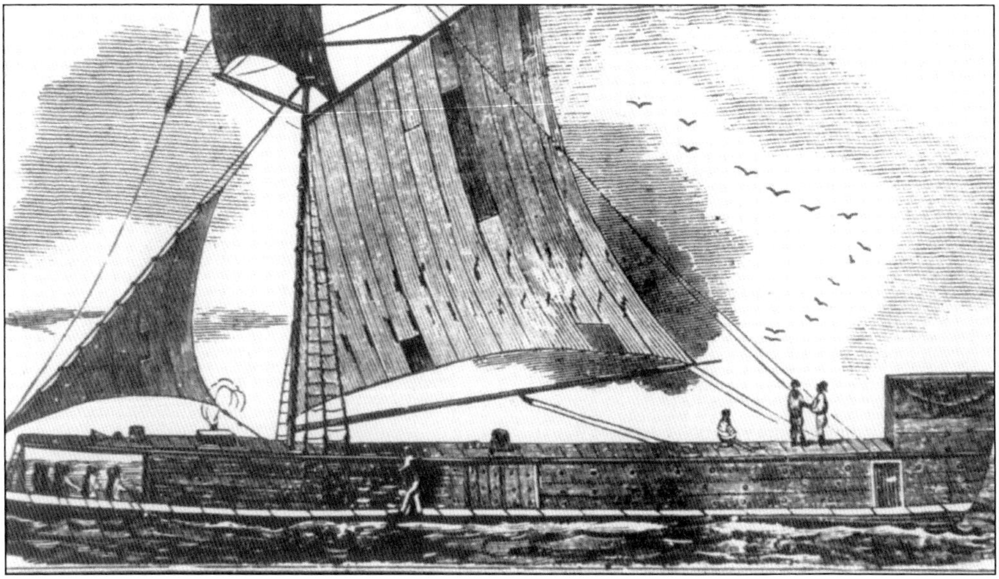

Flatboats and keelboats loaded with produce and goods for market pulled into the quiet waters of Bayou Sara for safe anchorage on trips downriver. Where the bayou emptied into the Mississippi River, in the late 1790s, a settlement sprang up to meet the needs of these boatmen, and it would grow into the most important port on the river between New Orleans and Natchez in the 19th century. (WFHS.)

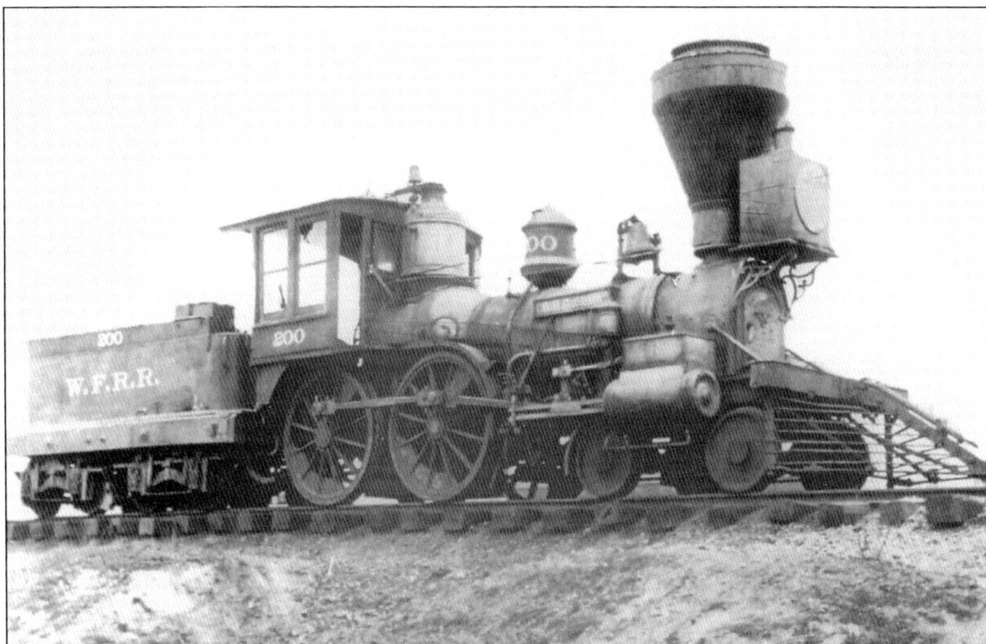

One of the country's earliest standard-gauge railroad lines transported cotton from plantations in West Feliciana and adjoining counties of Mississippi to the river packets docked at Bayou Sara for shipment to factors in New Orleans. Begun in the 1830s, the line cost $25,000 a mile, and it took years to construct 27 miles of track, with parallel wooden rails capped with thin strips of iron. (WFHS.)

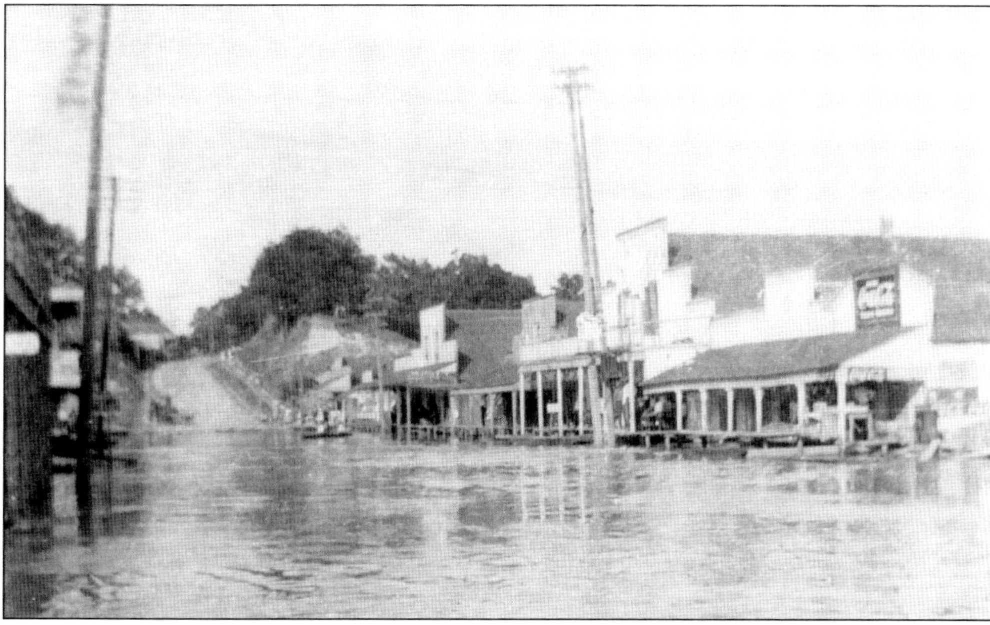

When the Mississippi River ran high in spring as northern snows melted, floodwaters inundated low-lying Bayou Sara. In some years, the waters reached all the way to the hill going up into St. Francisville, which sat high on a bluff. The above photograph shows water in the roadway. Below, muck and debris are left after the water receded from the same street. The great Mississippi flood of 1927, which finally sounded Bayou Sara's death knell, was one of the nation's greatest natural disasters, flooding out nearly a million people. At the height of the flood, the river carried more than three million cubic feet of water every second, and its strong current easily ripped apart buildings and wiped out entire towns in its path. (Both, WFHS.)

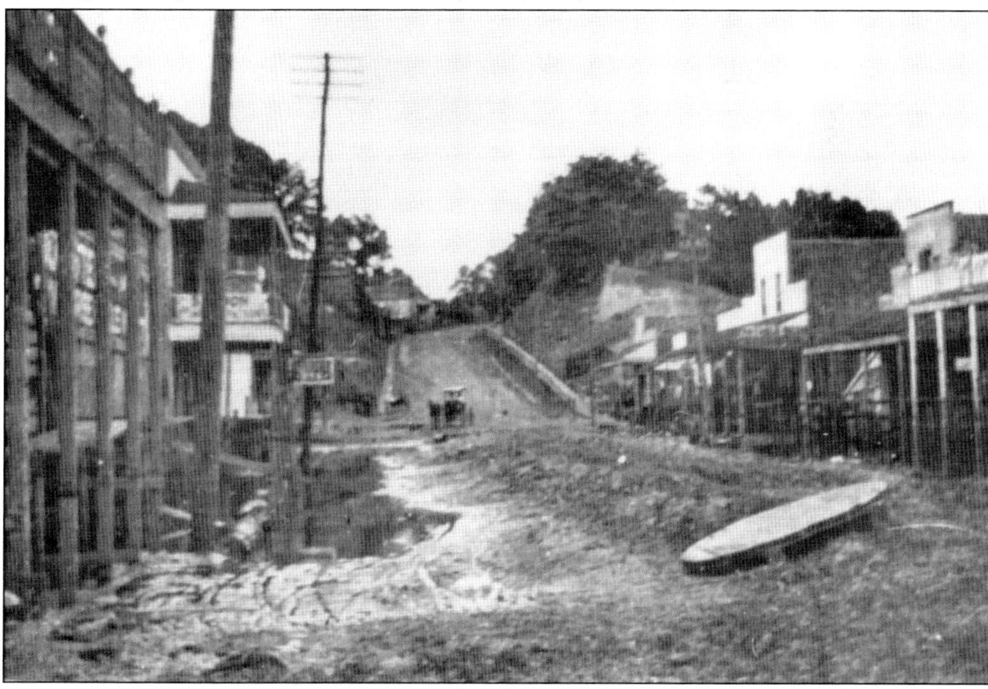

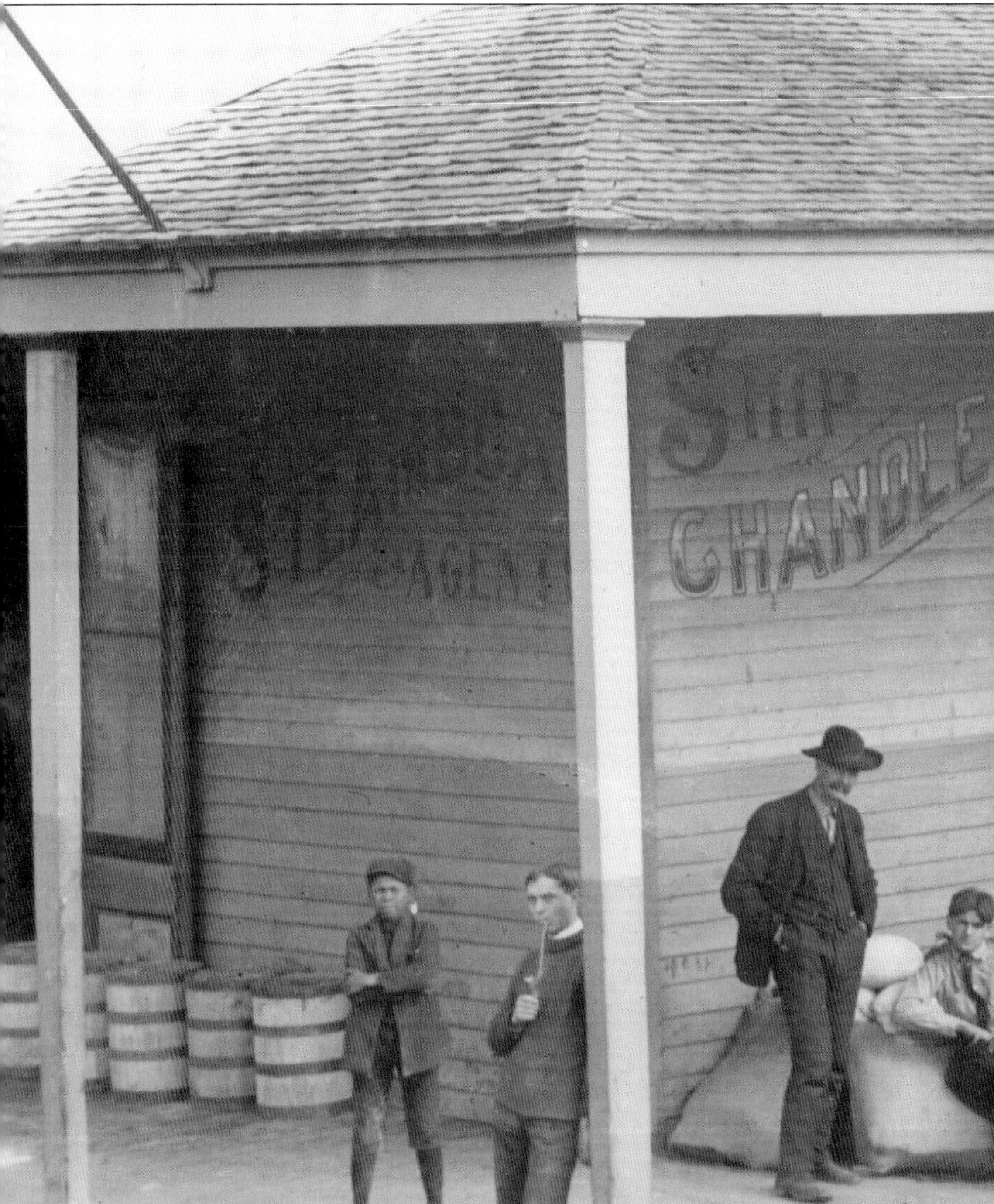

John Francis Irvine's Bayou Sara enterprises included a steam ferry and tugboat, icehouse, cotton compress, sawmill, hotel, coal company, liquor and tobacco distributorship, and a general mercantile. Born in 1828 in Jessamine County, Kentucky, John F. Irvine Sr. established himself in Bayou Sara before the Civil War, when the 1860 census recorded a population of 540 (360 whites, 152 slaves, and 28 free persons of color). From 1860 through the rest of his life, he dominated the

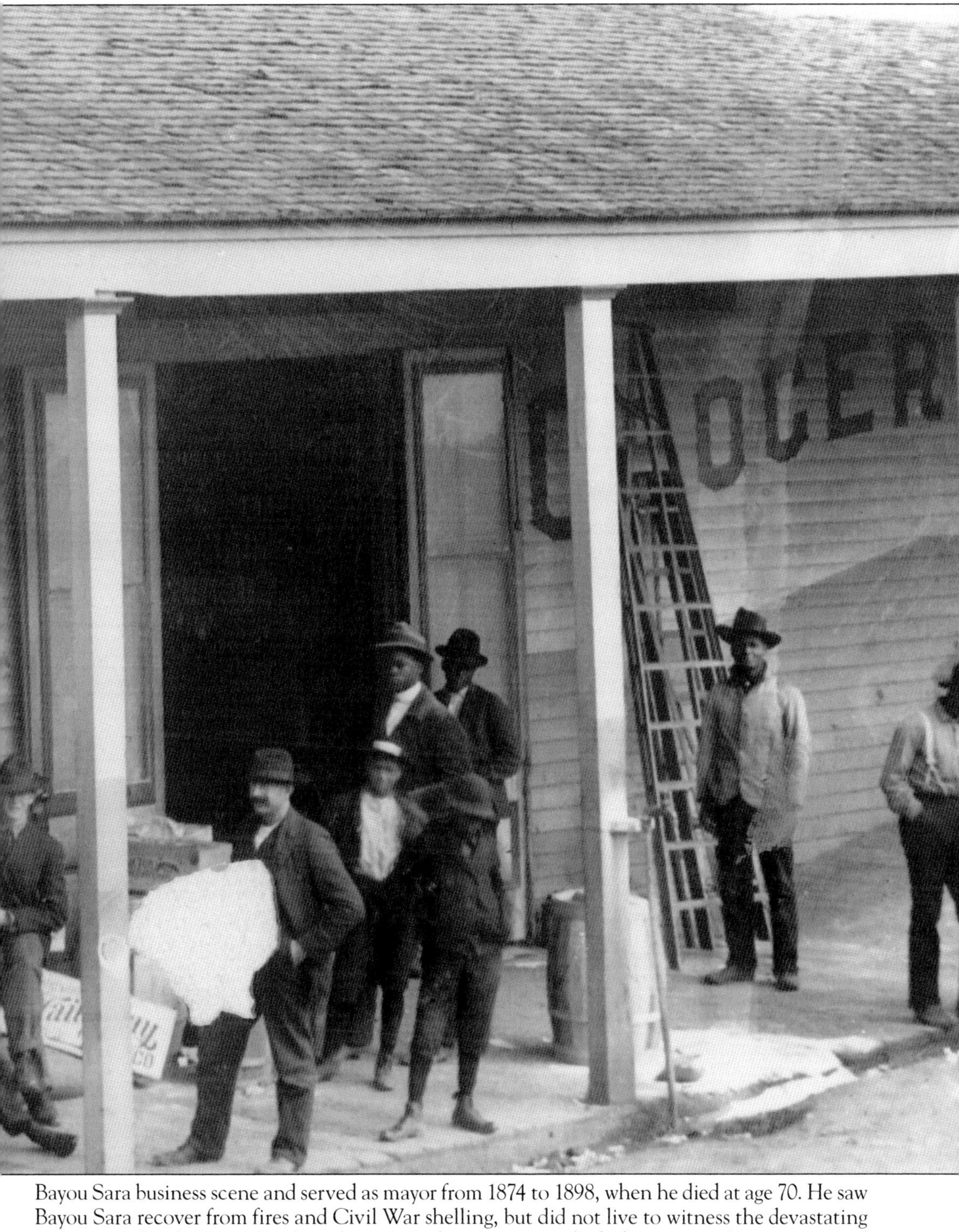

Bayou Sara business scene and served as mayor from 1874 to 1898, when he died at age 70. He saw Bayou Sara recover from fires and Civil War shelling, but did not live to witness the devastating early-1900s floods. By 1927, when the town's charter was revoked, there was only one registered voter in Bayou Sara. (WFHS.)

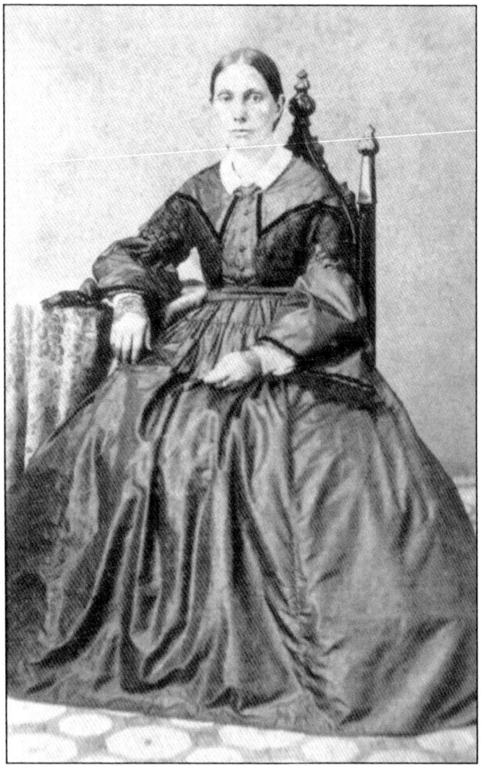

Theresa Ann Burton, born in 1834, was the first wife of John F. Irvine Sr.; her father, W.F. Burton, had a bustling hotel in Bayou Sara, and her husband would have his own new hotel on the riverfront called Irvine House. They were the parents of seven children, including a son born in 1863 and named for his father. (WFHS.)

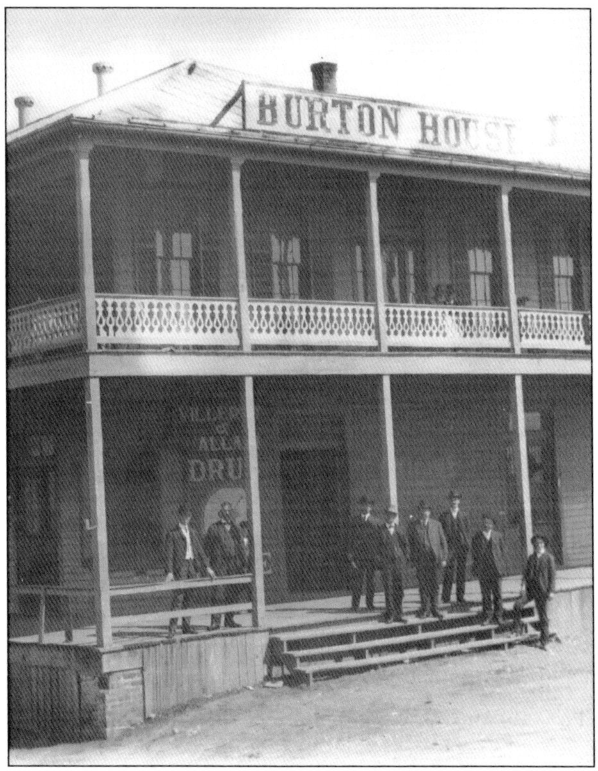

Drifters and drummers, steamboat passengers, and visitors of every stripe found Bayou Sara's hotels, including the double-galleried Burton House, accommodating. The busy cotton port had a thriving commercial center and residential areas, with boardinghouses, drugstores and apothecaries, sawmills and lumberyards, livestock traders, butchers, fish markets, fairgrounds, baseball fields, liveries and stables, grocers, dry-goods emporiums, post and express offices, clothiers, icehouses, banks, and other businesses. (WFHS.)

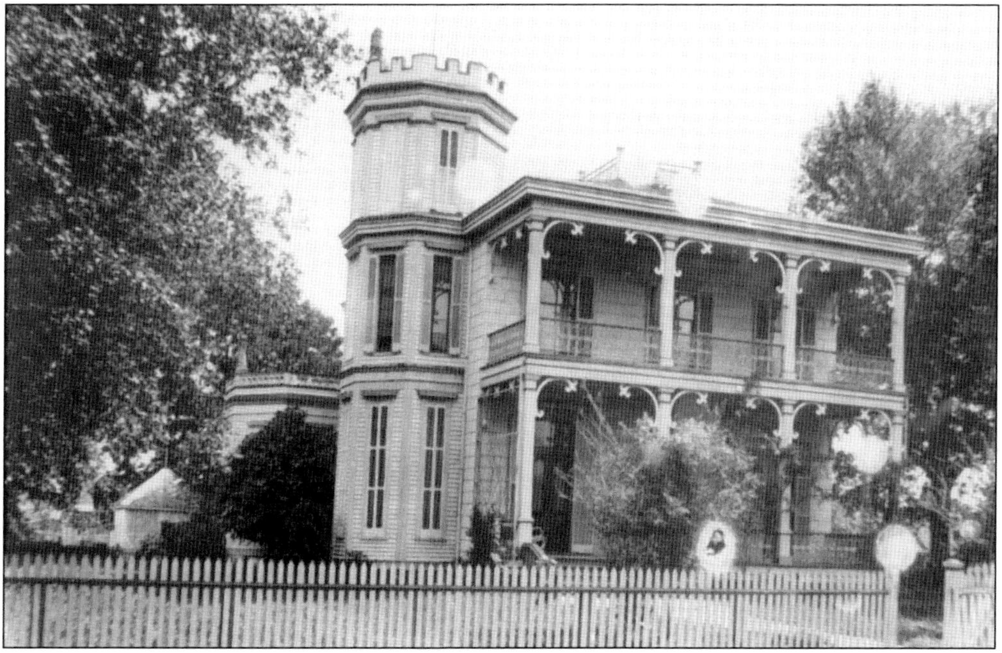

Bayou Sara mayor John F. Irvine Sr. and his second wife, Emma Henshaw, had two daughters and lived in this crenellated and turreted frame house. The home was located just off Bayou Sara's Principal Street and was enclosed by a picket fence. With its bay windows and fanciful trim, this was undoubtedly the finest house in town. (WFHS.)

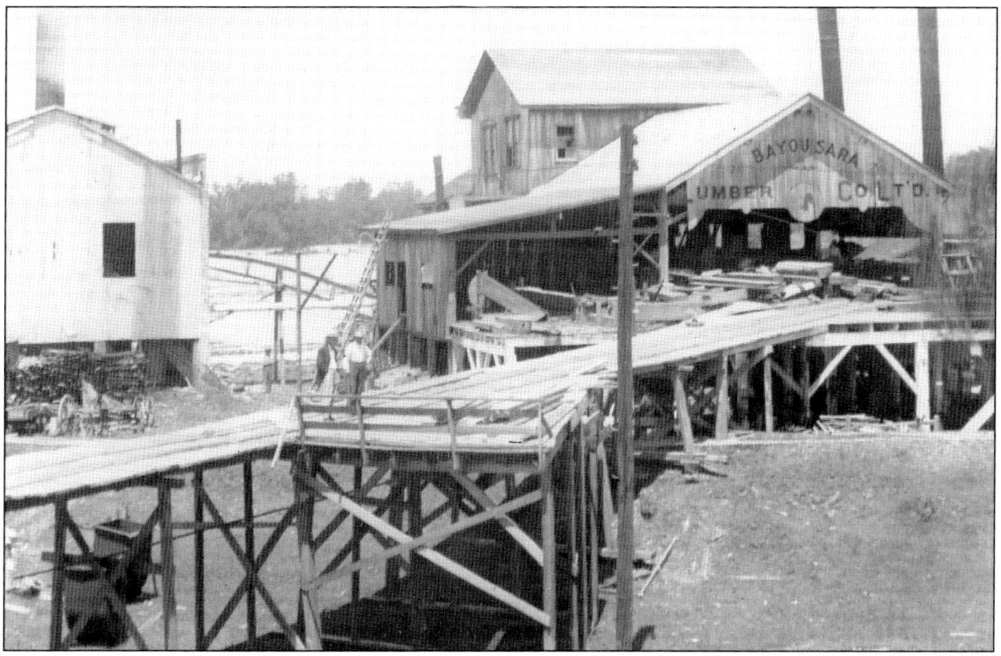

Lumber was in great demand as the port city of Bayou Sara expanded in the 19th century. John F. Irvine Jr. took over his late father's business empire, and by 1912, his sawmill was turning out 75,000 feet of lumber daily. That year saw a devastating flood from which the Irvine empire never recovered. (WFHS.)

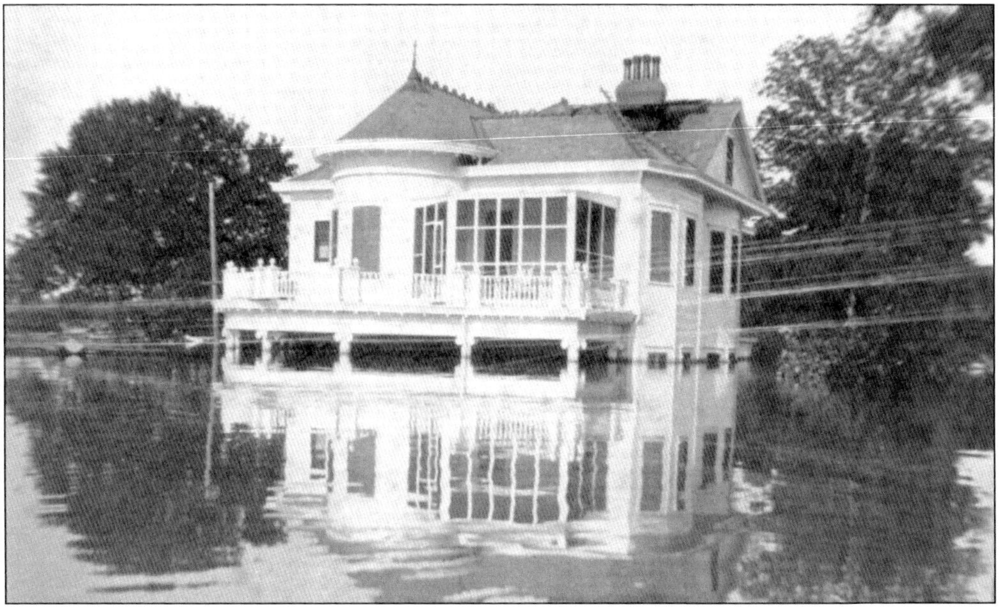

Irvinemoor was the late Victorian home of John F. Irvine Jr., called Cap'n Johnny, who succeeded his father as a successful businessman and politician. He married his stepmother's niece, Emma Raum Sherrard. Built in 1904 in Bayou Sara, the house was destroyed by the flood of 1912, which put a foot of water into the second story, just as his stepdaughter was about to be married in the home. (WFHS.)

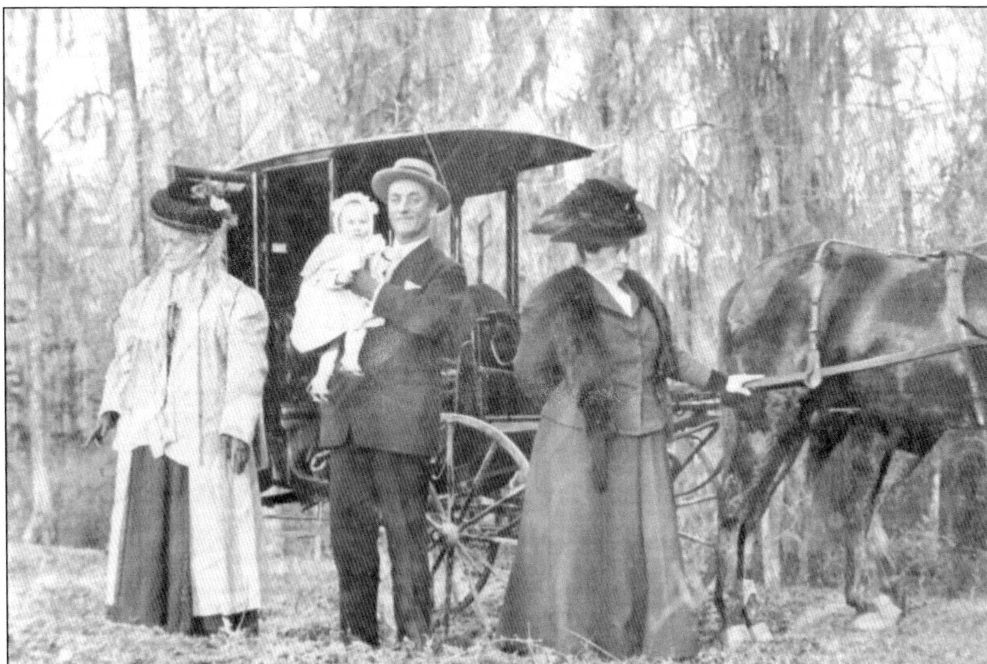

John F. Irvine Jr. (center) has disembarked from his two-horse carriage and is shown holding his infant daughter. Beside him are his wife, Emma Raum Irvine, wearing a dark riding outfit, and an unidentified older woman. This photograph was taken in 1910 in Bayou Sara. (WFHS.)

Jessamine Irvine Bentley made a lovely dark-haired bride when she wed a young Episcopal clergyman. Her modest, high-necked wedding gown featured lace inserts and elaborate sleeve treatments. The youngest daughter of John Francis Irvine Sr., she was named for the county in Kentucky where her father was born. On June 6, 1902, she died along with the twin sons she was delivering. (WFHS.)

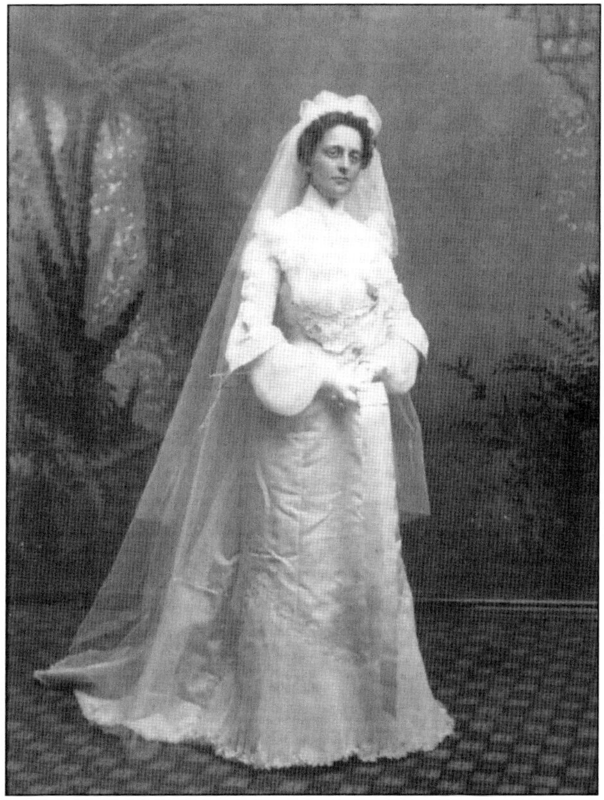

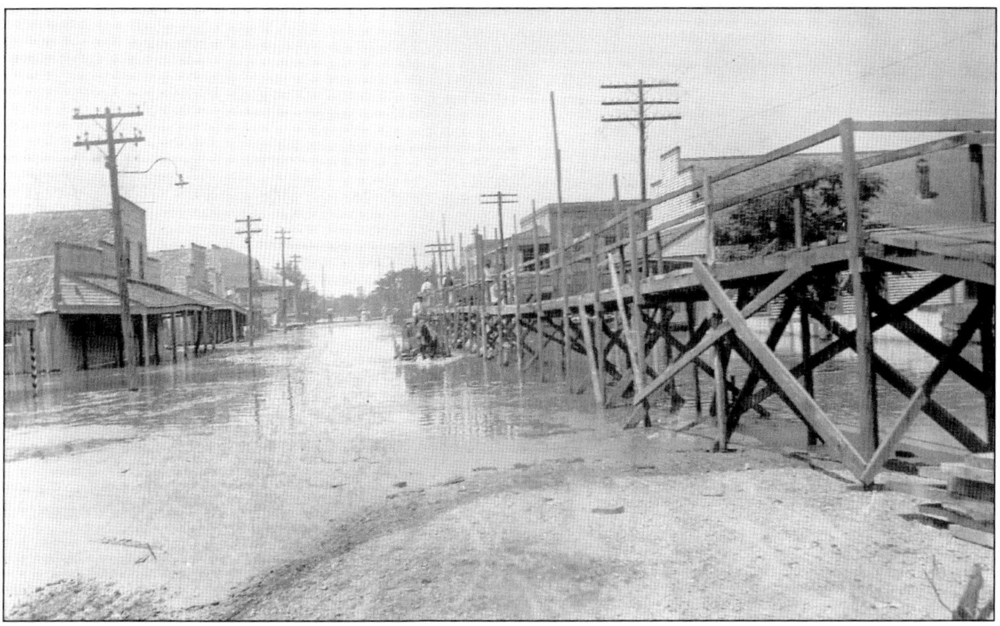

Horses and wagons had to plow through the flooded streets of Bayou Sara, but pedestrians could keep their feet dry and continue to patronize the stores via raised wooden walkways. In 1885, Mayor John F. Irvine Sr. implemented improvements like streetlights and raised wooden sidewalks, developments no doubt greatly appreciated by Bayou Sara residents. (WFHS.)

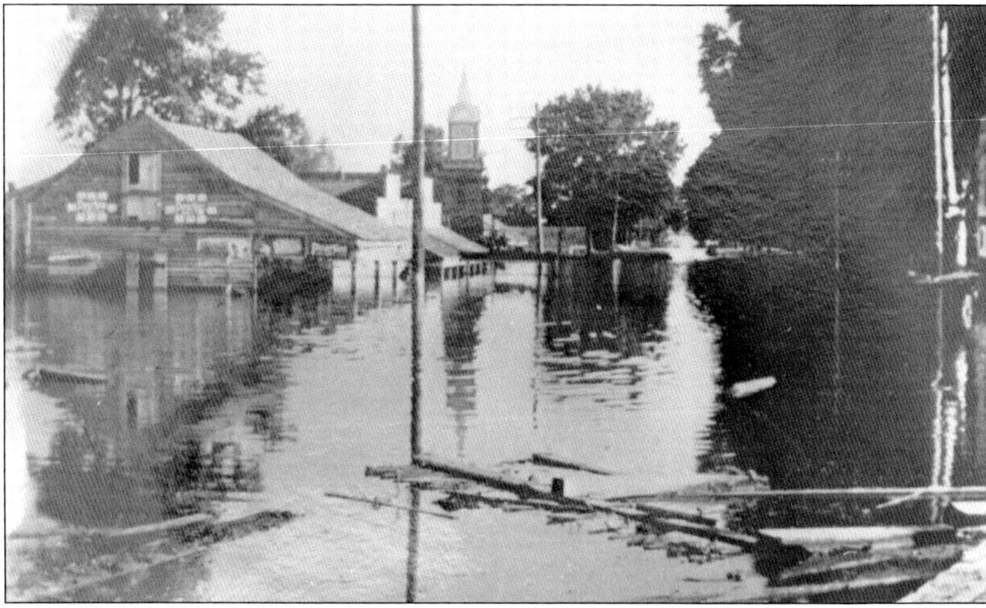

After a century of being inundated periodically by floodwaters from the Mississippi River, many Bayou Sara residents and businesses relocated to St. Francisville, located high atop a bluff. A few structures were hauled intact up the hill on rolling logs pulled by straining teams of oxen, and others were dismantled and rebuilt on high ground. (WFHS.)

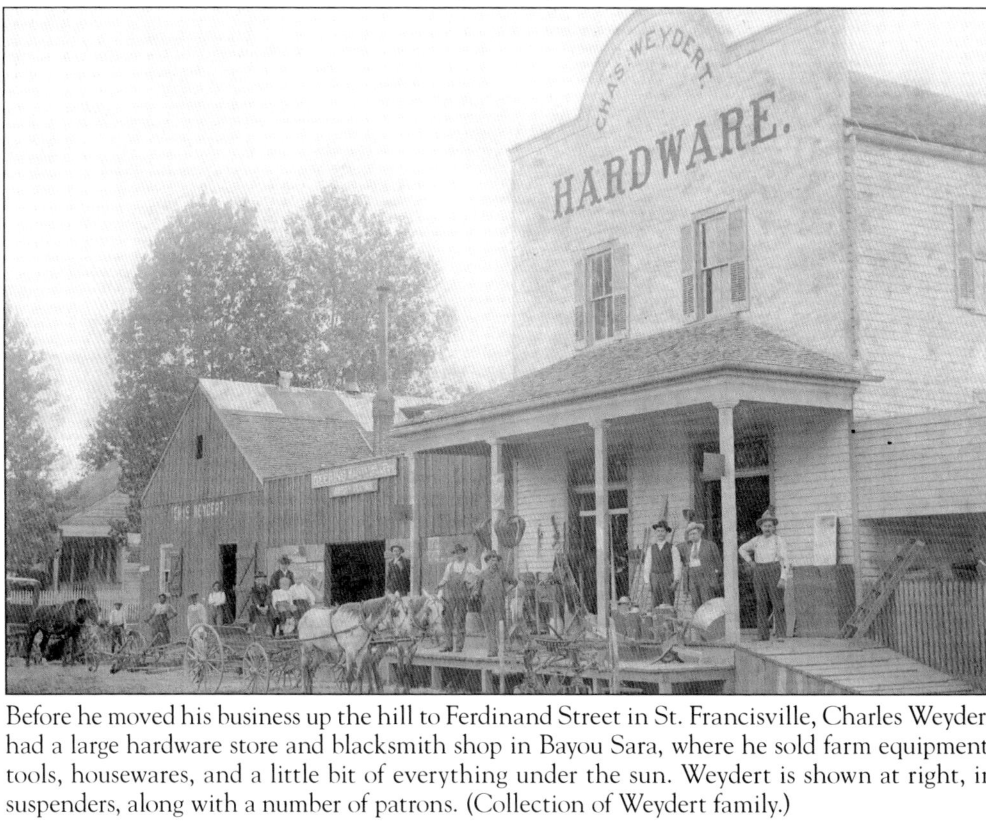

Before he moved his business up the hill to Ferdinand Street in St. Francisville, Charles Weydert had a large hardware store and blacksmith shop in Bayou Sara, where he sold farm equipment, tools, housewares, and a little bit of everything under the sun. Weydert is shown at right, in suspenders, along with a number of patrons. (Collection of Weydert family.)

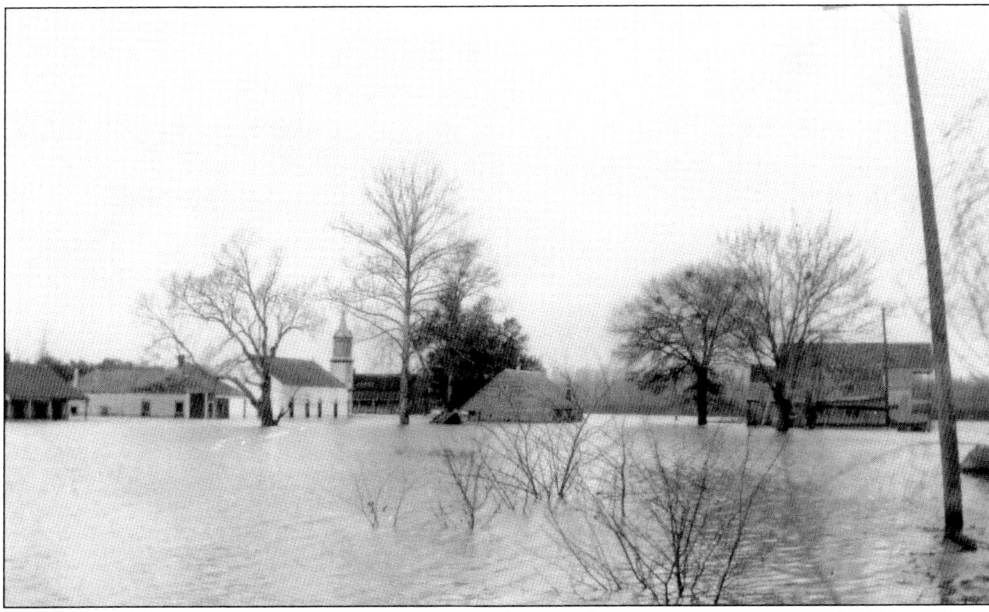

Bayou Sara had its share of houses of worship. The Jewish congregation met in the Meyer Hotel and Julius Freyhan's Opera House until Temple Sinai was erected in St. Francisville in 1902. In 1844, a Methodist church (shown here) was built on the main street, its upper galleries providing refuge during floods. In 1899, the Methodists built a beautiful wooden church on Royal Street in St. Francisville, utilizing the original bell. (WFHS.)

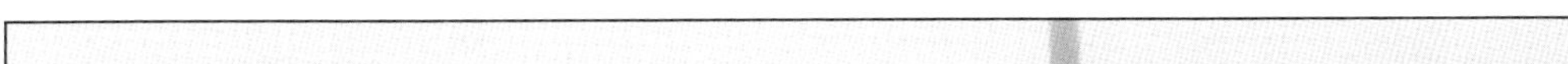

A flat-bottom skiff is loaded with supplies, perhaps being salvaged from a Bayou Sara store that has taken on water during flooding. Or, perhaps these are necessities being transported to flood victims unable to get to markets. The jewelry store in the background is typical of the stepped-parapet frame structures with overhanging shed-roof porches found throughout Bayou Sara. (Collection of Myrtle A. Brasseaux.)

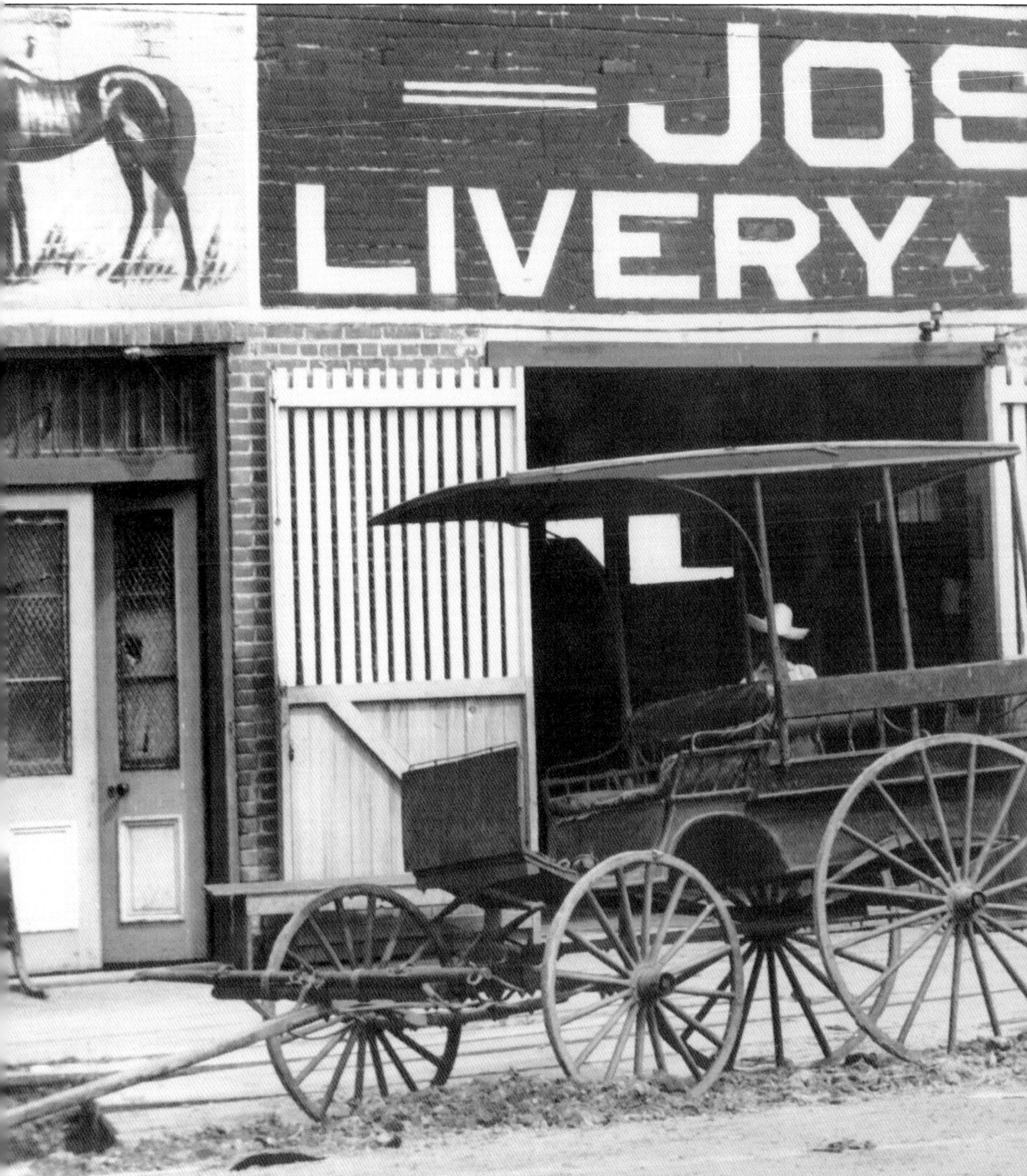

The livery business and horse and mule market of Joseph Stern, who came to this country in 1867 at age 19, did a booming trade in the days before automobiles. Many businesses were owned by Jewish immigrants, who had arrived in the middle of the 19th century, escaping religious persecution in the old country and lending much-needed merchandising and business skills to agrarian societies along the Mississippi River corridor. They often arrived penniless and began

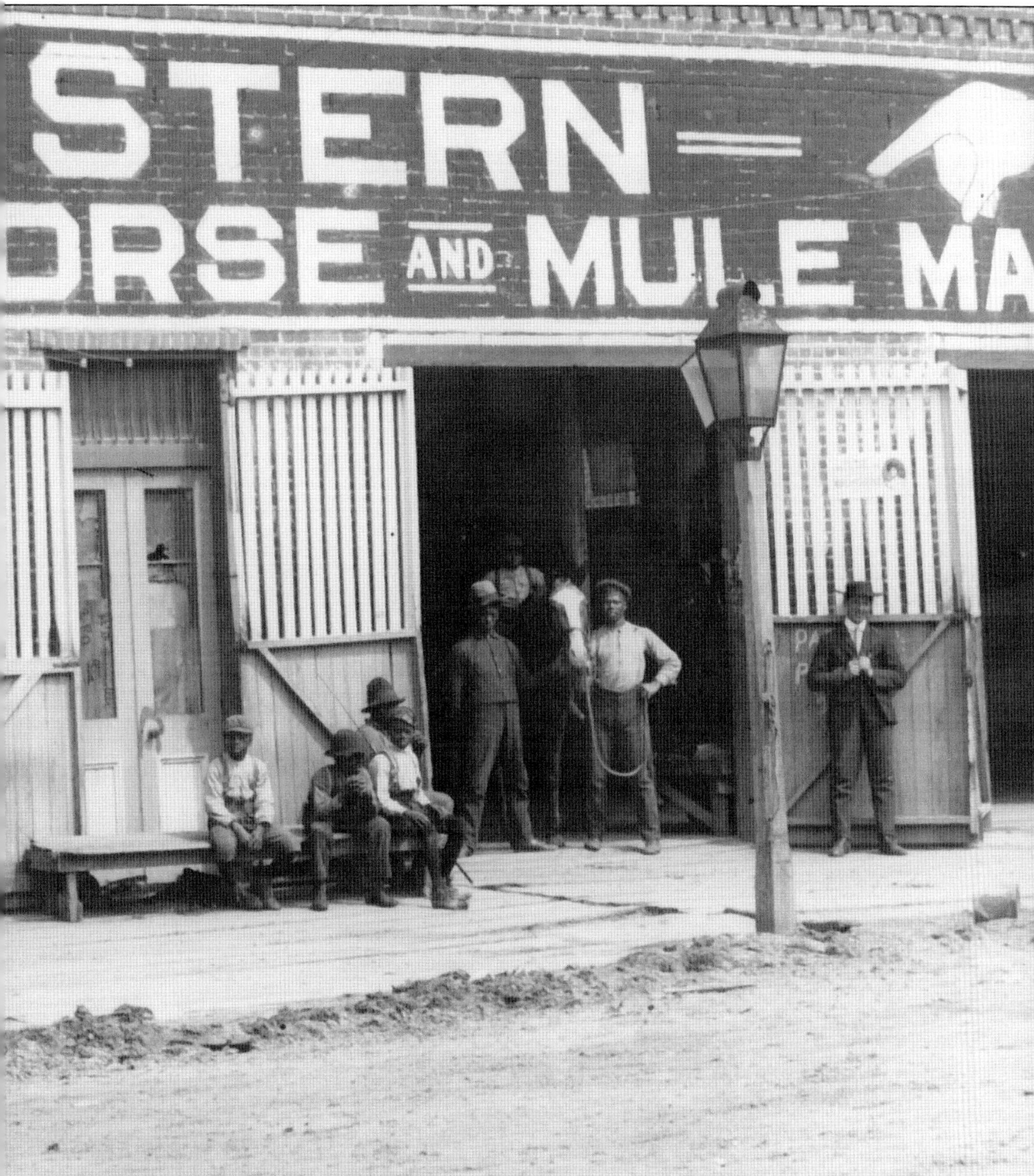

as peddlers with packs on their backs, selling small housewares to isolated housewives. As they prospered, they purchased horses and wagons, then clerked in stores until they could afford to start their own businesses. After the Civil War, when banks failed and cotton factorages went broke, Jewish merchants got into the cotton market, and as they prospered, they provided credit to help struggling farmers recover. (WFHS.)

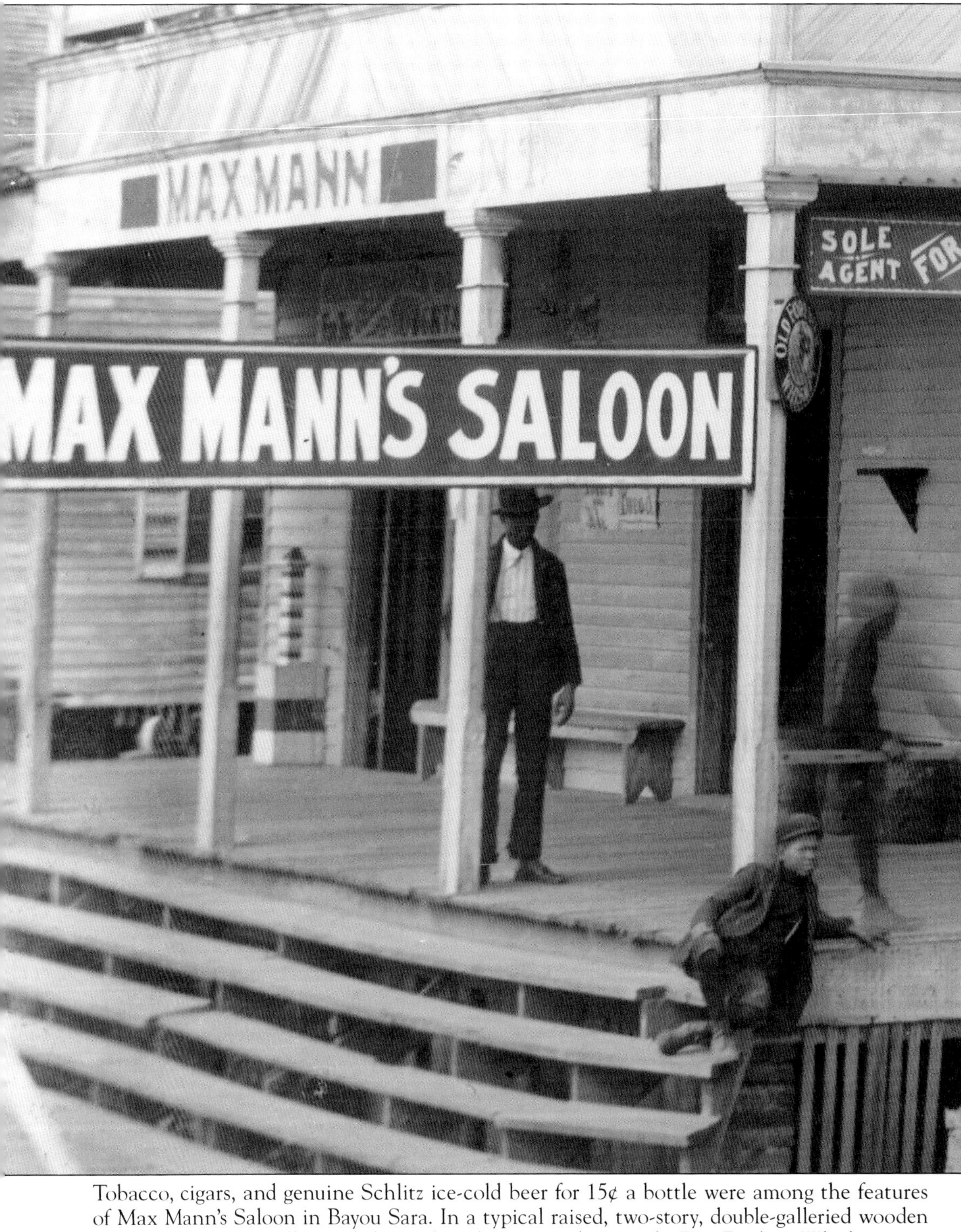

Tobacco, cigars, and genuine Schlitz ice-cold beer for 15¢ a bottle were among the features of Max Mann's Saloon in Bayou Sara. In a typical raised, two-story, double-galleried wooden building with fancy gallery rail above, the saloon was sole agent for Five Feathers Whiskey, a jug of which is held by the gentleman at right, standing near the underground cistern. Bayou Sara had lots of saloons, especially in the early years, when the rowdy flatboat men overnighted in

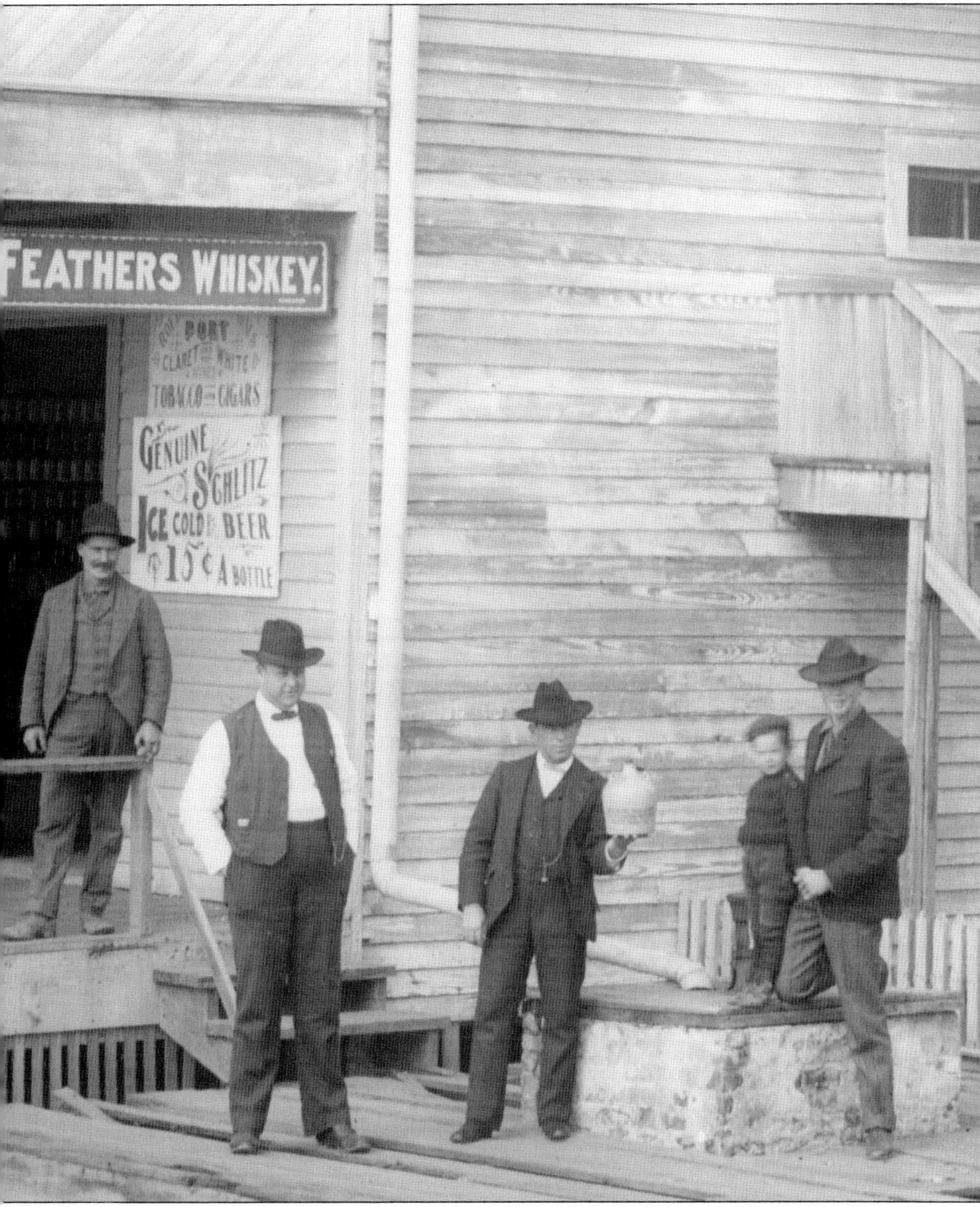

the calm waters of the bayou. After the disastrous flood of 1893, Max Mann moved his saloon to Ferdinand Street in Upper St. Francisville and built a nice house for himself on Royal Street. It is thought that the double-galleried structure across from the current post office was his saloon, moved from Bayou Sara. (WFHS.)

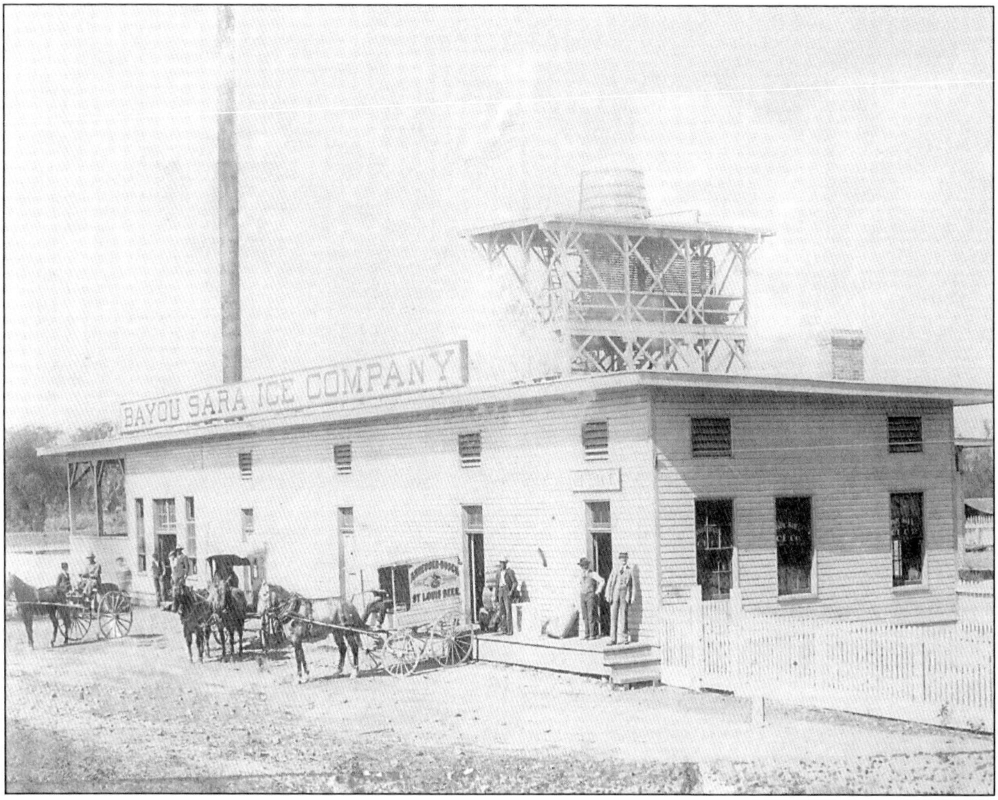

The enormous Bayou Sara Ice Company, with its all-important rooftop cooling system, did a bustling business in the days when reliable electrical refrigeration systems were rare or nonexistent. Note the one-horse, four-wheel Anheuser-Busch/St. Louis Beer delivery wagon. One of Mayor John F. Irvine Sr.'s major business ventures was this icehouse. Ice was a highly valued commodity in this hot climate, and even isolated plantations devised methods of keeping perishables cool, utilizing cool springwaters, dairy rooms, sawdust pits, and other innovations. Town residents, of course, could easily patronize Irvine's Ice Company. After Bayou Sara was abandoned to the floodwaters and the Irvine business empire was essentially wiped out by the late 1920s, there continued to be an icehouse in St. Francisville on Commerce Street into the mid-1950s, and old-timers recall little Eudora Ard stopping there to load her red wagon with blocks of ice to take home. (WFHS.)

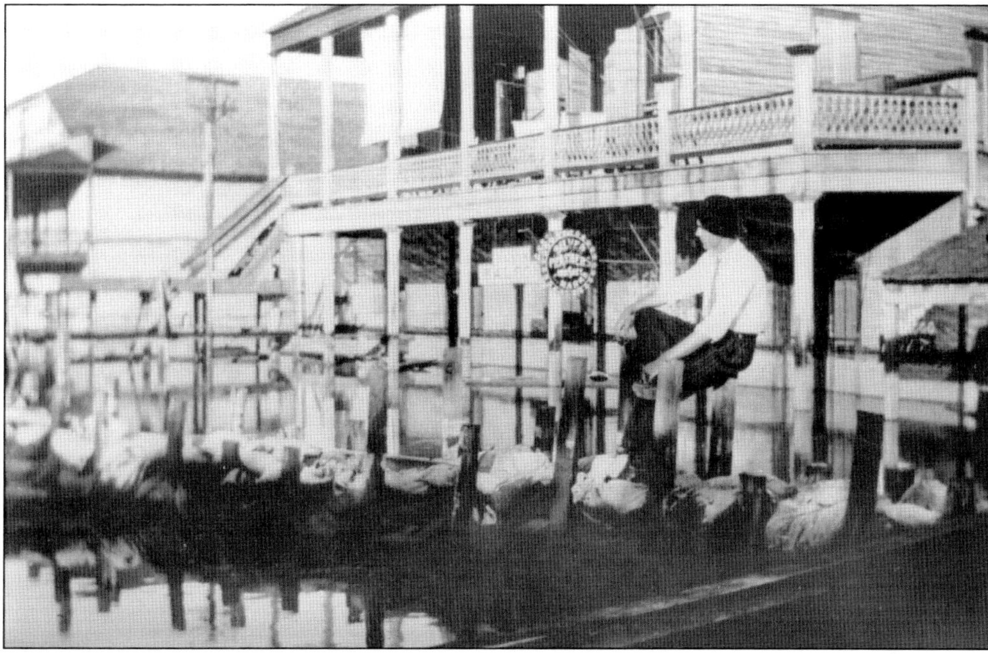

This Bayou Sara gentleman, sitting patiently on a sandbagged walkway outside one of many saloons, may be waiting for the floodwaters to recede so he can sample the advertised Silver Feathers Whiskey, specialty of the house. The upper floor probably has rooms to let or houses living quarters for the business owner. (WFHS.)

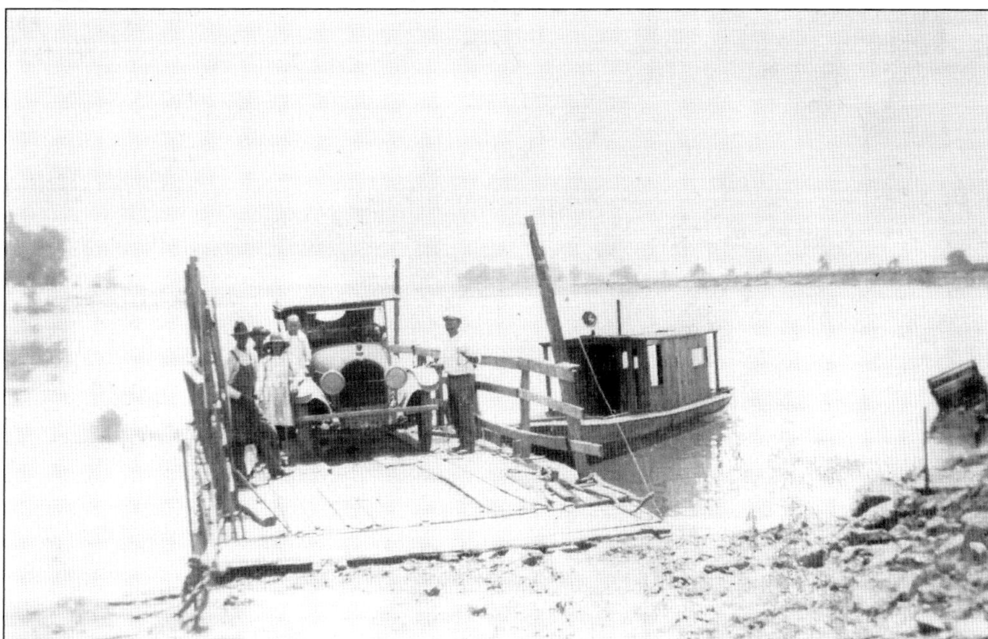

In 1919, passage across the Mississippi River, from West Feliciana to Pointe Coupee Parish, was achieved aboard a wooden, one-car barge propelled by a small, attached boat. Throughout the 20th century, this crossing featured an operational ferry, increasingly larger, motorized, and able to transport multiple vehicles, including large trucks and buses. (WFHS.)

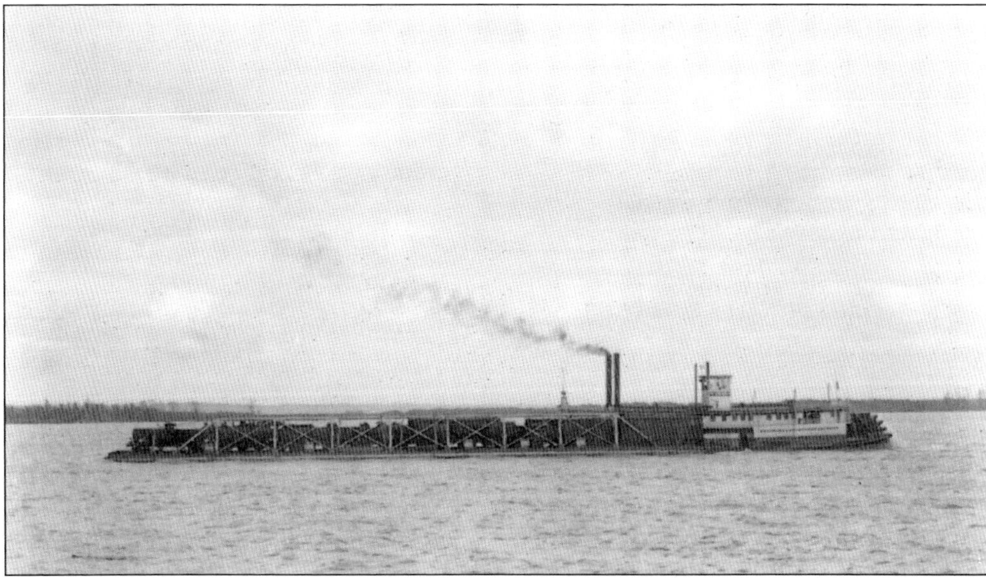

Before bridges, even trains had to cross the river on barges, this one propelled by a steam-powered stern-wheeler. Today, the crossing is made on the beautiful new Audubon Bridge, the country's longest cable-stayed structure. Its approach roads are named to recognize homegrown heroes from each side of the river, Gen. Robert H. Barrow on the east and Gen. John A. Lejeune on the west. Both were commandants of the US Marine Corps. (WFHS.)

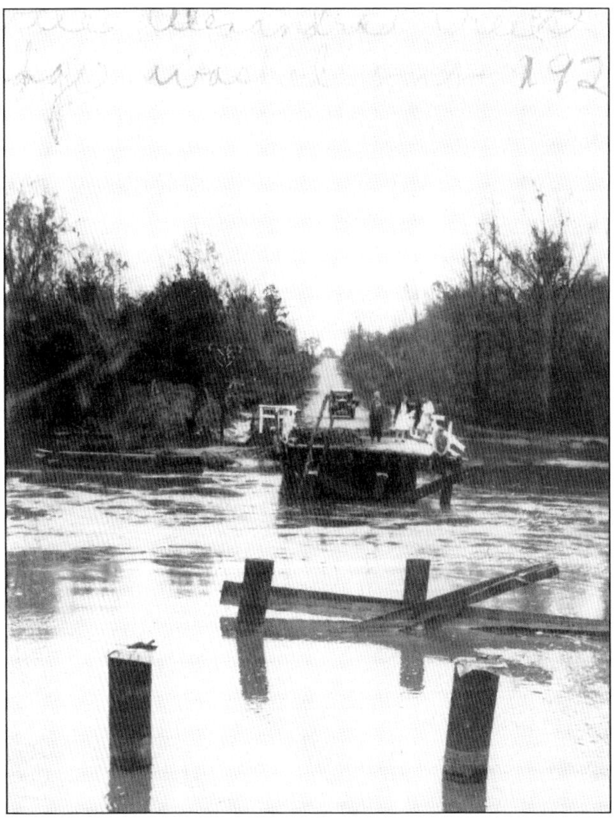

The bridges built across streams and bayous were rudimentary affairs that often washed out in spring floods. In the 1920s, the Alexander Creek bridge was completely washed away, making it difficult to reach St. Francisville's downtown area from some points; many smaller creeks were crossed only by low-water bridges, impassable when water was high. (WFHS.)

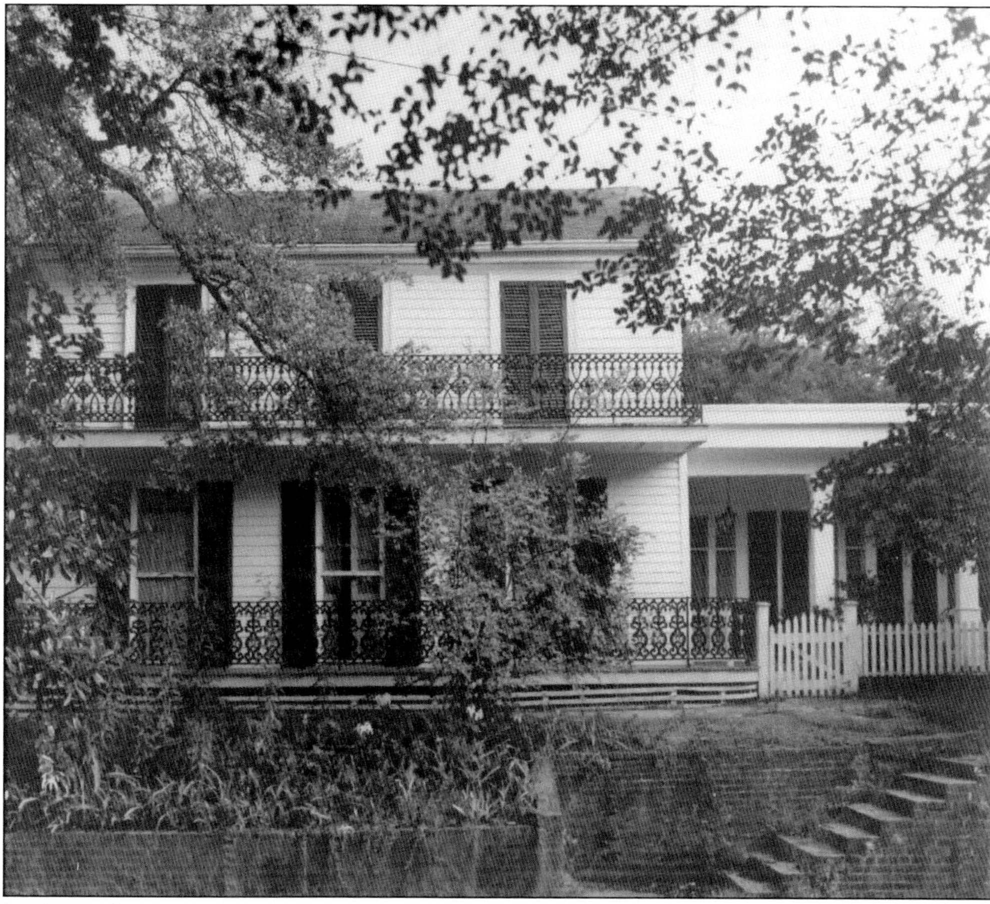

In the mid-1800s, Barrow House was home to W.W. Leake, an attorney, Confederate cavalry officer, and senior warden of St. Francisville's Masonic lodge. He was instrumental in stopping the Civil War for a few brief moments to bury a Union gunboat commander and fellow Mason in the cemetery of Grace Episcopal Church, a touching tribute to the universality of brotherhood and civility in the midst of a bloody war. This act is commemorated yearly as the Day the War Stopped. Leake's daughter Camilla married Dr. A. Feltus Barrow of Highland Plantation in 1892. Dr. Barrow, a horse-and-buggy doctor, made exhaustive trips into remote regions to treat the sick, fording creeks that often rose and stranded him away from home for days at a time. When he found time to relax, he relished his bath. When patients dripping with blood were brought by at inopportune times, he was known to lean out the window, still soaking in his tub, to give instructions for their admission to the sanitarium he built next door. (WFHS.)

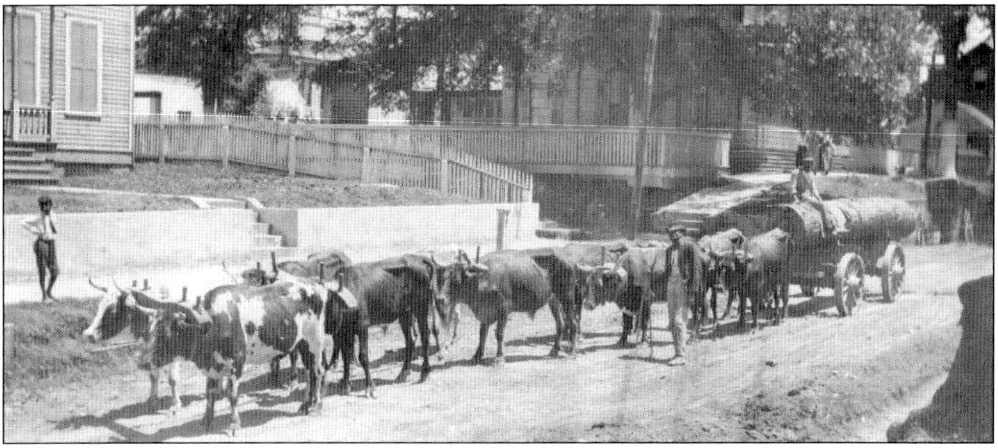

St. Francisville has only two main thoroughfares, Ferdinand Street and, shown here, Royal Street. A team of oxen hauls a huge log along the dirt track in front of one of the town's earliest homes, historic Barrow House, visible behind the cart. The home, a two-story saltbox with side additions, was begun in 1809 and is now a popular bed-and-breakfast. (WFHS.)

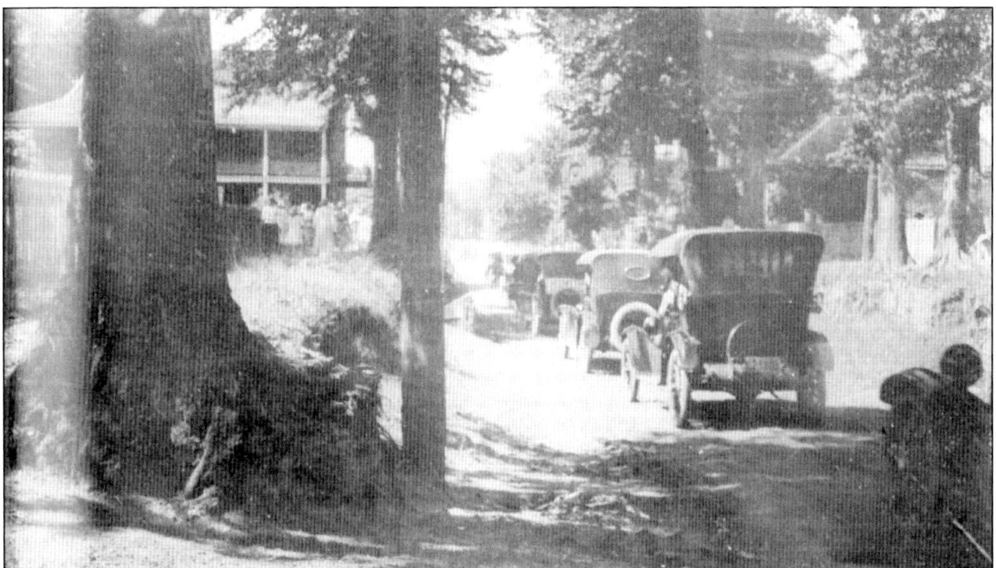

Cars, including the Model T at the back of this line, transport a big group of people past the historic townhouse called Propinquity (left) on Royal Street. Propinquity is one of St. Francisville's earliest homes, built of brick in 1809 by John Mills, founder of Bayou Sara. The community was so prone to flooding that Mills had the good sense to establish his own residence up the hill in St. Francisville. (WFHS.)

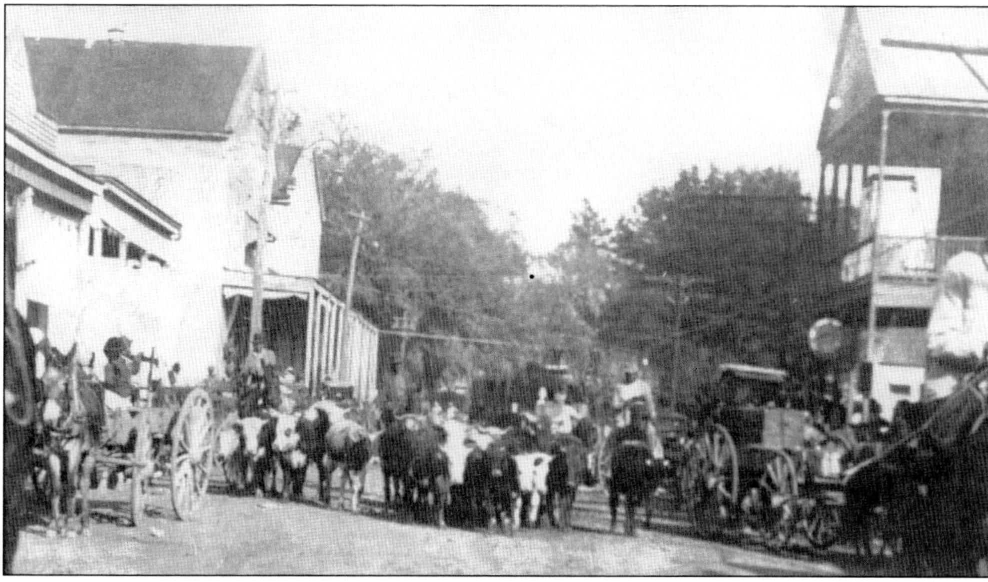

St. Francisville, laid out in 1807 while under Spanish control, called its main street Ferdinand to honor the Spanish king. Throughout the 19th century, this dirt thoroughfare bustled with cattle drives and horse-drawn cotton wagons en route to the river port at Bayou Sara. The large, columned building at left is Freyhan & Co.'s enormous emporium; the double-galleried structure on the right is the Vinci grocery. The upstairs was a residence. (WFHS.)

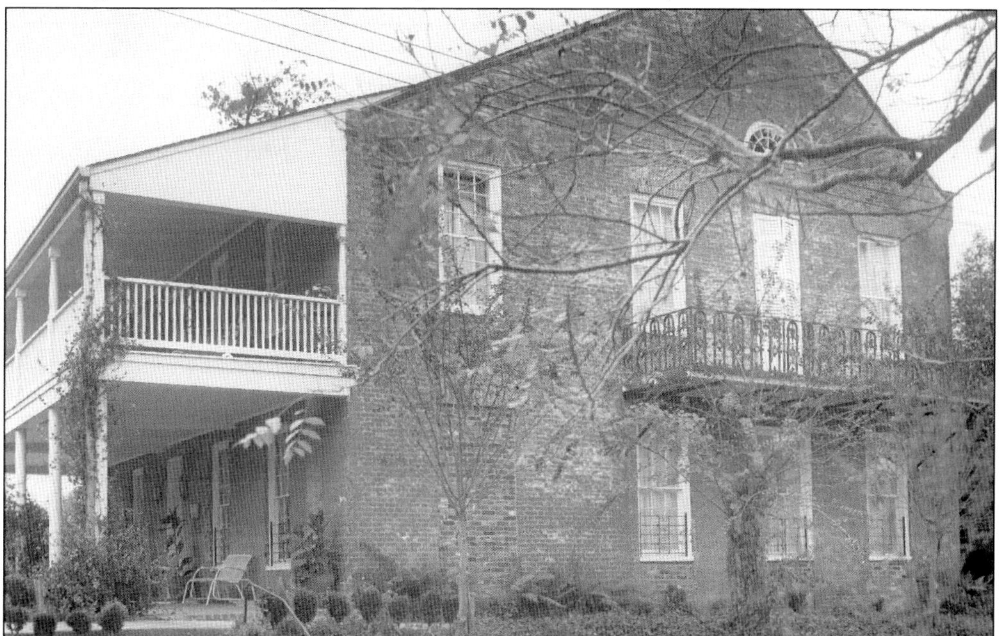

In 1822, Propinquity was operated as a store by German immigrant Dietrich Holl. Upon his death, his nephew Maxmillian Nubling took responsibility for both the store and Holl's young widow, whom he soon wed. She had been the ward of the owner of Beech Woods Plantation, where both John James Audubon and his wife, Lucy, worked as tutors for area children. Consequently, both Audubons patronized the store at Propinquity. (WFHS.)

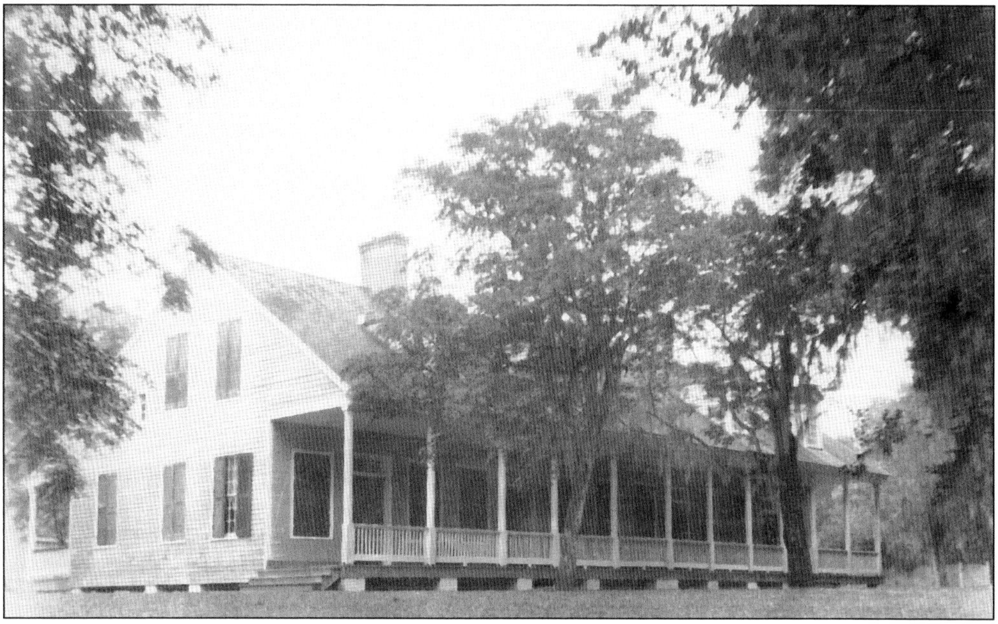

St. Francisville was the cultural and commercial center for surrounding plantations, one of the earliest of which was the Cottage, begun on a 1795 Spanish land grant and still surrounded by original dependencies: kitchen, dairy, commissary, law office, stable, carriage house, and slave quarters. Andrew Jackson stayed there, the home of his chief of staff's brother, after the Battle of New Orleans. (Collection of Louisiana Office of State Parks.)

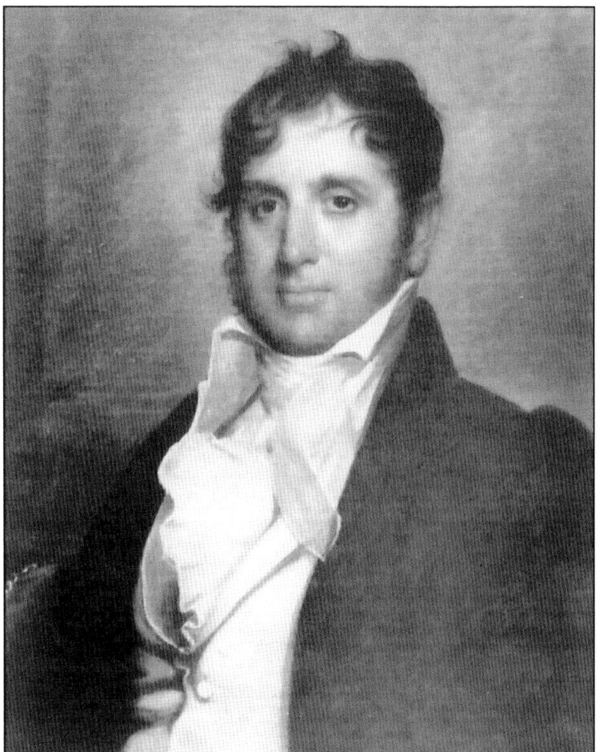

Father of a dozen children and first judge of the Feliciana parishes after Louisiana became a state in 1812, distinguished judge Thomas Butler, resident of the Cottage Plantation, was elected to Congress in 1818. He found Washington "nothing like the agreeable social society we have here in Louisiana." (Collection of Anne Butler.)

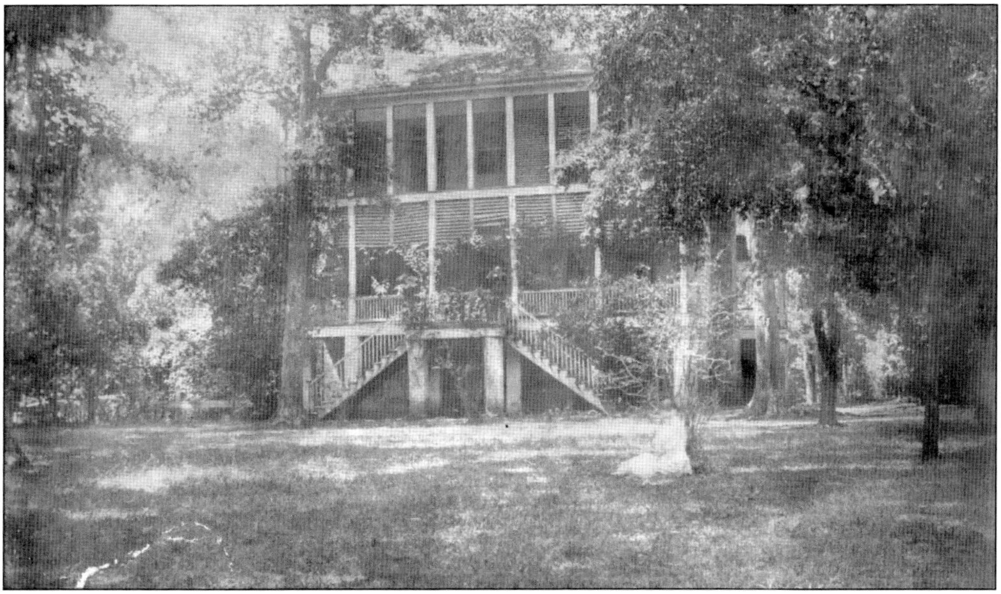

Lucretia Alston and her husband, Ruffin Gray, received a Spanish land grant of 600 acres. In 1799, they began construction of the Oakley Plantation house, a simple and sensible three-story structure with divided Spanish-style steps to the front gallery. Within a year, Gray was dead; in 1801, his widow married James Pirrie, described by Audubon as "when sober, truly a good man." (Collection of Louisiana Office of State Parks.)

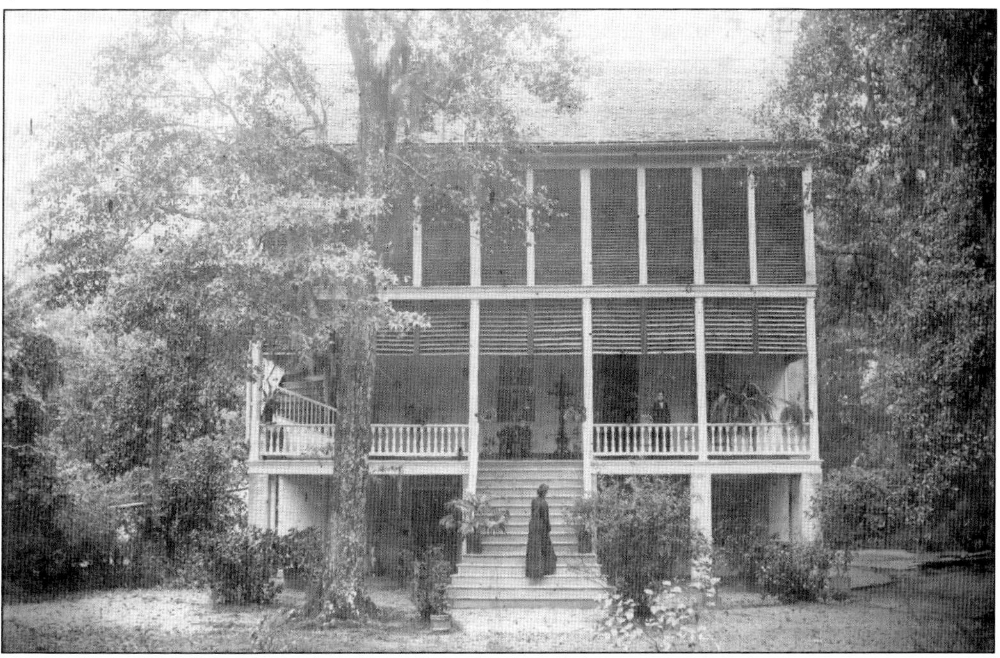

By 1879 or 1880, as seen here, the front entrance steps at Oakley, leading from ground level to the main living space on the second floor, had been changed to a single central stair. The galleries, however, remained shaded by jalousies that blocked the harsh, hot sunlight while permitting cool breezes to blow through the rooms, all of which opened onto the porch. (Collection of Louisiana Office of State Parks.)

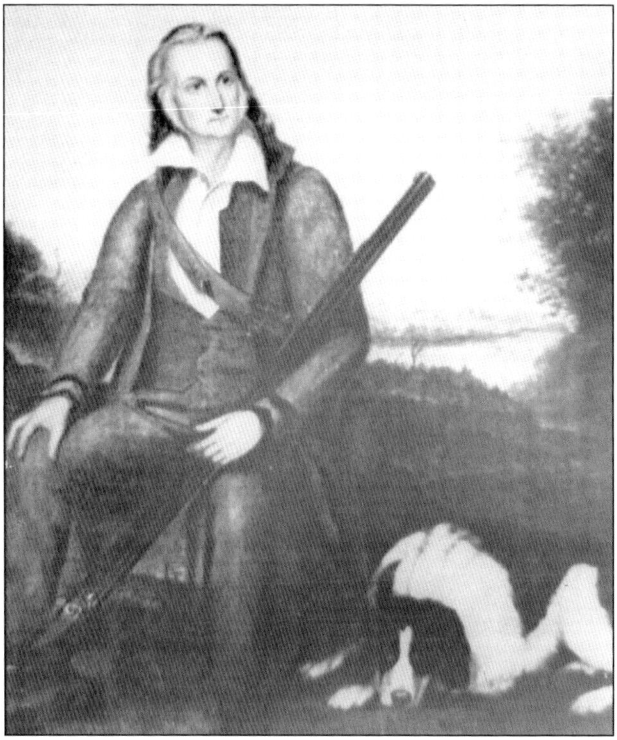

The artist-naturalist John James Audubon, who set for himself the staggering task of painting all the birds of this immense, fledgling country, was hired by Lucretia Pirrie to tutor her daughter Eliza in 1821. He received room and board plus $60 a month, and he had half the day off to pursue his own painting and bird studies in the surrounding woods. (Collection of Louisiana Office of State Parks.)

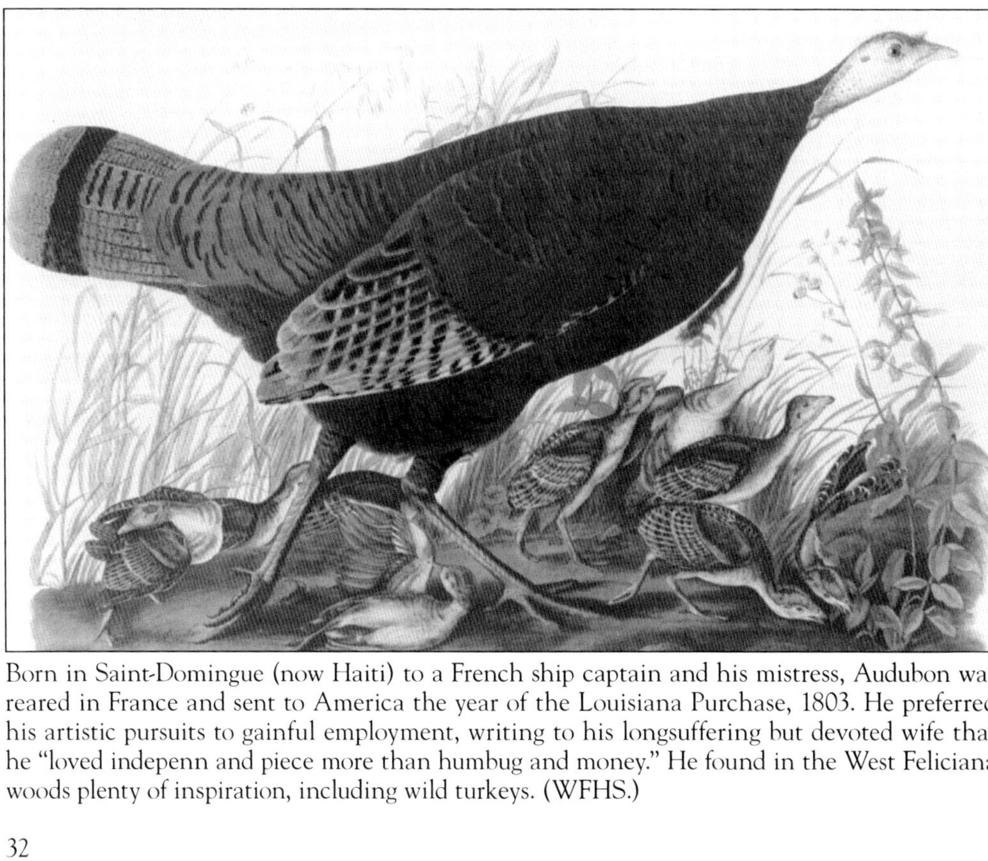

Born in Saint-Domingue (now Haiti) to a French ship captain and his mistress, Audubon was reared in France and sent to America the year of the Louisiana Purchase, 1803. He preferred his artistic pursuits to gainful employment, writing to his longsuffering but devoted wife that he "loved indepenn and piece more than humbug and money." He found in the West Feliciana woods plenty of inspiration, including wild turkeys. (WFHS.)

Beautiful, young Eliza Pirrie of Oakley Plantation is shown here in a portrait by Chester Harding. Her need of a tutor drew the artist John James Audubon to West Feliciana in 1821. Pirrie's three subsequent marriages would entwine the histories of some of the area's earliest planting aristocracy. (Collection of Louisiana Office of State Parks.)

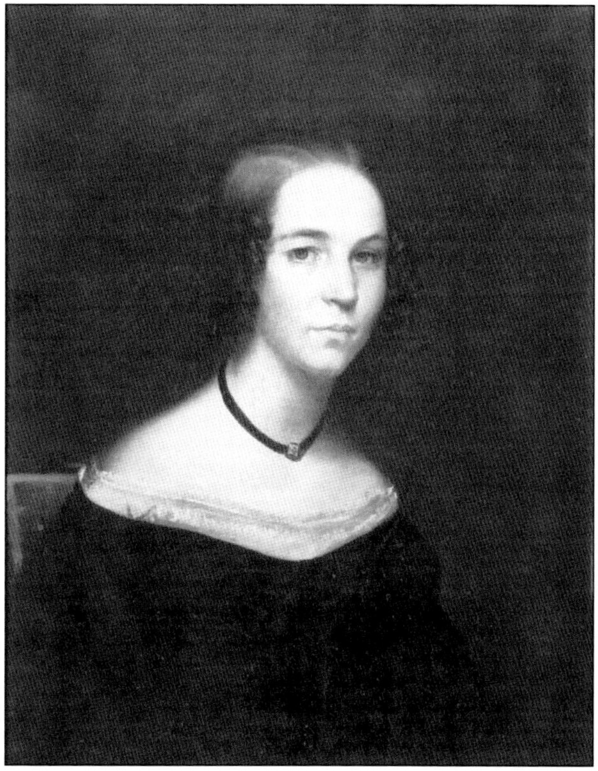

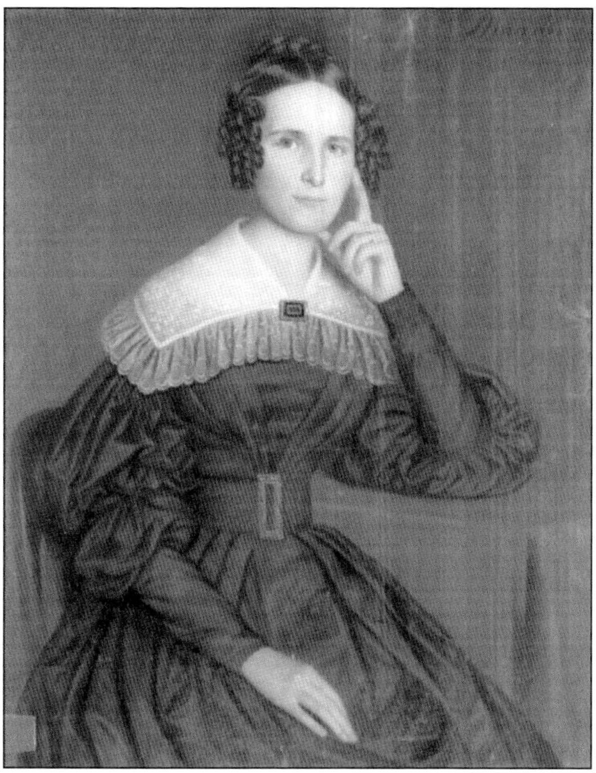

Audubon was at Oakley for only four months. Lucretia Pirrie had already buried five children and one husband, so, when Eliza fell ill, her mother stopped her lessons with Audubon and resisted paying him for that period, generating ill will. Another factor was the presence at Oakley of Lucretia's daughter by her first marriage, Mary Ann Gray (pictured), who despised the flamboyant artist. (Collection of Louisiana Office of State Parks.)

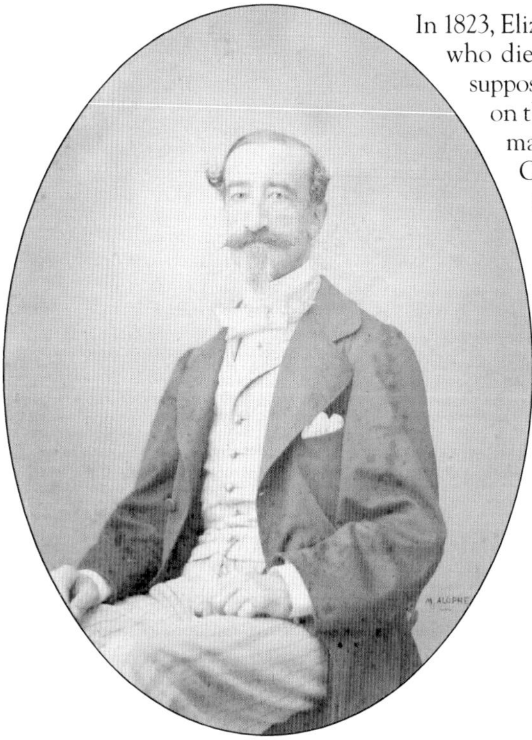

In 1823, Eliza Pirrie eloped with cousin Robert H. Barrow, who died six weeks after contracting pneumonia, supposedly from carrying her across a flooded stream on their honeymoon. Twice widowed, in 1841, she married a third husband, Henry Lyons (shown). Called a "trifling sponge," Lyons went off to the Mexican War and then the Gold Rush in 1849, leaving Eliza to die of childbirth fever. (Collection of Louisiana Office of State Parks.)

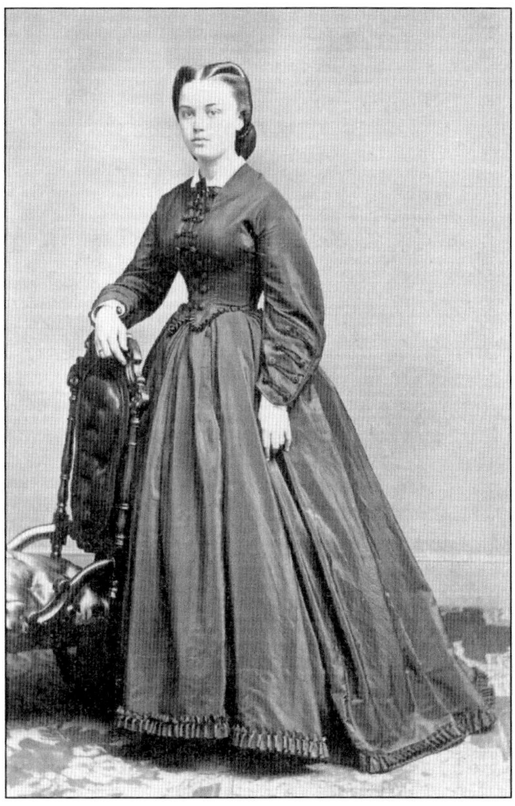

By her third husband, attorney Henry Lyons, Eliza Pirrie had daughters Cora (pictured), Lucy, and Eliza. Lyons returned from California after his wife died in 1851, but he left his daughters at Oakley in the care of Isabelle Bowman, daughter of Eliza's second marriage, who was married to William Wilson Matthews. The Matthews heirs sold Oakley to the state in 1947. (Collection of Louisiana Office of State Parks.)

Eliza Pirrie's second husband was the Reverend William Robert Bowman (pictured), first rector of Grace Episcopal Church in St. Francisville. The couple was married in 1828. Their daughter Isabelle remained at Oakley; their son James Pirrie Bowman married the beautiful Sarah Turnbull of Rosedown Plantation. (Collection of Louisiana Office of State Parks.)

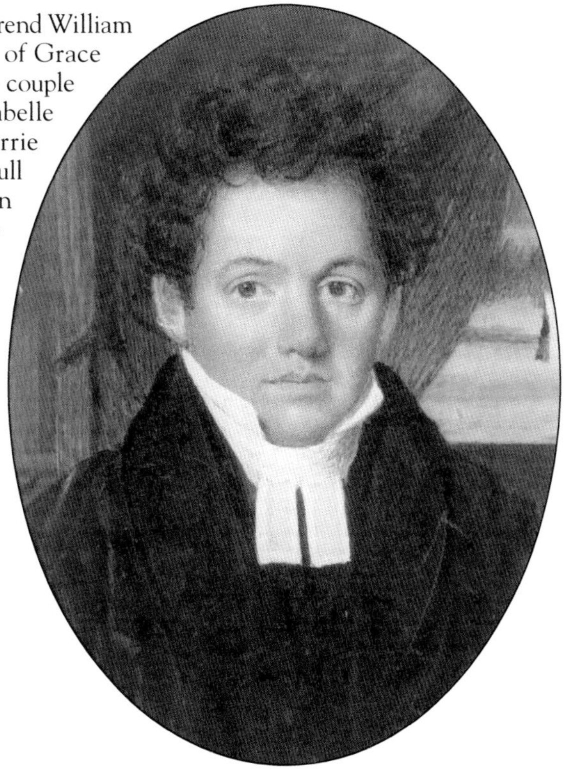

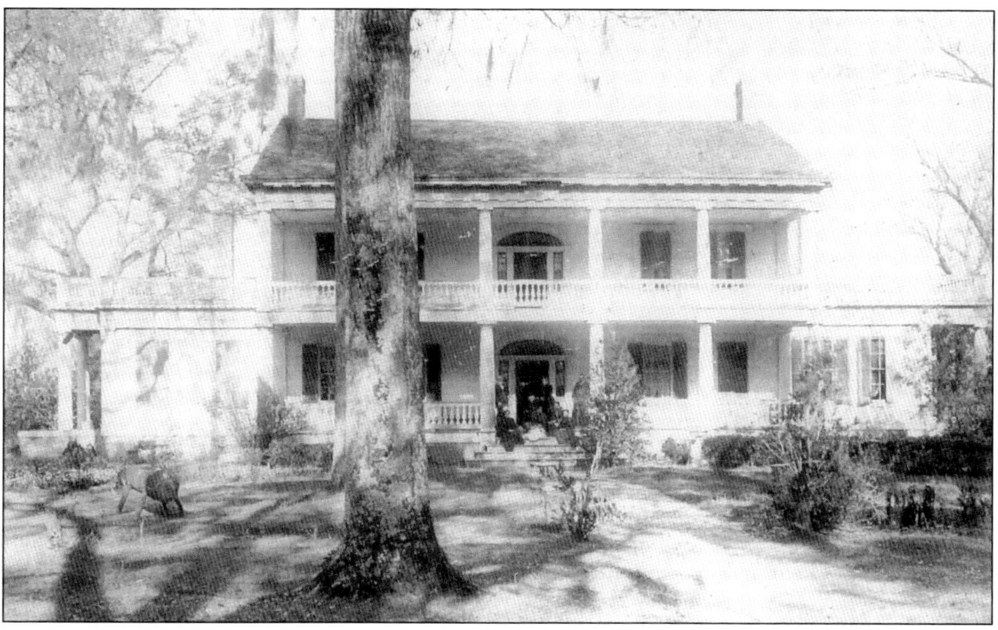

Surrounded by 27 acres of formal gardens and approached by a fine oak allée, the grand Greek Revival home Rosedown was built in 1835 by planter Daniel Turnbull and his young bride, Martha Barrow. Their only son drowned; their daughter married Eliza Pirrie's son James Pirrie Bowman. This photograph shows that generation with at least some of their ten children, including eight daughters. (Collection of Louisiana Office of State Parks.)

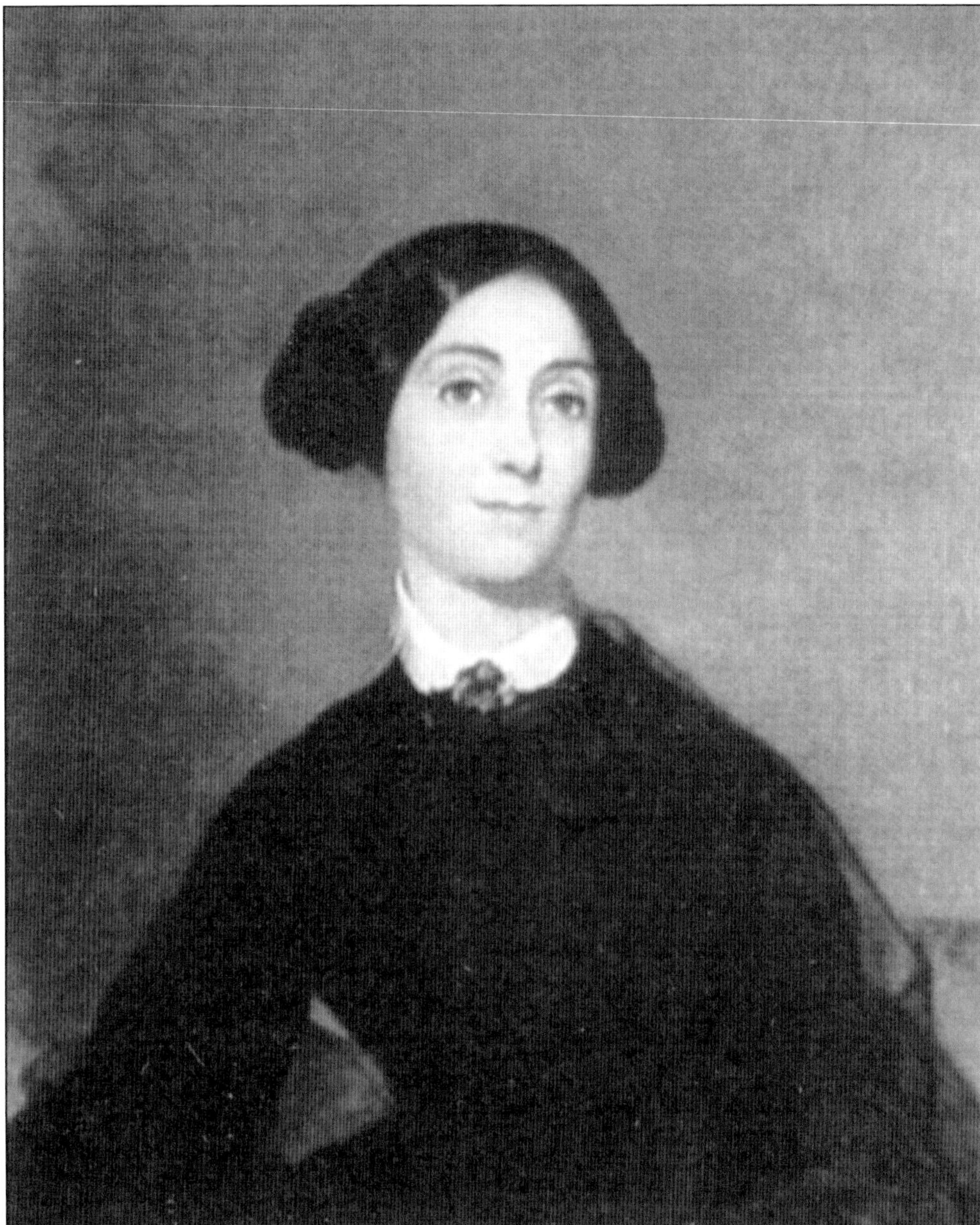

Beautiful Martha Barrow Turnbull, seen here in a painting by Thomas Sully, was only 18 when she married Daniel Turnbull and left on a honeymoon grand tour of Europe. She was so inspired by the gardens of Versailles and other European landscapes that she became a remarkable horticulturist, one of the first to import camellias and azaleas. She experimented and kept a detailed diary of six decades of gardening that proved useful in the restoration of her 27 acres of formal plantings surrounding the house. Her father, William Barrow, and her grandmother Olivia Ruffin Barrow of Highland Plantation were some of Feliciana's earliest Anglo settlers. Both Rosedown and Oakley are now preserved as state historic sites, open for touring and often hosting special events and demonstrations of early skills, like down-hearth cooking. Rosedown is also a National Historic Landmark. (Collection of Louisiana Office of State Parks.)

Two

AGRICULTURE AND LUSH LANDSCAPE

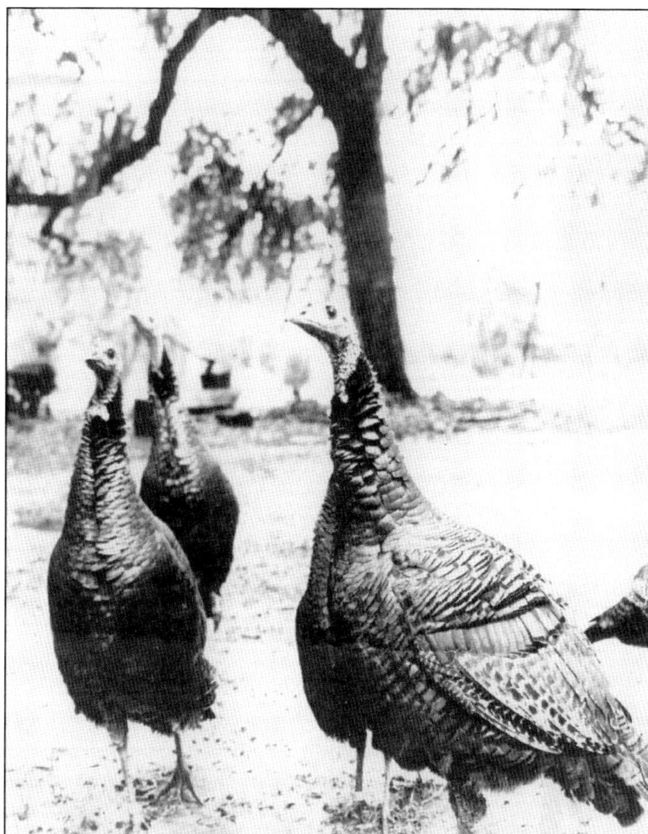

Left over from the glacial age, which carved out steep hills and deep, shady hollows harboring plants and animals found nowhere else in Louisiana, the unspoiled wilderness areas of the Tunica Hills support large populations of wildlife and birdlife, including white-tailed deer and wild turkeys (pictured). (Collection of Anne Butler.)

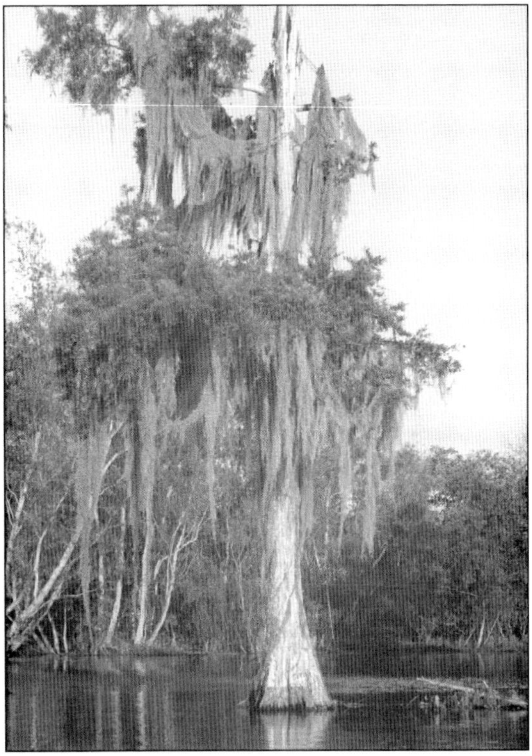

The 10,473-acre Cat Island National Wildlife Refuge preserves one of the largest tracts of virgin wetland forest not protected by levees from cyclical flooding. Spring floods can put upward of 20 feet of Mississippi River water into this unique habitat area. Among the refuge's old-growth bald cypress trees is the 85-foot-tall National Champion (not shown), thought to be over 1,000 years old. (WFHS.)

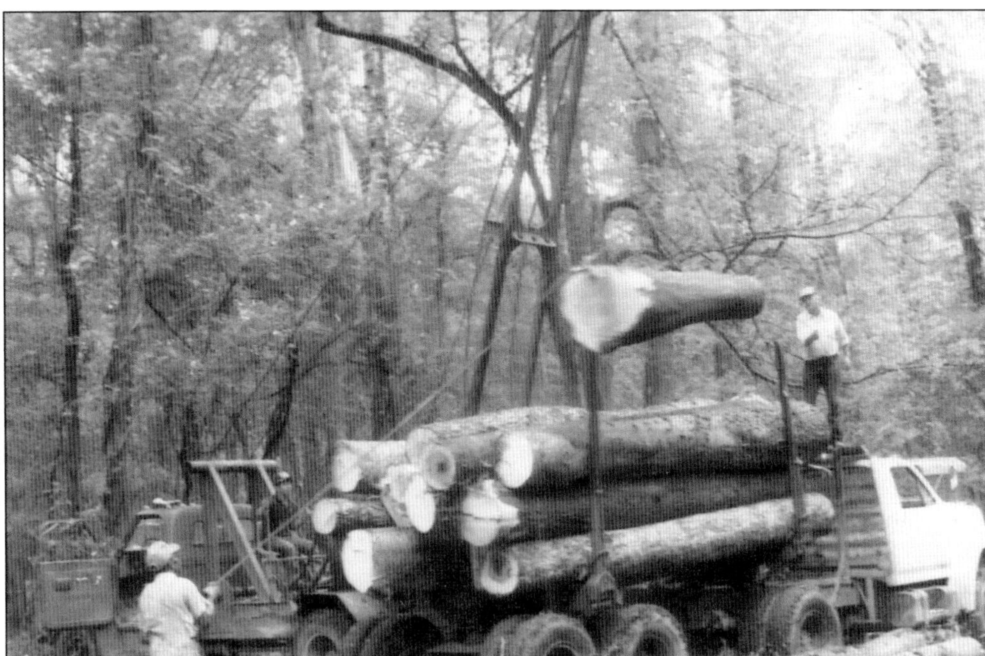

Along this southernmost un-leveed stretch of the lower Mississippi River, the dynamic cycles of wetting and drying as the river rose and fell created ideal growth conditions for cypress. Logging was an important early industry. Shown here are Julius Metz on the truck and young Randy Metz sitting in the loader. The man at left is unidentified. (Collection of Metz/Imahara family.)

An old logging family of German descent included Jesse Metz and his six handsome, rugged sons and two daughters. They lived near Cat Island along the Mississippi River. They logged, farmed, raised cattle, ground cornmeal, made cane syrup, and otherwise lived in nearly total self-sufficiency. This truck is a 1938 model. (Collection of Metz/Imahara family.)

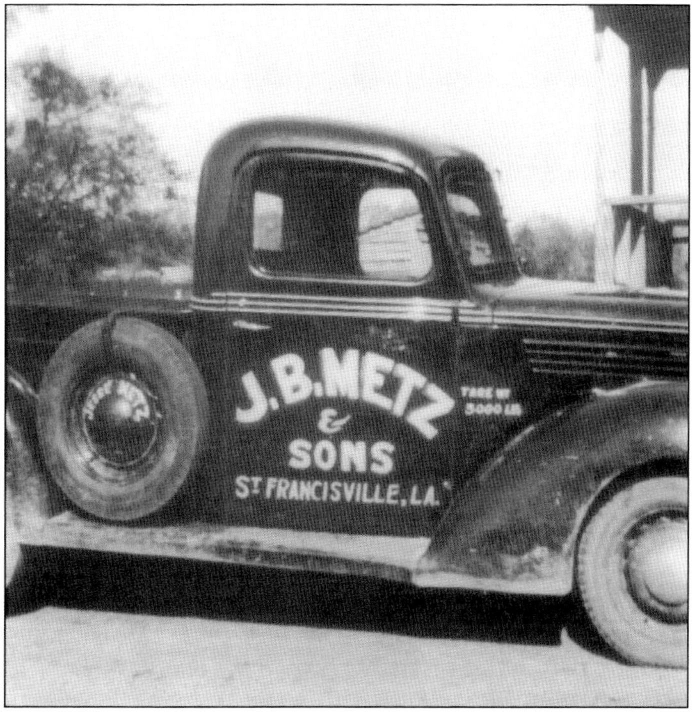

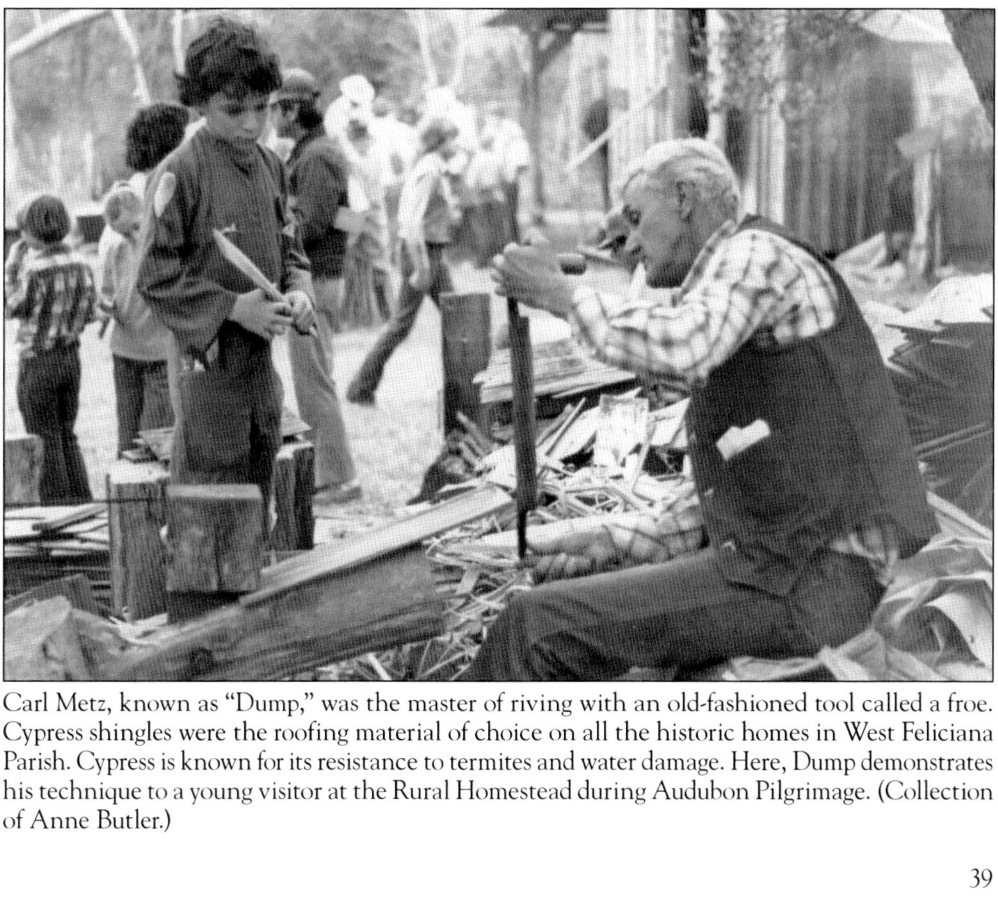

Carl Metz, known as "Dump," was the master of riving with an old-fashioned tool called a froe. Cypress shingles were the roofing material of choice on all the historic homes in West Feliciana Parish. Cypress is known for its resistance to termites and water damage. Here, Dump demonstrates his technique to a young visitor at the Rural Homestead during Audubon Pilgrimage. (Collection of Anne Butler.)

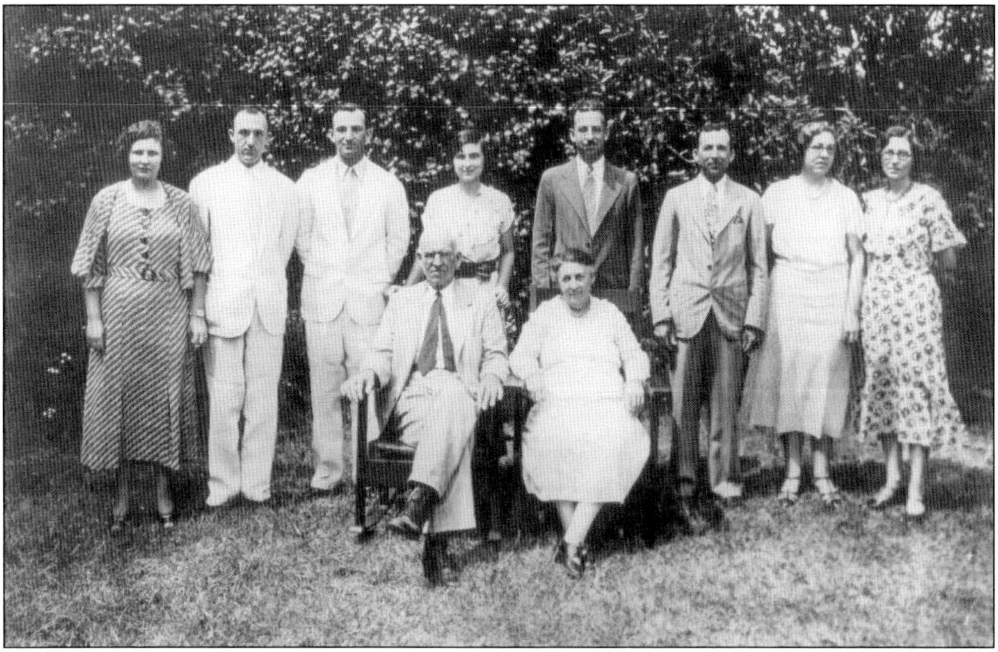

Thomas DeWitt Bickham and his wife, Sallie Harvey, pose here with their eight grown children. Thomas arrived by wagon in West Feliciana in 1889 with a mule and colt, rented a farm from his father, and began growing cotton. When the devastating boll weevil forced farmers to diversify after the soil was depleted by one-crop cotton farming, Bickham was one of the first to rotate crops and raise cattle. (Collection of Beryl Bickham Eisworth.)

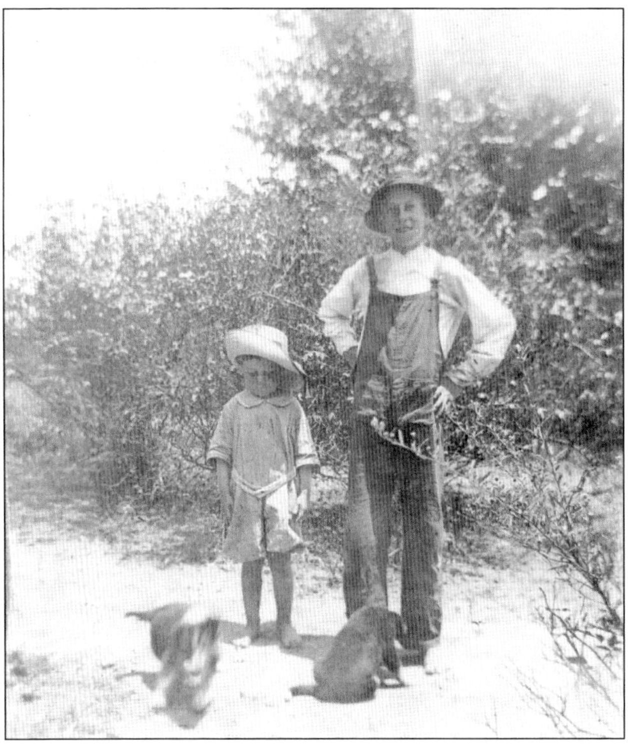

Elvin (right) and Dennis Bickham benefited from the industry of their father, Thomas DeWitt Bickham. He was a farmer, country storekeeper, and postmaster for over half a century in the Thompson Creek delta. The Bickhams diversified their initial cotton operations by adding cattle, hay, corn, potatoes, vegetables, pigs, and chickens after expanding over several thousand acres. (Collection of Beryl Bickham Eisworth.)

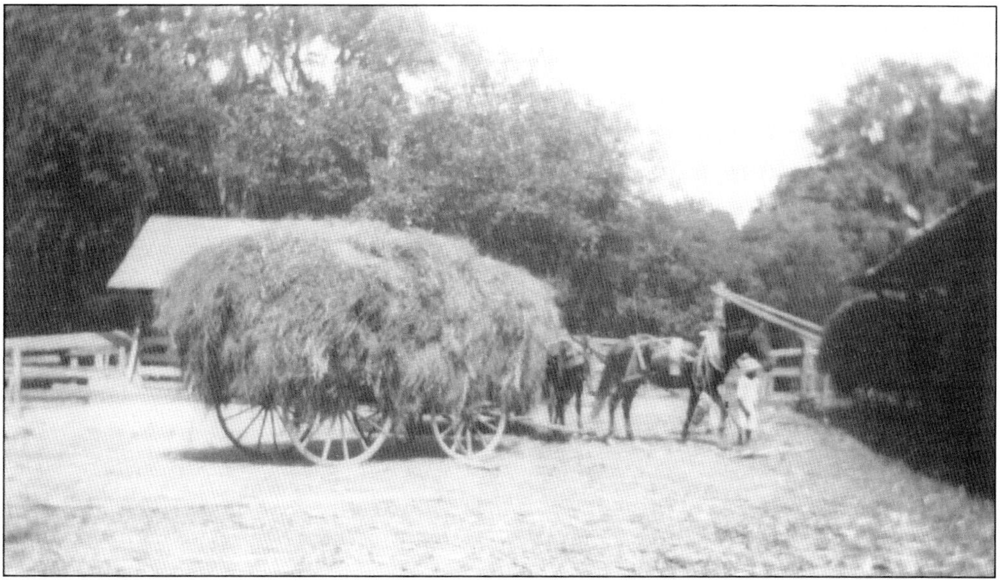

Peak 19th-century years saw annual cotton yields of more than 20,000 bales, but by the early 20th century, agricultural authorities estimated that land in the Felicianas was divided roughly fifty-fifty between agriculture and cattle-raising, a condition unique in the state. The rich lands and long summer growing season produced bountiful crops of hay, even before the introduction of mechanized equipment like tractors and balers. (Collection of Louisiana Office of State Parks.)

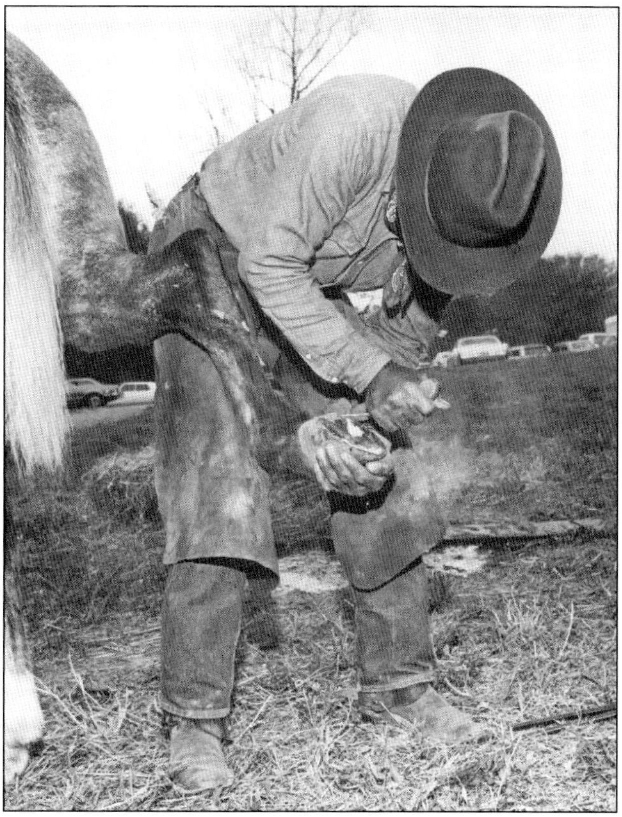

A 1937 issue of the *Progress* magazine quotes forward-thinking farmer Thomas D. Bickham as saying that cattle-raising would be the industry of the future for the Felicianas. Soon, the rolling hills and verdant pasturelands were dotted with herds. Horses were needed to work the cattle, of course, so farriers and experienced cowboys like Oliver "Preacher" McNabb (pictured) were in great demand. (WFHS.)

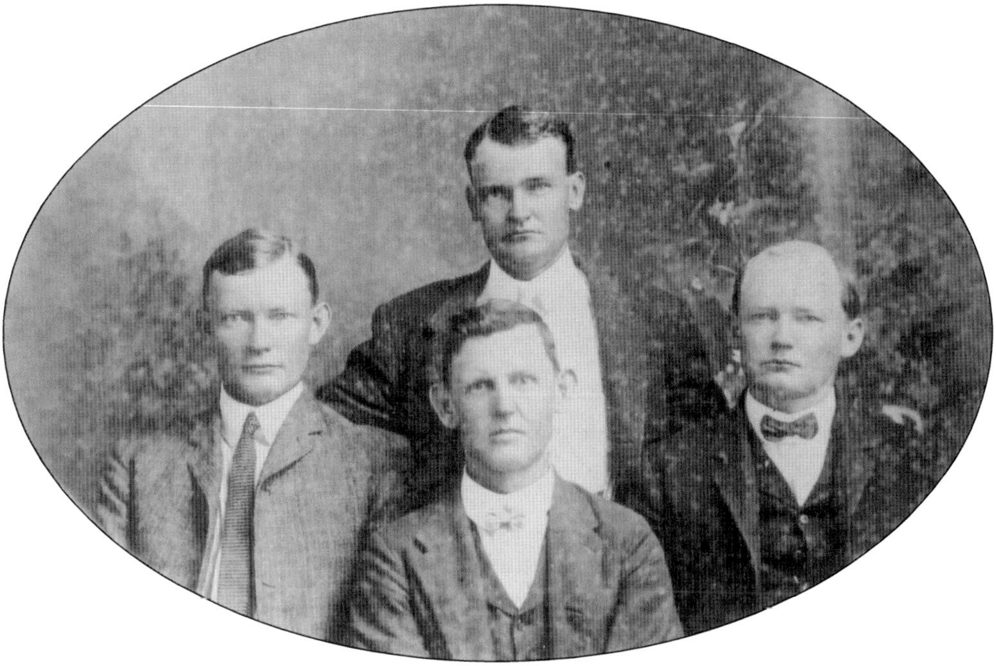

Progenitors of one of the most innovative agricultural dynasties in West Feliciana were "the Daniel boys," as this old photograph is labeled. E.I. Daniel (front, center) was a parish resident since 1882 and an early advocate of stock raising and crop diversification. His focus was on Hereford cattle, lespedeza, sweet and Irish potatoes, and corn. (Collection of Bank of St. Francisville Calendar.)

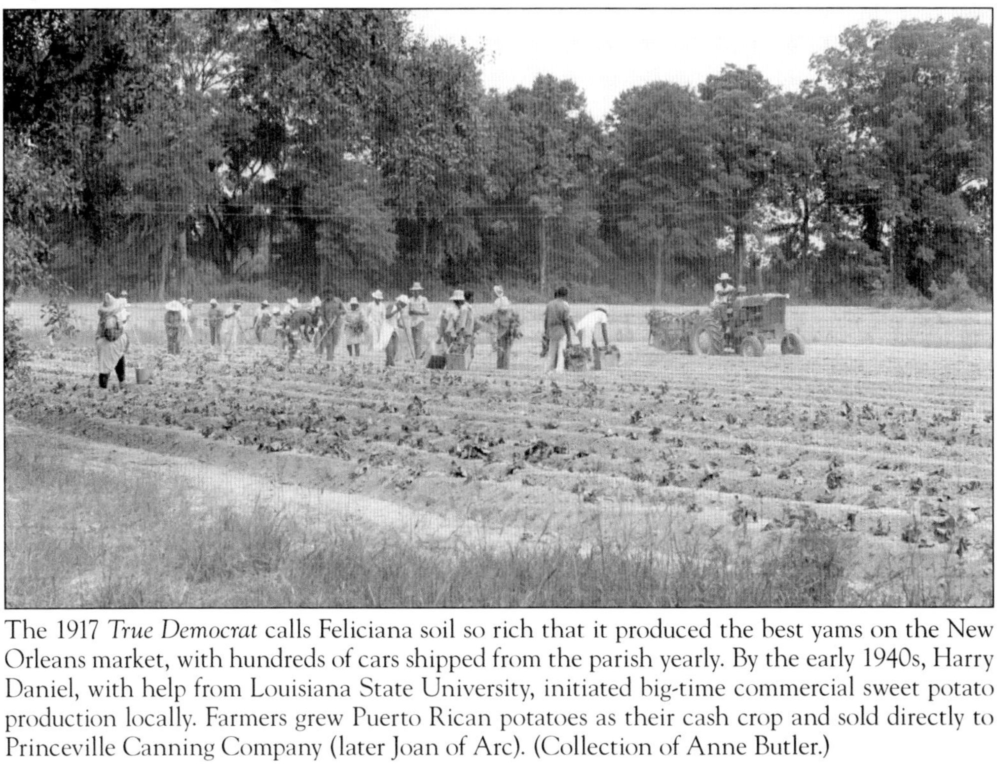

The 1917 *True Democrat* calls Feliciana soil so rich that it produced the best yams on the New Orleans market, with hundreds of cars shipped from the parish yearly. By the early 1940s, Harry Daniel, with help from Louisiana State University, initiated big-time commercial sweet potato production locally. Farmers grew Puerto Rican potatoes as their cash crop and sold directly to Princeville Canning Company (later Joan of Arc). (Collection of Anne Butler.)

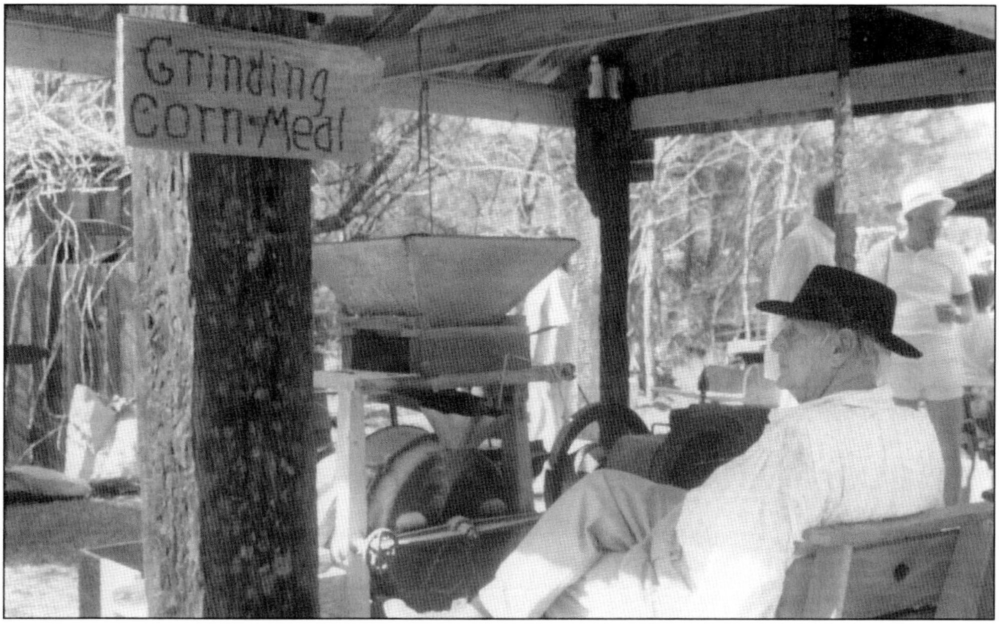

While indigo, cotton, and sugarcane were the early cash crops, corn was also planted. It was an important food not only for the farm family but for the livestock as well. It was often dried and ground into cornmeal with a 19th-century steam-powered gristmill, like this one being demonstrated by Danny Magee at the Rural Homestead. (WFHS.)

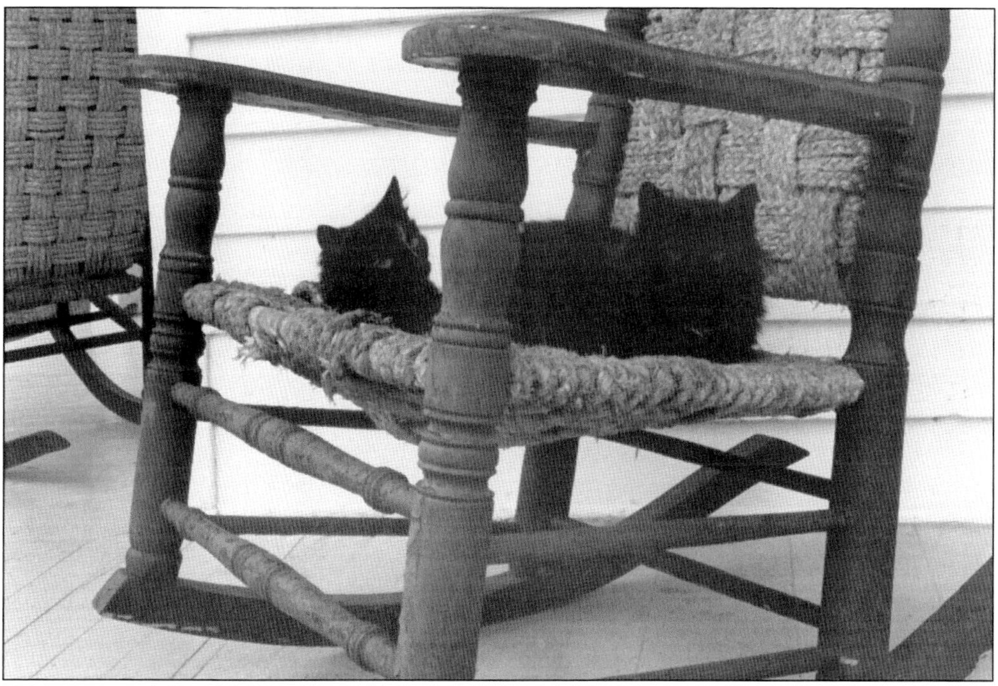

Once removed from the ripe ear of corn, even the shucks were used, and not just as livestock fodder. They could also be soaked until pliable and then plaited into long strands that were woven into useful items like horse collars, doormats, bags, and the back and seat of this old rocking chair being enjoyed by two black cats. (WFHS.)

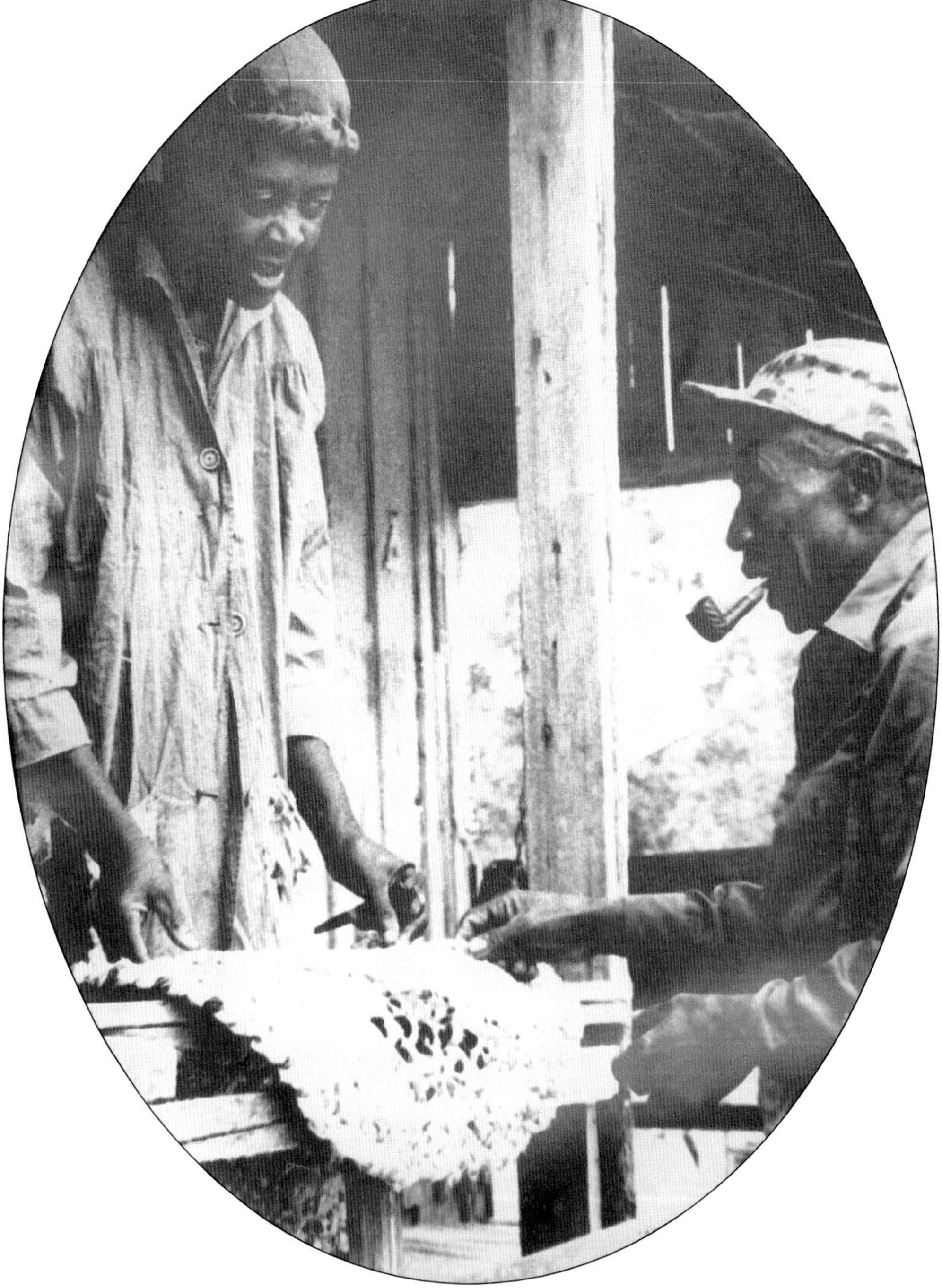

Levy Ruth and his wife, Lucinda "Sugardoo" Cavalier, lived in a field behind the big house on Highland Plantation, the earliest home of the Barrow family. Sugardoo, a deaf mute, skillfully twisted corn shucks into delicate, lacy placemats, something she learned as a child in the little school on Cat Island. (Collection of Anne Butler.)

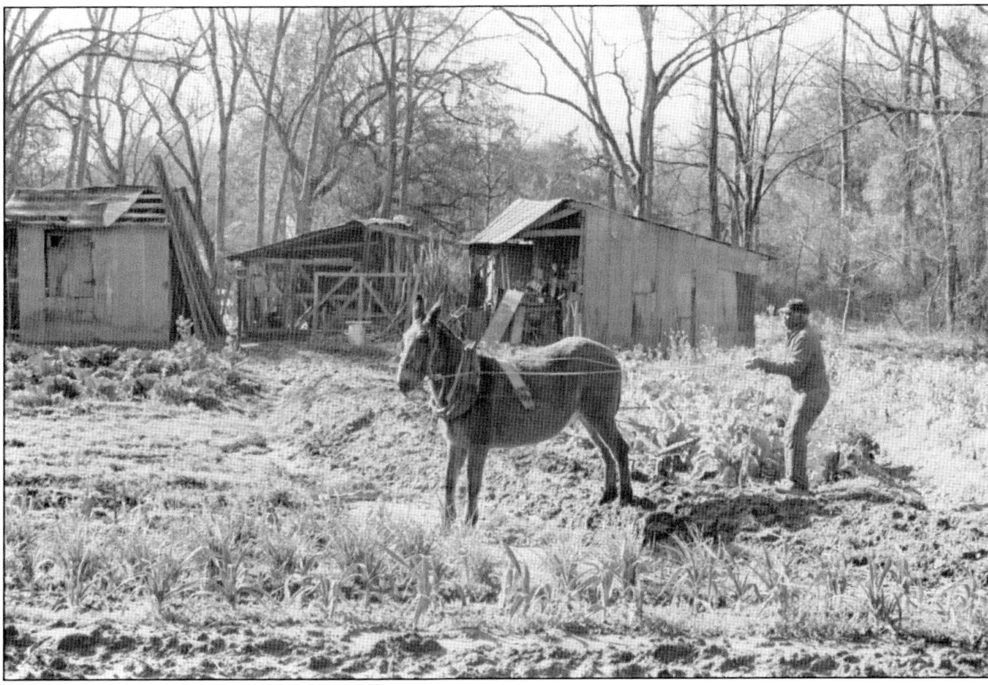

Until the turn of the 20th century, progress was impeded by all-dirt roads and unbridged streams. For these reasons, automobiles and mechanized farming equipment were late to arrive in West Feliciana. Small farm fields were worked by a hand plow and mule, as Noah Thomas is doing here in his truck patch. (Collection of Anne Butler.)

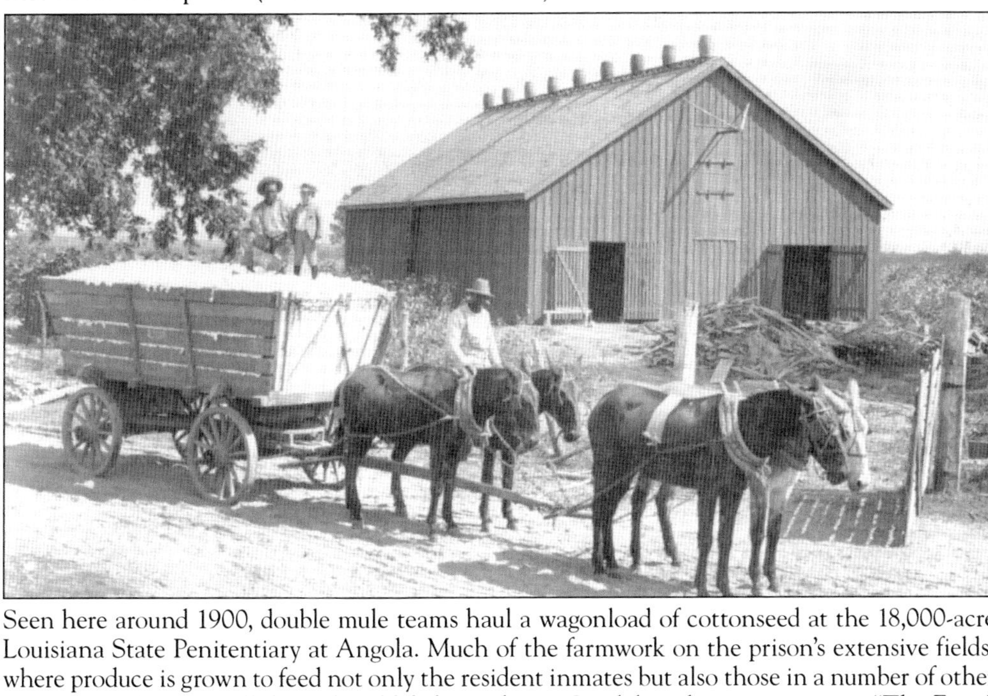

Seen here around 1900, double mule teams haul a wagonload of cottonseed at the 18,000-acre Louisiana State Penitentiary at Angola. Much of the farmwork on the prison's extensive fields, where produce is grown to feed not only the resident inmates but also those in a number of other state institutions, is still done the old-fashioned way. Stock-breeding programs on "The Farm" produce fine blooded work- and show horses. (Collection of Louisiana State Penitentiary.)

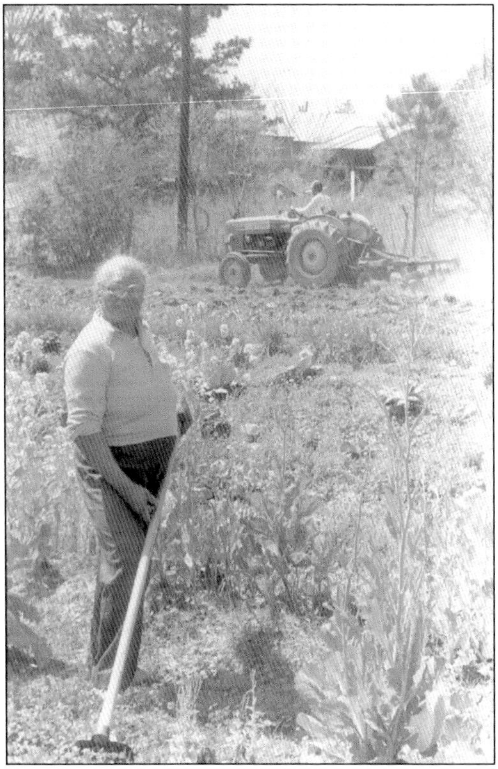

One of 14 children, Ethel Metcalf learned early the importance of the vegetable patch to feed the family. She attributed the success of her bountiful gardens to planting by the moon and following almanacs' advice as to when the moon would be in the right phase. She said that seeds planted in the wrong zodiac signs, the "barren" signs, produced plants deficient in health and growth. (Collection of Anne Butler.)

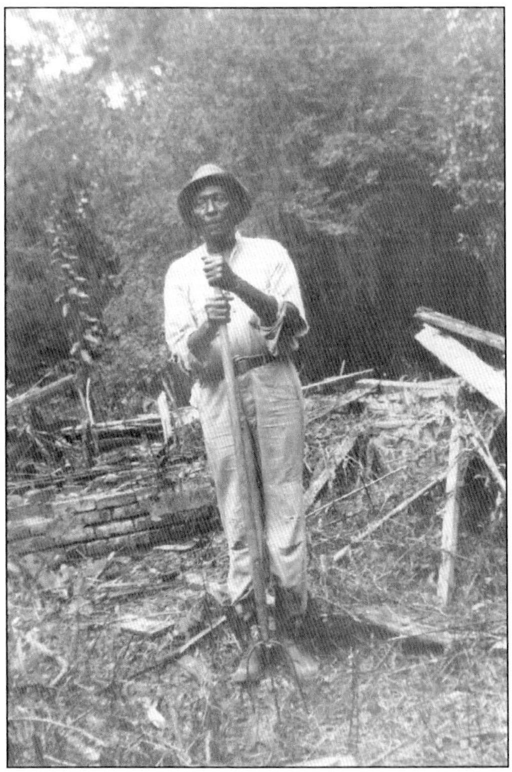

Shown holding his pitchfork in 1948 is Sam Scott, longtime gardener and groundskeeper at Oakley Plantation, which had just been purchased by the state and would be opened to the public as what is now called Audubon State Historic Site. Gardeners like Scott were enormously important in the daily maintenance of the gardens and extensive grounds surrounding all of the early plantation homes. (Collection of Louisiana Office of State Parks.)

California born and of Japanese descent, James Imahara, shown here at age four, was hired in 1950 to move to Afton Villa Plantation and restore the acres of gardens that had been laid out in the 1800s but neglected for years. Wallace and Dot Percy renovated the main house, while the Imahara family reclaimed the terraced plantings and formal parterres on the grounds. (Collection of Metz/Imahara family.)

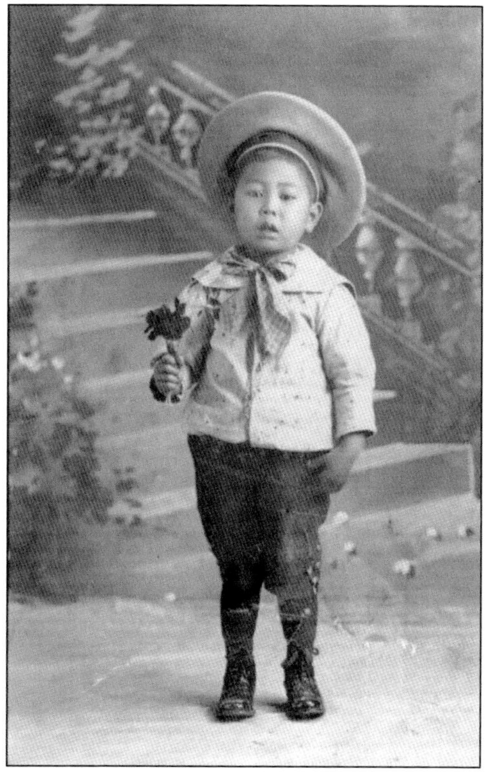

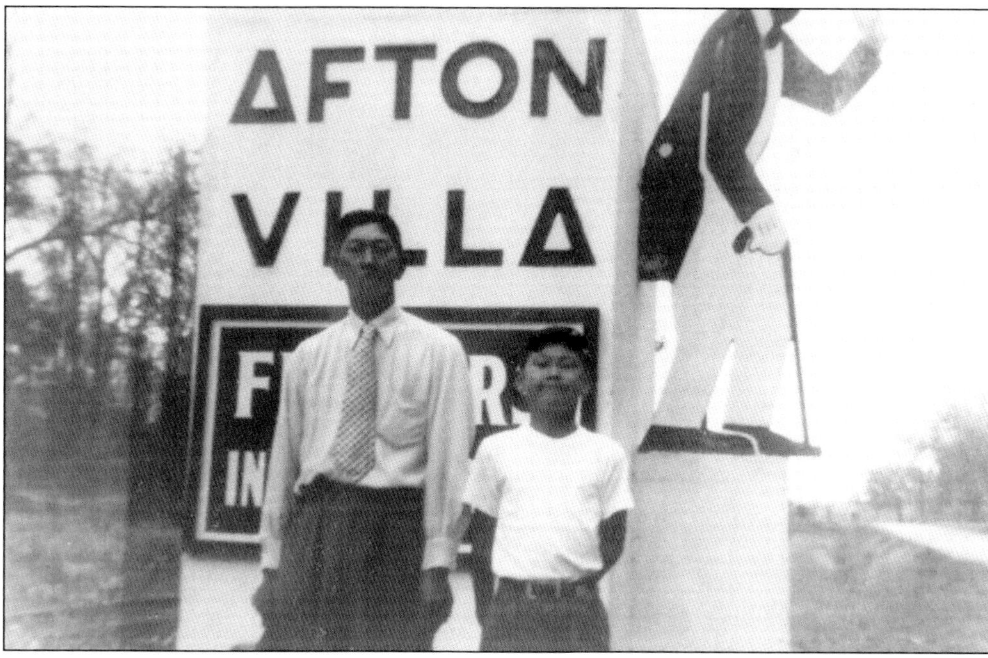

Expert horticulturist James Imahara and his son John stand at the entrance to Afton Villa Plantation in 1951. After returning the gardens to their original splendor, James moved to Baton Rouge, where he began the nursery that grew into a very profitable business, responsible for much of the city's corporate landscaping. (Collection of Metz/Imahara family.)

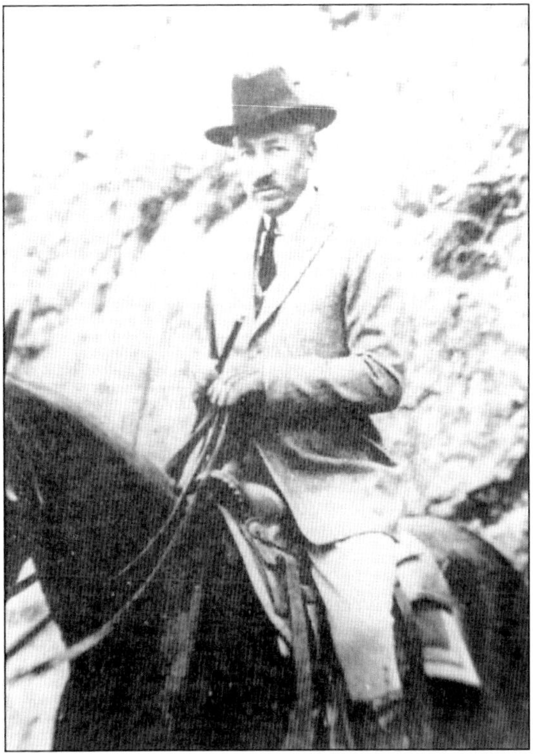

Before 1901, when Louisiana purchased 18,000 acres for the country's largest maximum-security prison, Louisiana State Penitentiary, the state had been leasing out its convicts to private, profit-motivated lessees. By leasing state criminals to operations like that run by Maj. S.L. James (pictured) on Angola Plantation, the state divested itself of the responsibility for inmates and even made money on their labors. (Collection of Louisiana State Penitentiary.)

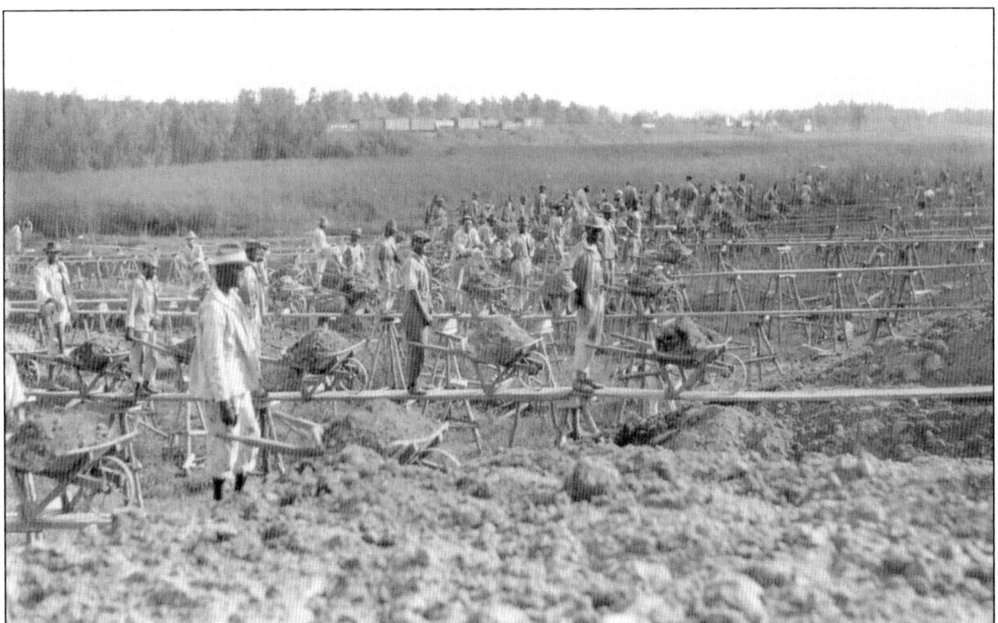

Angola's rich river bottomland and fertile farm fields are surrounded by the Mississippi River and the rugged Tunica Hills—virtually escape-proof but also vulnerable to floodwaters every spring. Over the years, inmates carried out the backbreaking work of building and stabilizing levees to hold back the waters, one wheelbarrow of dirt at a time. (Collection of Louisiana State Penitentiary.)

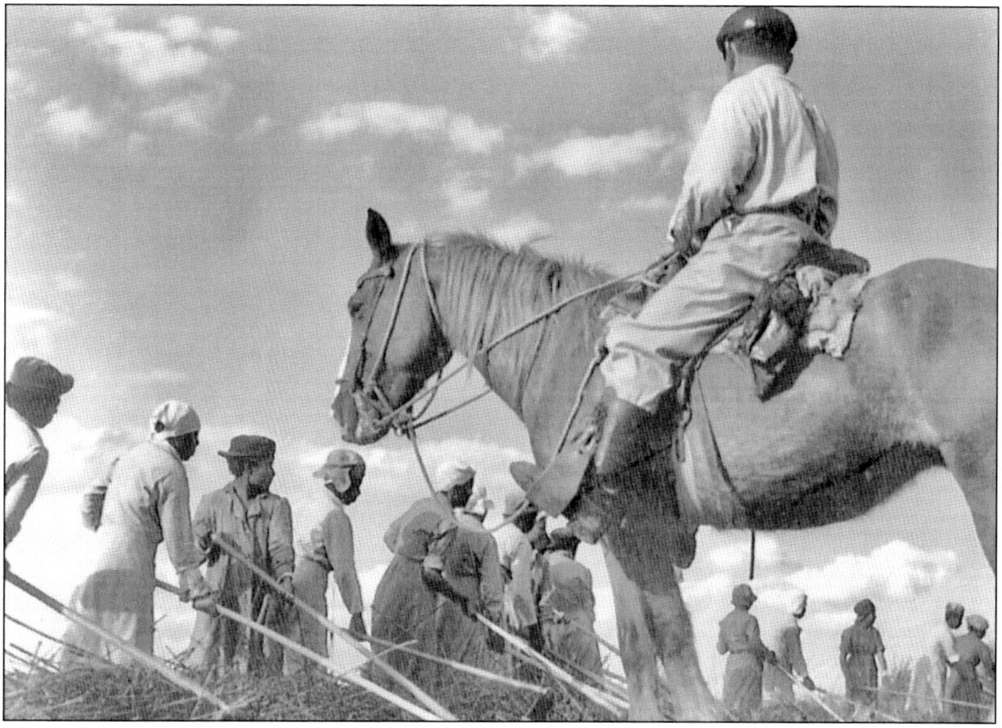

The Louisiana State Penitentiary at Angola, now an all-male facility, housed female inmates in a wooden dormitory, built in 1901, until 1958, when they were moved to another camp and then relocated to the women's prison at St. Gabriel in 1961. Here, women prisoners in 1938 hoe in the fields under the watchful eyes of a mounted guard. (Fonville Winans photograph; collection of Louisiana State Penitentiary.)

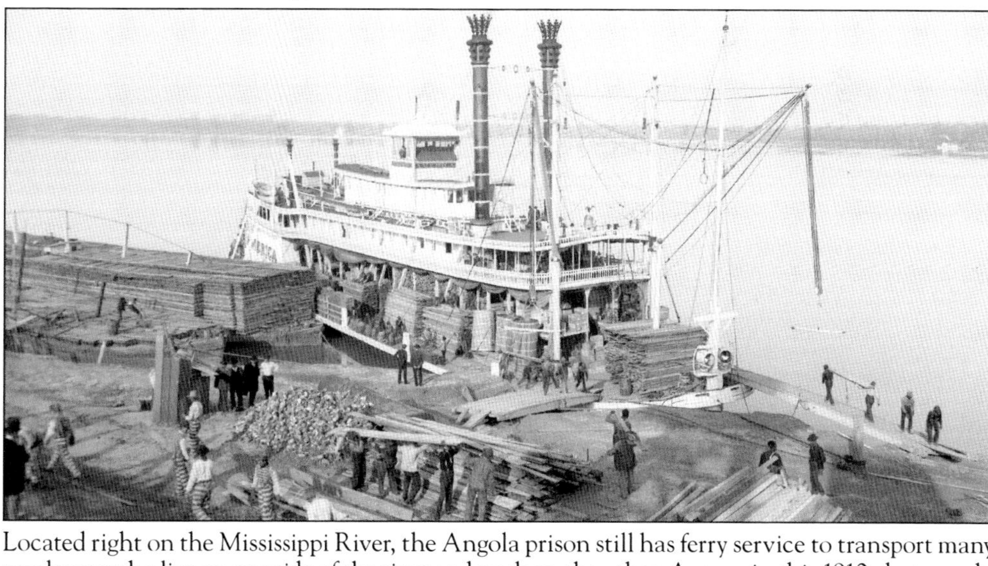

Located right on the Mississippi River, the Angola prison still has ferry service to transport many employees who live on one side of the river and work on the other. As seen in this 1910 photograph, there was a loading dock where steamboats like this one could take on loads of lumber, hogsheads of sugar, cabbages, and other produce. The Big Stripe inmates are identifiable by their striped pants. (Collection of Louisiana State Penitentiary.)

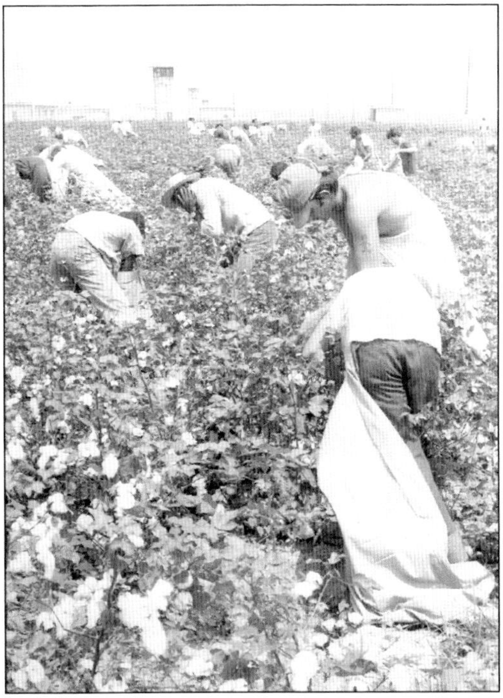

Cotton was the traditional cash crop at Angola, and inmates labored in the fields to fill long sacks with the snowy bolls. In the early years, conditions were horrendous and violent. Inmates were poorly clothed, barely fed, brutally punished, and forced to work long hours, often losing their feet from frostbite after working barefoot in frozen fields. One inmate said of early prison conditions, "It ain't fit for hogs." (Collection of Louisiana State Penitentiary.)

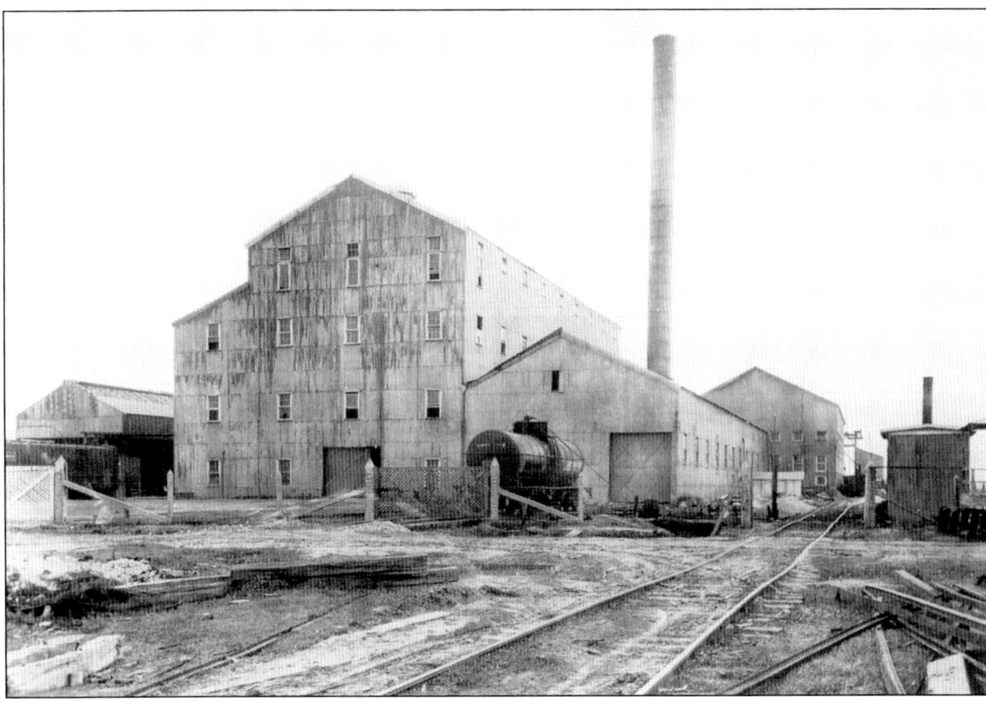

The sugar mill at Angola, seen here in 1916, was the last one operating in West Feliciana, processing cane grown on 5,000 acres. Grinding season was the busiest time of year at the prison, when work continued without interruption 24 hours a day to maintain the high temperature required to keep the sugar flowing. In the 1970s, the sugar mill was dismantled and shipped to Brazil. (Collection of Louisiana State Penitentiary.)

Three

Amazing Architecture

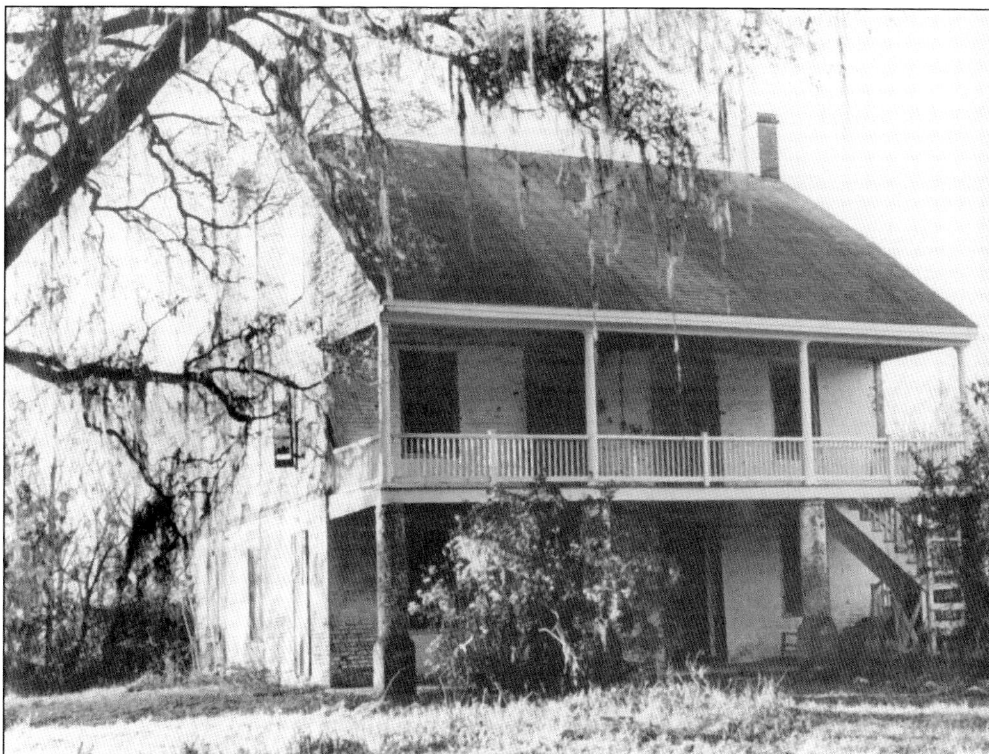

Live Oak Plantation, built by Elijah Adams around 1808 on a Spanish land grant, shows both Spanish and Anglo American influences. In 1928, Kate Towles LeSassier had a little school for neighborhood children upstairs while her husband ran the post office downstairs. The home fell into disrepair until it was purchased in 1975 by Sue and Bert Turner, great preservationists who meticulously restored the house and grounds. (Collection of Grady Smart.)

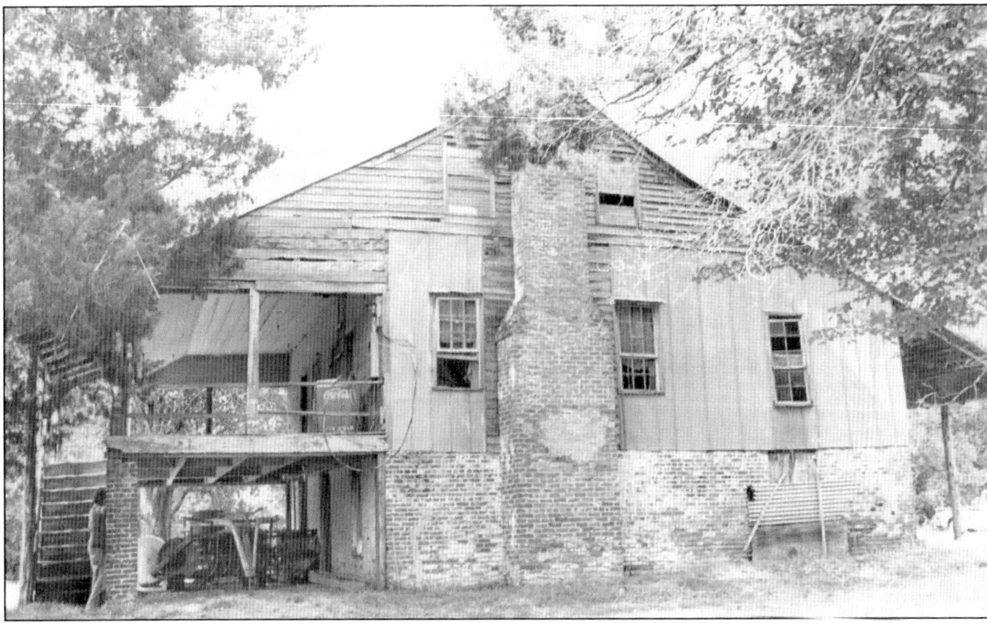

Trudeau House, a raised French Louisiana cottage with touches of Spanish and American influence, is one of the oldest structures in West Feliciana. It was built near the mouth of Tunica Bayou on land granted to Spanish surveyor general Carlos Trudeau. Sold by Trudeau's widow in 1789 for 1,000 pesos to Revolutionary War financier Oliver Pollock, it has been uninhabitable for many years. (Collection of Anne Butler.)

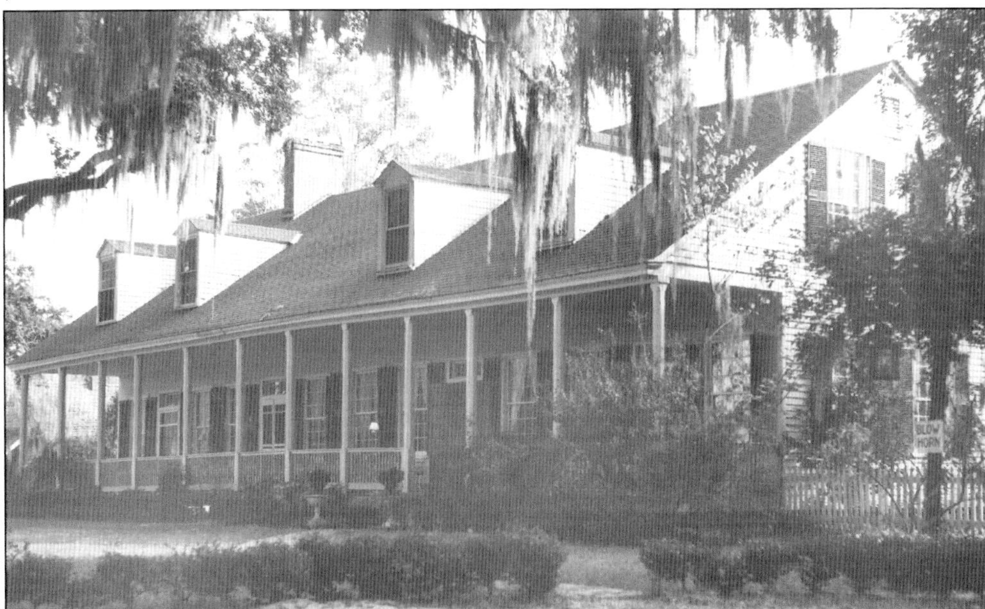

Built on a 1790s land grant from Baron de Carondelet, the Cottage Plantation in 1811 was the home of Thomas Butler, first judge of the Feliciana parishes and member of Congress. His descendants remained in residence for the next century and a half. Surrounding the home is one of the most complete collections of original outbuildings in the area, enhancing an understanding of the operation of plantation communities. (WFHS.)

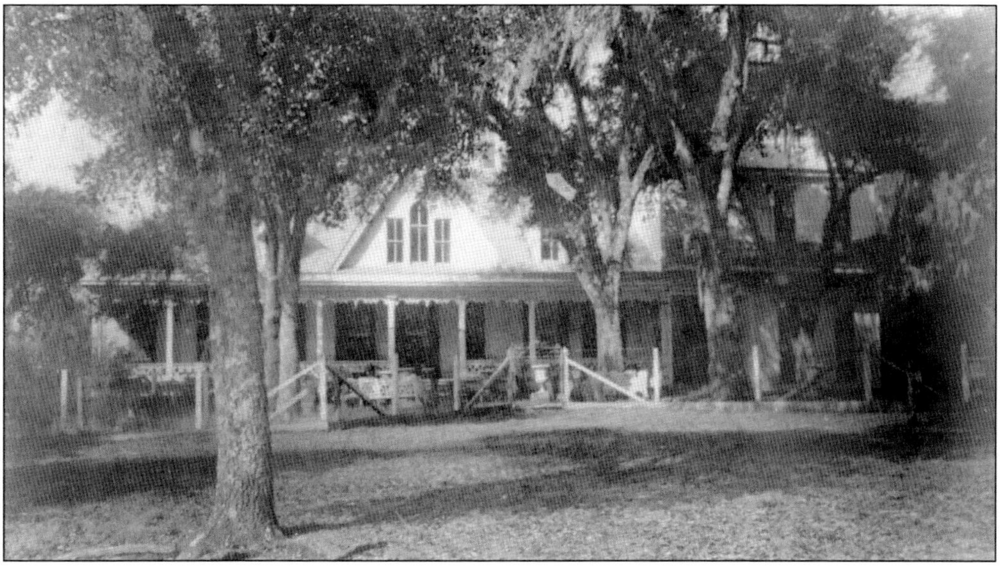

Butler Greenwood Plantation, shown with Victorian trim added in the 1850s and since removed, was the property of early physician Dr. Samuel Flower beginning in the 1770s. His daughter Harriet and her husband, Judge George Mathews of the first Louisiana Supreme Court, were among the top nine percent of planters in the state in the 1850s, growing indigo, cotton, and cane. The home remains in the original family. (Collection of Anne Butler.)

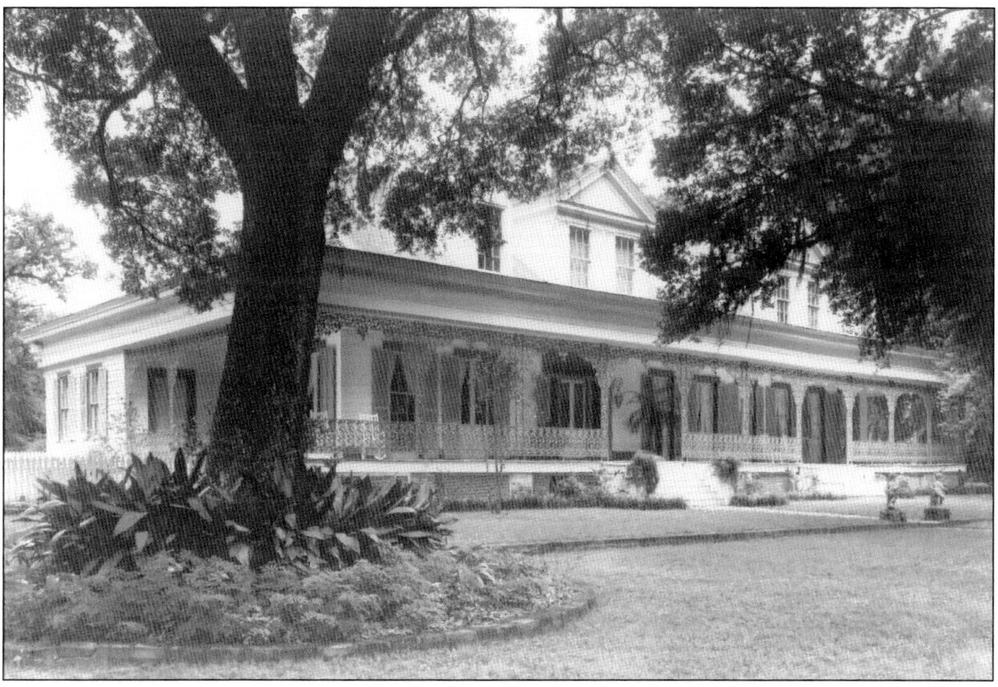

The Myrtles, called one of American's most haunted houses, was established in the 1790s by Judge David Bradford, leader of the Whiskey Rebellion. In the 1850s, owner Ruffin Gray Stirling expanded the house and added elaborate trim. It was Gray's son-in-law, attorney William Drew Winter, who was murdered on the front gallery in 1871 during Reconstruction unrest, fodder for the popular candlelight mystery tours. (WFHS.)

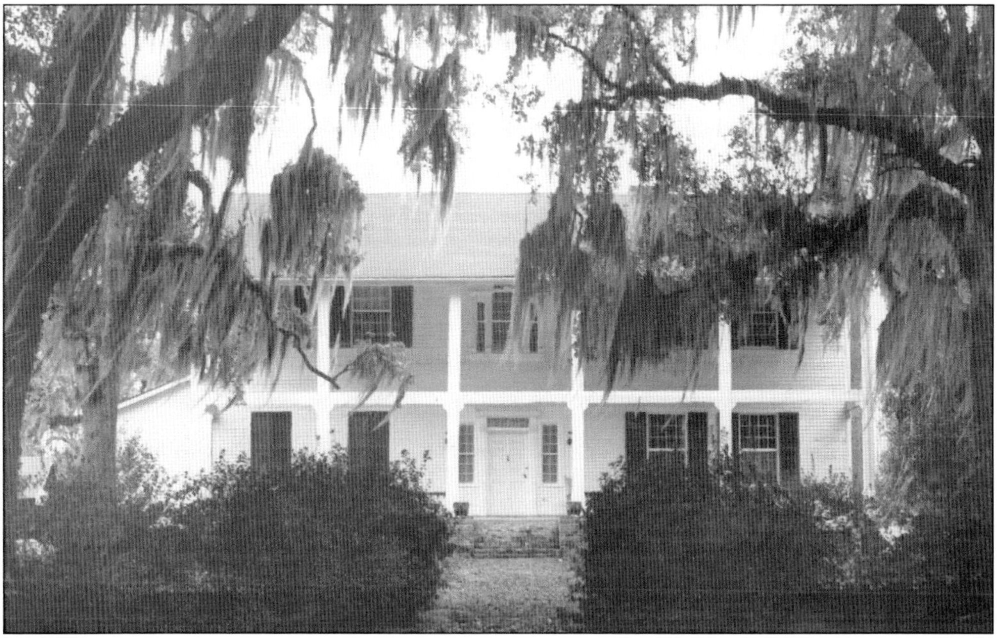

In the 1790s, widowed Olivia Ruffin Barrow traveled from the Carolinas by covered wagon and riverboat, accompanied by grown sons and daughters, to claim a large Spanish land grant along Little Bayou Sara. Her son William, one of the leaders of the West Florida Rebellion, supervised construction of this stately, Federal-style home. Completed in 1805, this residence began the Barrow dynasty that would produce a number of exceptional plantation homes. (WFHS.)

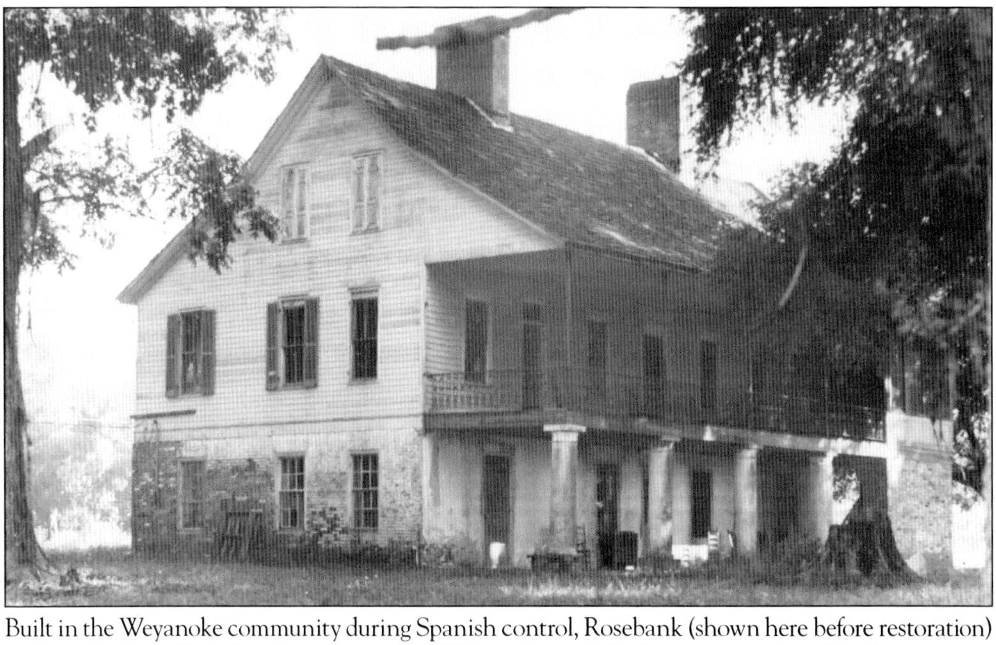

Built in the Weyanoke community during Spanish control, Rosebank (shown here before restoration) and nearby Live Oak date from the early 1800s and are of similar construction. The homes were two stories, with sturdy brick columns across the lower gallery and slender, simple columns above. Both houses had exterior stairs, giving rise to conjecture that the Spanish authorities taxed interior ones, although there is little compelling evidence for this theory. (WFHS.)

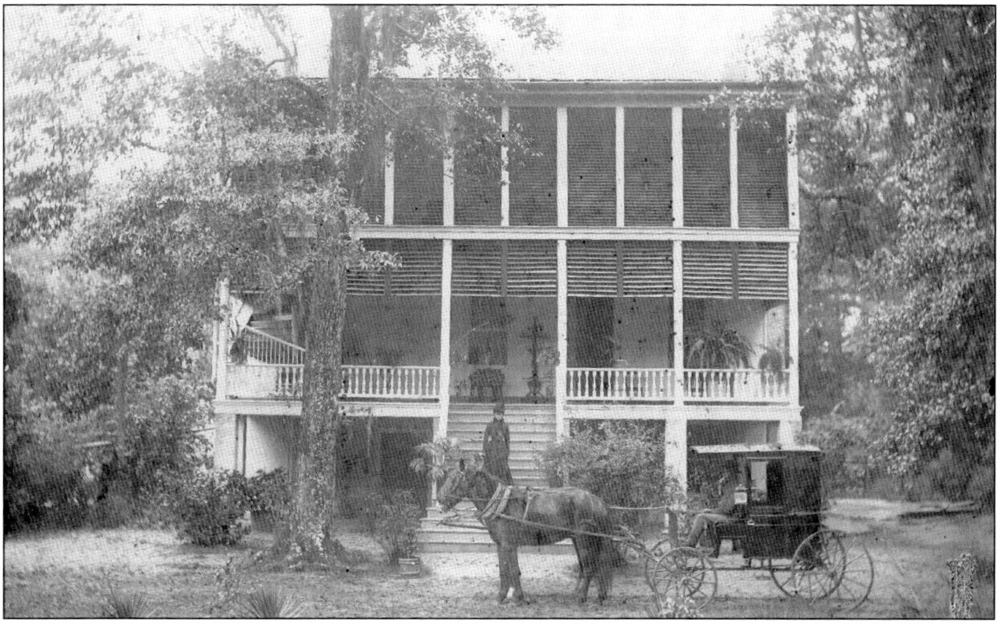

In 1887, the Oakley Plantation coachman has brought the covered buggy around to transport one of the Matthews women, shown descending the central stair from the second-floor living quarters. Perhaps she intended to visit friends or relatives, or to ride into St. Francisville or Bayou Sara for some marketing. The respite from the isolation of these early plantations was surely welcome. (Collection of Louisiana Office of State Parks.)

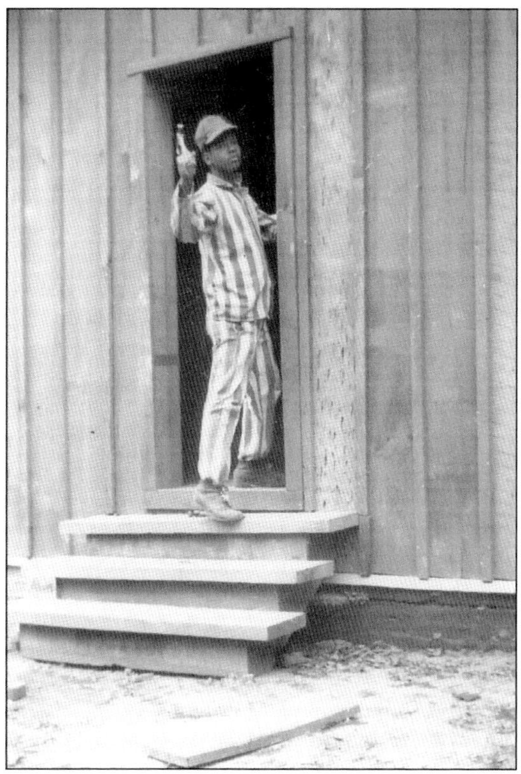

Oakley in 1947 was in disrepair, without running water or electricity, when the state acquired the house and 100 acres for $10,000. The unmarried grandchildren of Eliza Pirrie through her daughter Isabelle did the best they could, but when the last heirs, Ida and Lucy Matthews, died, massive restoration work was required. Some labor was provided by prison inmates like "Little Red," pictured here. (Collection of Louisiana Office of State Parks.)

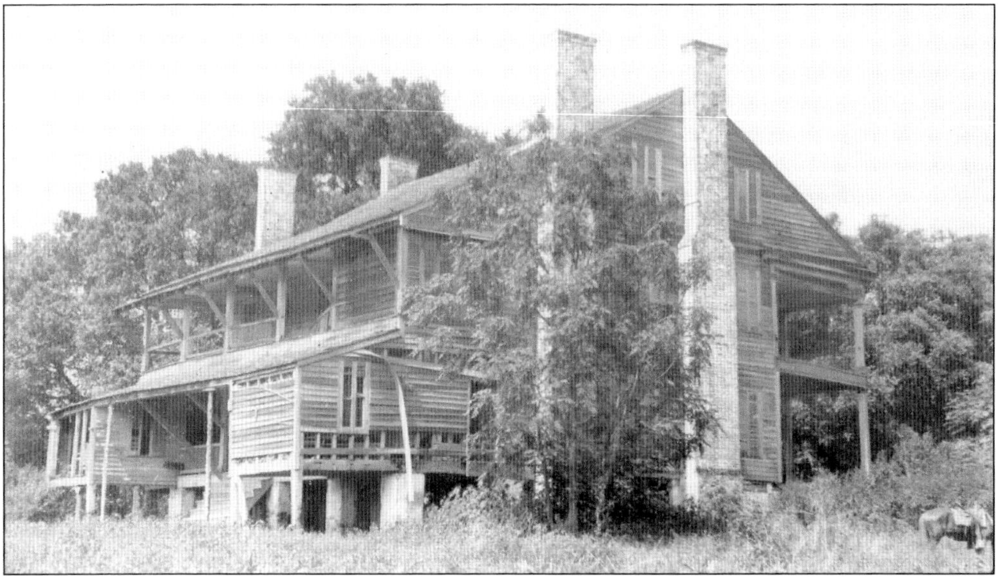

When he retired from the British navy in 1802, Robert Percy acquired Beech Woods, a 2,200-acre plantation on Big Bayou Sara. The house is shown here from the rear. John James Audubon's wife spent the years 1823 through 1826 in residence to tutor the Percy girls and children of neighboring plantations, with the artist a frequent visitor who found great inspiration in the surrounding woodlands rich with birdlife. (Collection of Louisiana Office of State Parks.)

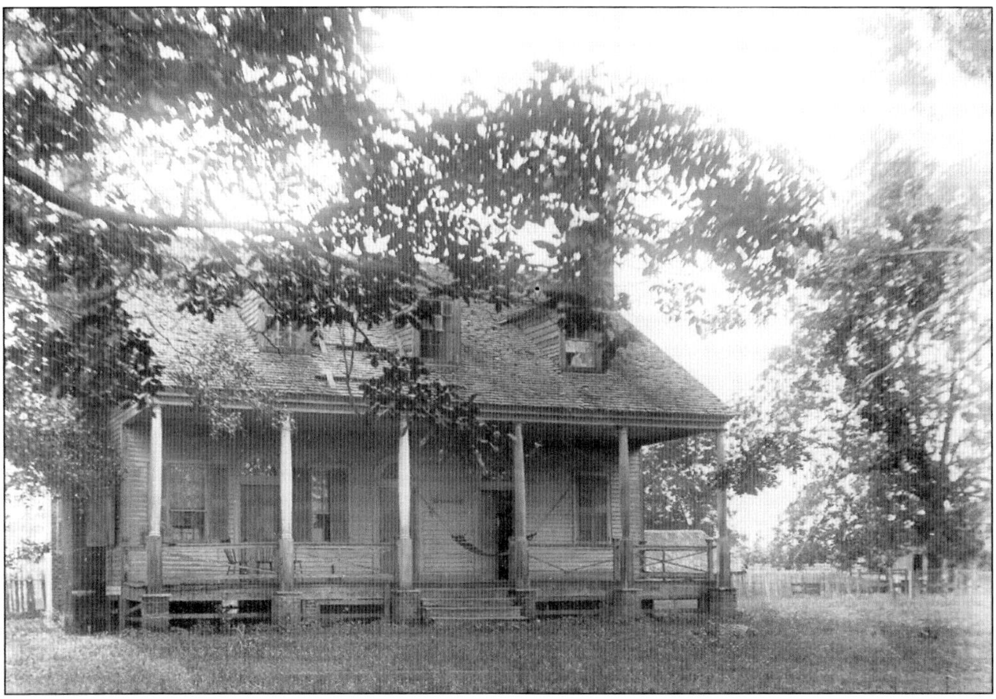

William Garrett Johnson of Beech Grove Plantation employed Lucy Audubon from 1827 to 1830 as his children's tutor, and this is where she remained while the artist worked on publication of his bird prints in England. The house was destroyed by fire. (Collection of Louisiana Office of State Parks.)

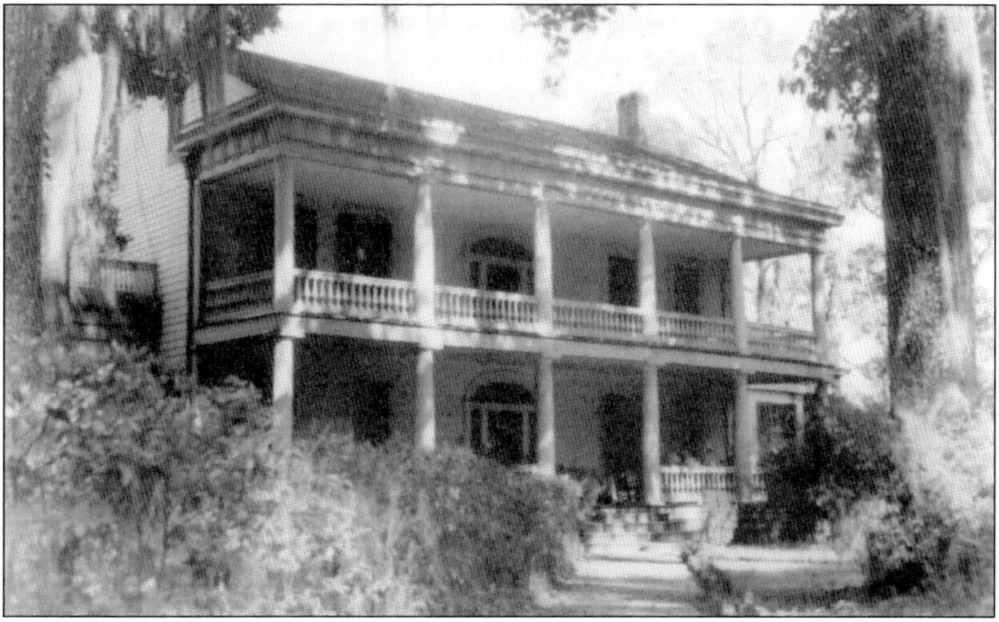

Wealthy planter Daniel Turnbull built stately Rosedown in the 1830s. His wife, Martha, was a dedicated horticulturist who surrounded the double-galleried house with the 27 acres of gardens that still enfold it. In 1934, Civil War novelist Stark Young referred to Rosedown thusly: "Of all the houses in the world it seemed to be the beloved of its own trees and gardens." (Collection of Louisiana Office of State Parks.)

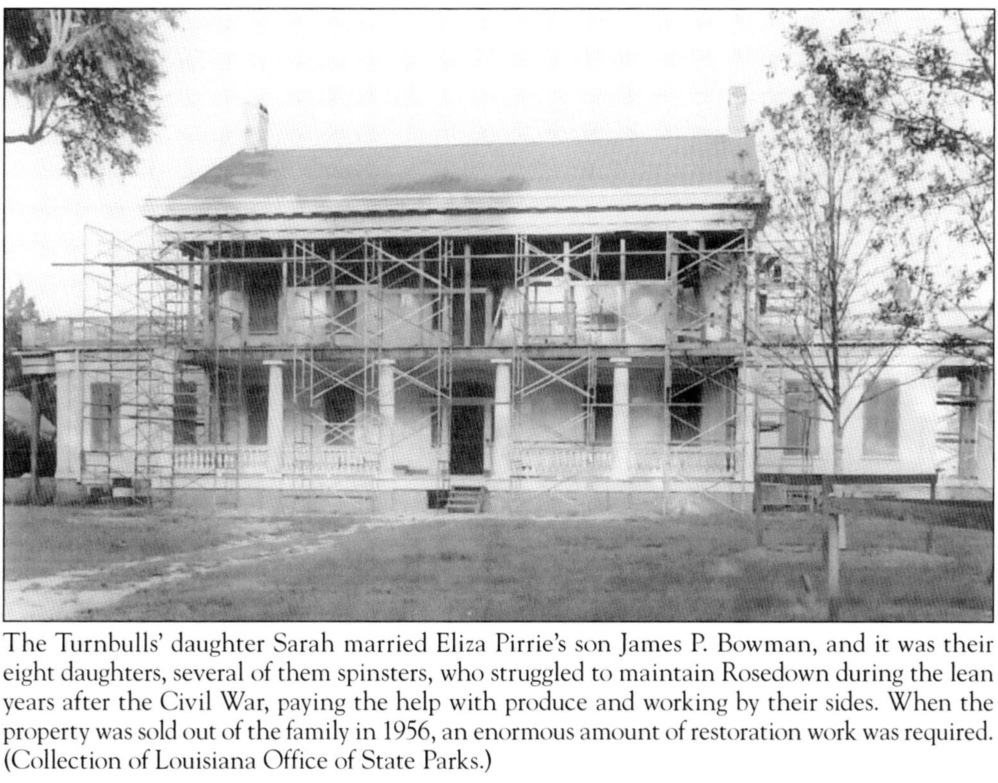

The Turnbulls' daughter Sarah married Eliza Pirrie's son James P. Bowman, and it was their eight daughters, several of them spinsters, who struggled to maintain Rosedown during the lean years after the Civil War, paying the help with produce and working by their sides. When the property was sold out of the family in 1956, an enormous amount of restoration work was required. (Collection of Louisiana Office of State Parks.)

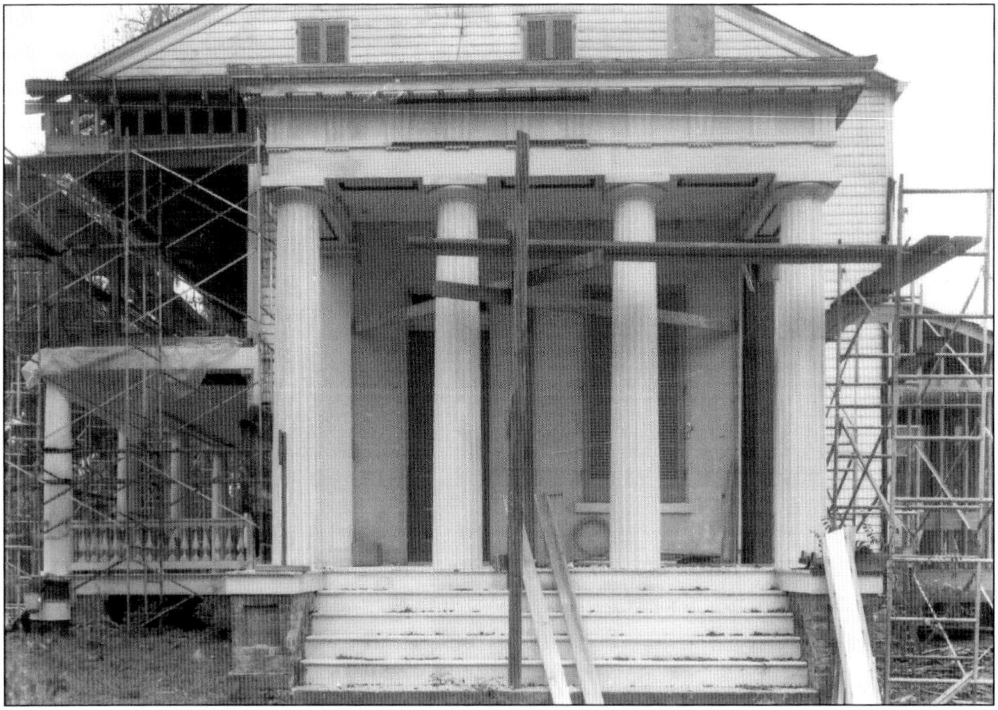

In 1956, oil heiress Catherine Fondren Underwood purchased Rosedown. Through the creeping undergrowth and peeling plaster, her keen eye recognized the lush beauty of the formal gardens and the haunting dignity of the house. An extensive 10-year restoration was meticulously carried out. Here, work commences on the library wing, added in the 1840s, its black mourning stripes memorializing William Turnbull, who drowned in 1856. (Collection of Louisiana Office of State Parks.)

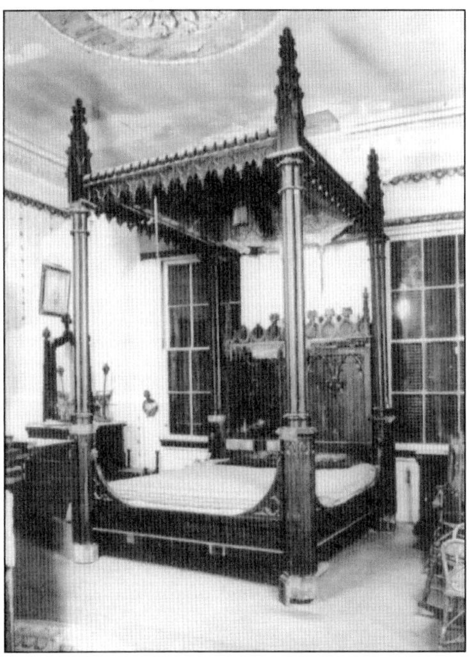

When Henry Clay ran for president in 1844, friends had a magnificent Gothic bedroom suite made in Philadelphia for his use in the White House. After he lost, Daniel Turnbull bought it. The suite was so large, Turnbull had to construct a wing on the north end of the house to accommodate it. He balanced this with a library wing to the south. (Collection of Louisiana Office of State Parks.)

Considered one of the finest examples of Greek Revival architecture in the South, Greenwood Plantation was built in 1830 by William Ruffin Barrow and surrounded by 12,000 acres. His 750 slaves planted crops of cotton and then sugarcane ground in his own sugar mill. Designed by prominent architect James Coulter, the house had a 70-foot center hall, 14-foot ceilings, and a belvedere from which the Mississippi River was visible. (WFHS.)

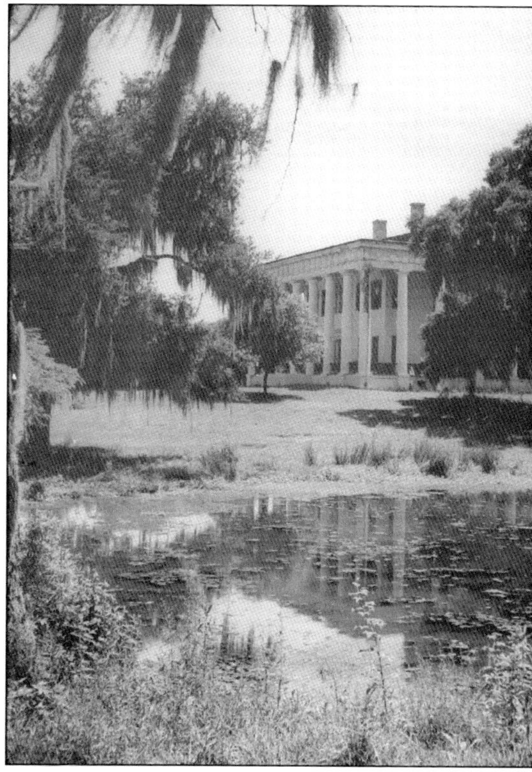

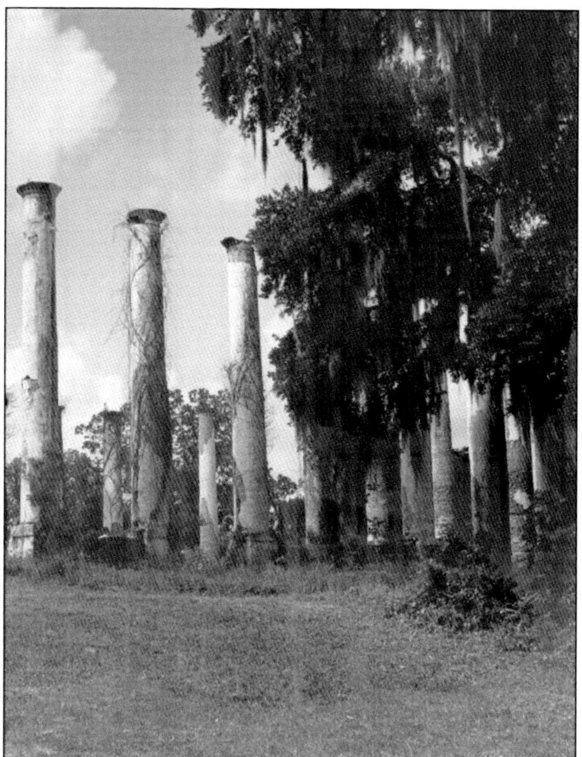

Greenwood Plantation was surrounded by 28 Doric columns that rose more than 30 feet from a porch five feet above ground. In a fate all too common for historic structures, Greenwood was struck by lightning in August 1960 and burned to the ground, leaving only the columns and chimneys. Just enough of the structure remained to touch the hearts of new owners, the Barnes family. It has been rebuilt exactly as it was. (WFHS.)

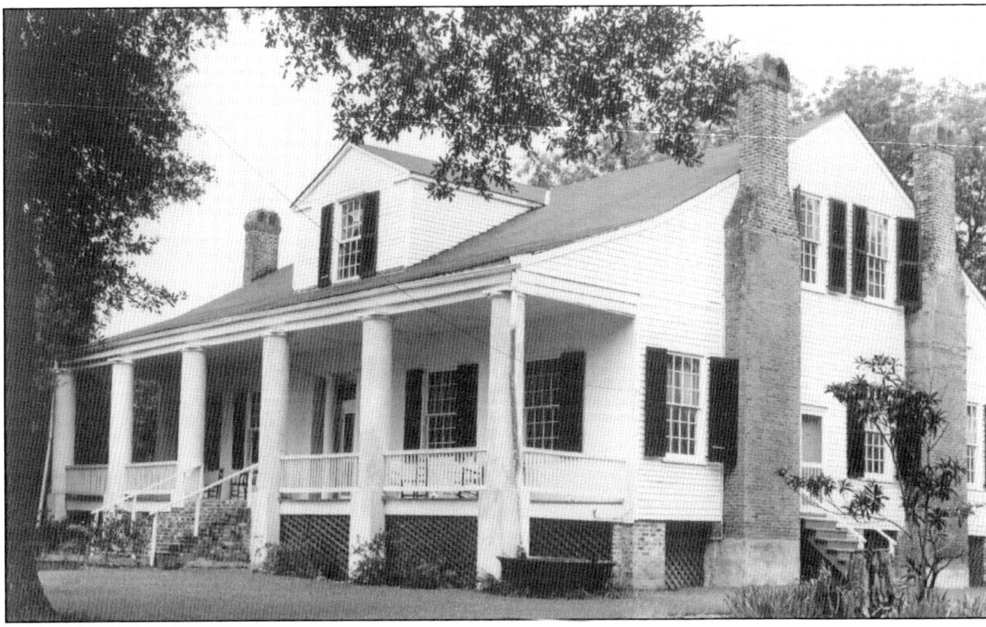

Constructed in the 1830s for Lewis Stirling, the two-and-a-half-story Greek Revival Wakefield had its roof raised and second story removed as his heirs effected a strange property division. Lewis's father, Alexander Stirling, called "an old Scotchman, plain and blunt . . . but possessed of an immense fortune," arrived in America in the late 1770s and acquired 10 square miles of property; his wife was the sister of Lucretia Pirrie of Oakley. (WFHS.)

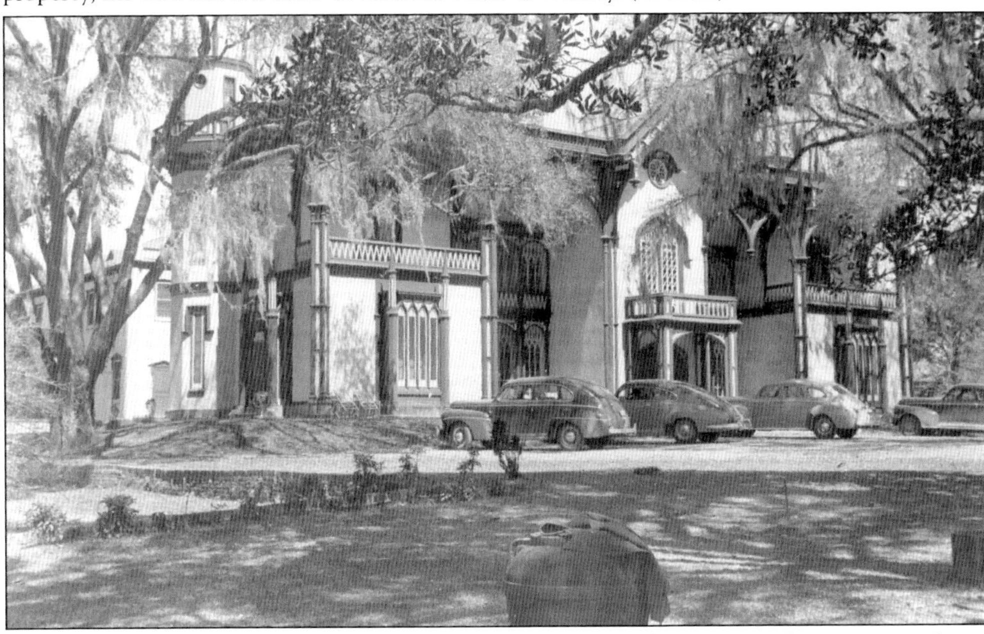

Constructed in 1848 to incorporate a simpler home that was on the property when it was purchased in 1820 by Bartholomew Barrow, Afton Villa was an extravagant French Gothic Revival–Victorian affair planned to please the Kentucky widow he had just wed. It was named for the fondness of Barrow's daughter Mary for the song "Flow Gently, Sweet Afton"; Mary would become the wife of Eliza Pirrie's son Robert H. Barrow Jr. (WFHS.)

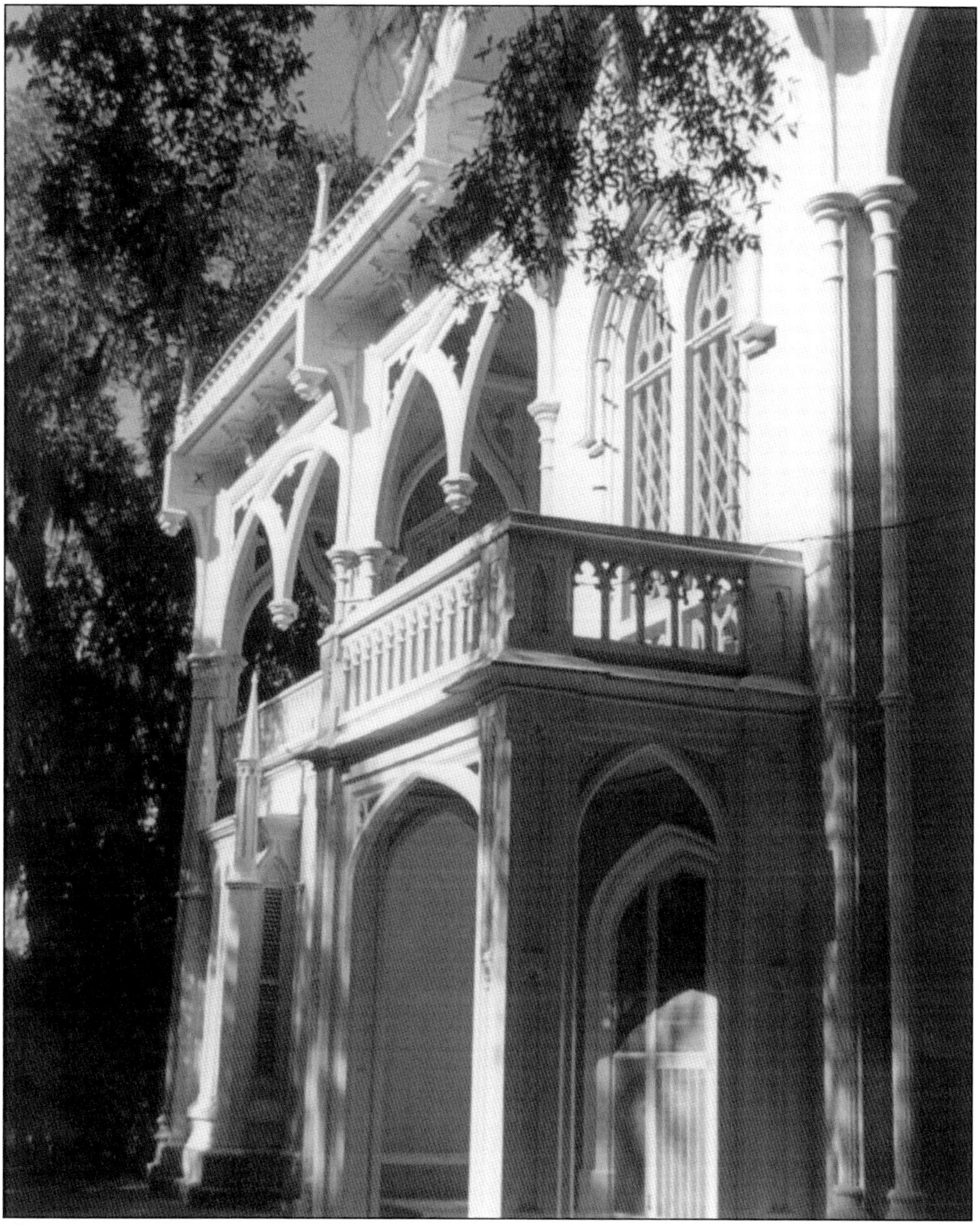

Like a European castle, the 1848 Afton Villa was resplendent with intricate woodcarvings, stained glass, Dresden china doorknobs, elaborate marble and plasterwork, towers, turrets, galleries, balconies, ballrooms, and cathedral windows. The house was approached by a splendid winding oak alley and surrounded by lush landscaping and formal parterre gardens. Afton Villa's Bartholomew Barrow was the uncle of Martha Barrow Turnbull of Rosedown Plantation, and he followed her 1830s example, hiring European landscape artists to sculpt the grounds into a series of seven terraces sweeping from the house and cemetery. After the house burned in 1963, Genevieve and Morrell Trimble meticulously restored the grounds and transformed the ruins into a glorious garden of thousands of flowering bulbs and imported marble statuary, a veritable celebration of the hardiness of early plantings and the dedication of contemporary garden preservationists. (WFHS.)

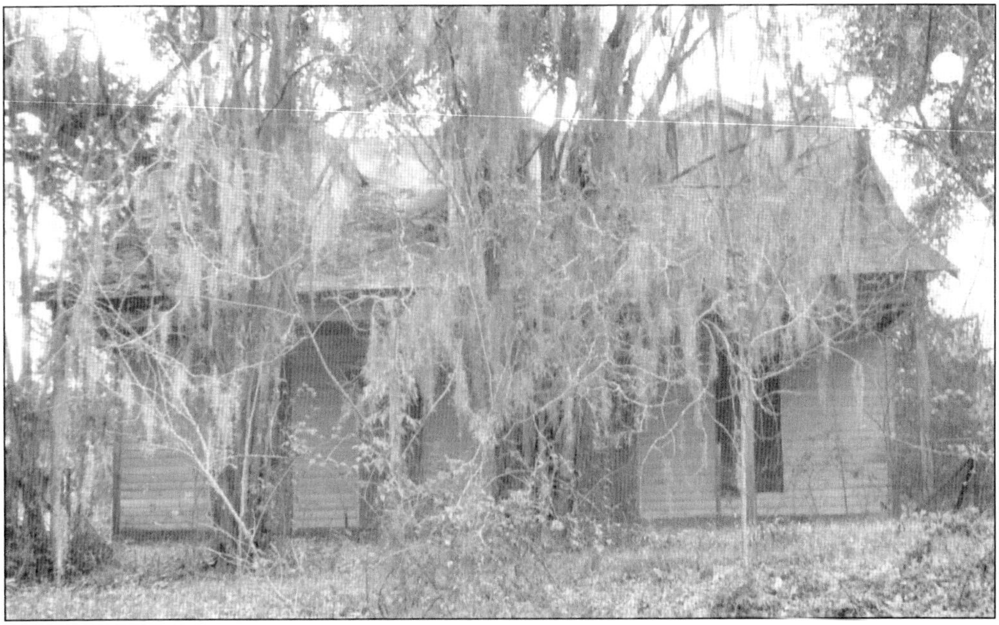

Educated at Afton Villa Finishing School, orphaned Rose Ker was raised by spinster cousins at Ouida and Ellerslie Plantations. On April 20, 1881, Rose left Ouida for her marriage at Grace Church to Murphy J. Foster, a future Louisiana governor, and she would blessedly not live to see the charming little Ouida house abandoned to hay storage, as pictured here. It has since been beautifully restored. (WFHS.)

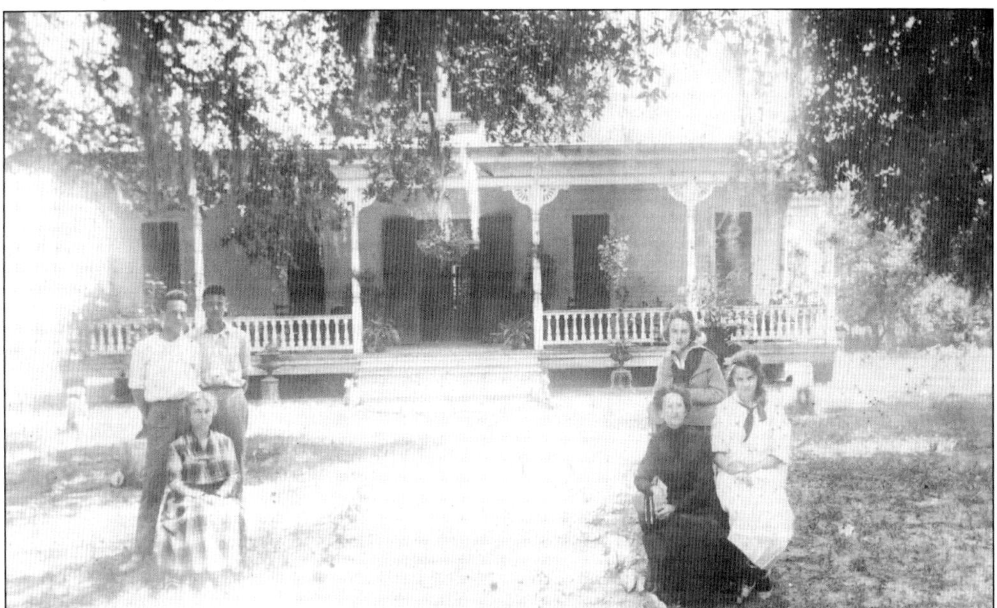

William J. Fort arrived in West Feliciana around 1800 to establish Catalpa Plantation, noted for cotton and cane crops and also for hospitality; "there is always such a good time to be had at the Forts," the saying went. When the main house burned in 1885, it was replaced by this pleasant raised Victorian cottage, pictured around 1915 with Fort family and staff. (Collection of Mary Thompson.)

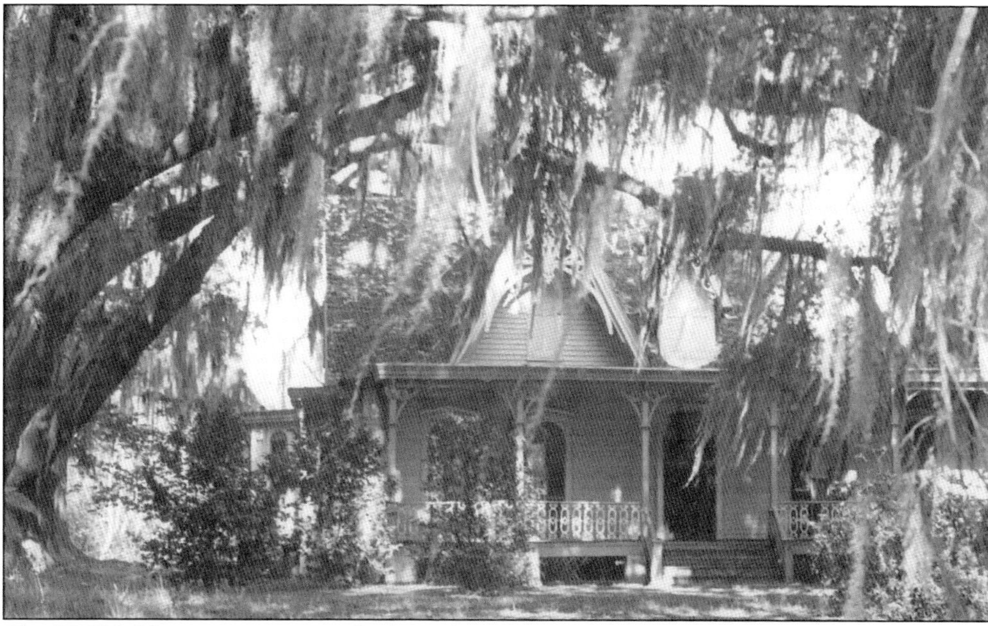

The Wolf-Schlesinger House was built in the 1880s by prosperous merchant and cotton broker Morris Wolf right across the street from his commercial interest, M&E Wolf's General Store and Cotton Gin (formerly Freyhan & Co.). His brother Emmanuel built a similar house next door, but, sadly, this has been demolished. The structure shown here survives as the St. Francisville Inn, a bed-and-breakfast. (WFHS.)

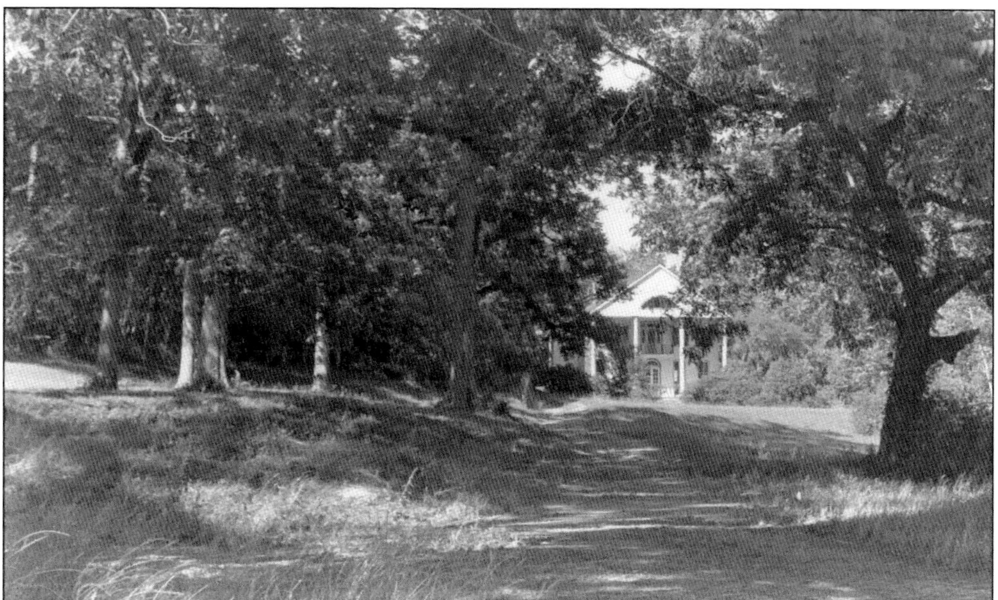

Erected in the 1890s to replace an earlier home that burned down, Como is the only plantation house in West Feliciana located directly on the Mississippi River, whose floodwaters have threatened it for years. Set in splendid isolation in the rugged Tunica Hills, Como's clipped lawns and columned majesty thrill passing steamboat passengers and break the monotony of long stretches of barren riverbanks. (WFHS.)

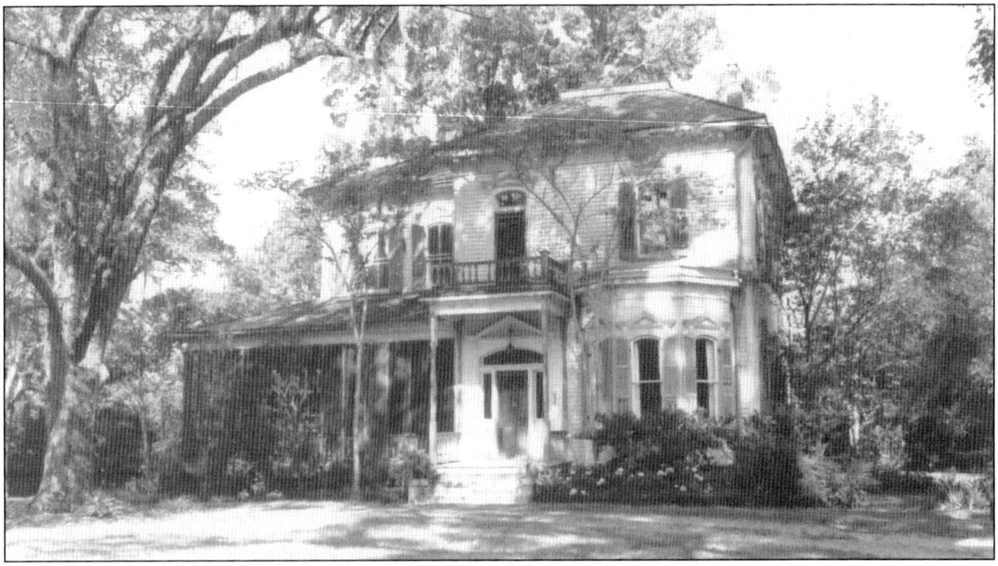

An 1890s structure built in Laurel Hill in the late Victorian period, but with Classical lines reminiscent of an earlier simplicity, the Rosemound house was surrounded by the rolling hills and fertile fields of a plantation begun a century before by the earliest arrival of the Jackson family. It is still occupied by direct descendants. The home's builder, V.M. Jackson, switched from cotton to cattle and hogs in the early 1900s. (WFHS.)

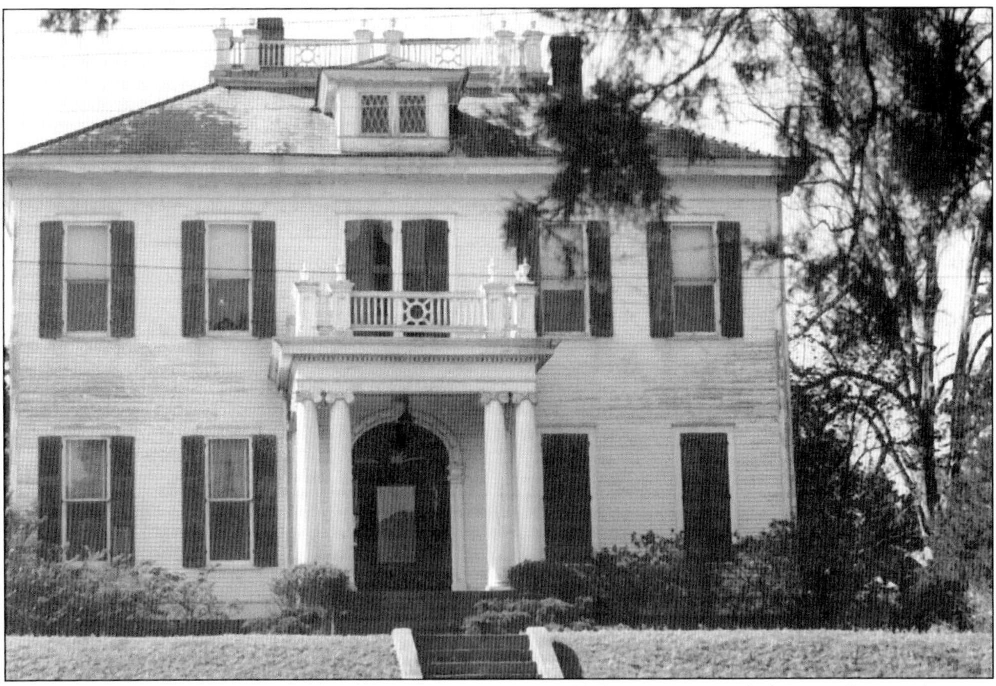

When Judge Samuel McCutcheon Lawrason of Clover Hill Plantation needed a townhouse closer to court duties in St. Francisville, this stately Neoclassical structure was built for $5,000, the funding coming from the family of his wife, Harriet Mathews. That family owned sugarcane operations in south Louisiana. The widow's walk overlooks Royal Street and the river. A carriage house was located down the hill, and there were beautiful gardens in the ravine beside it. (WFHS.)

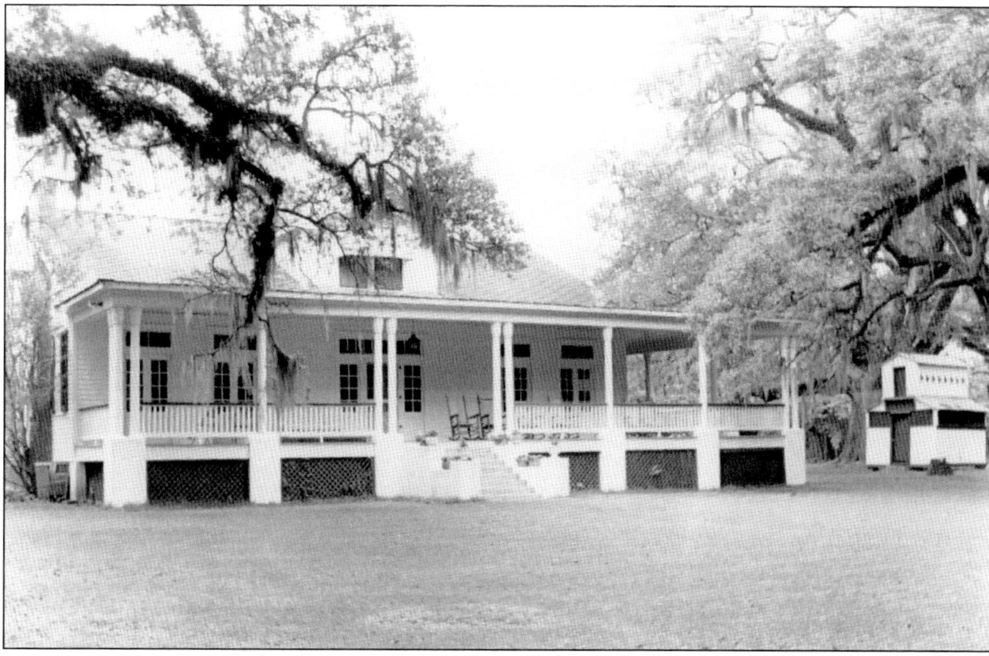

Built in 1918 with simple railings on the wraparound gallery, the raised cottage called Ambrosia was the third house on this site. It retains original outbuildings, like the dovecote (right), where squab were raised as delicacies for 19th-century dinner tables. In the early 1900s, Sarah Barrow was mistress of Ambrosia and Independence Plantations. (WFHS.)

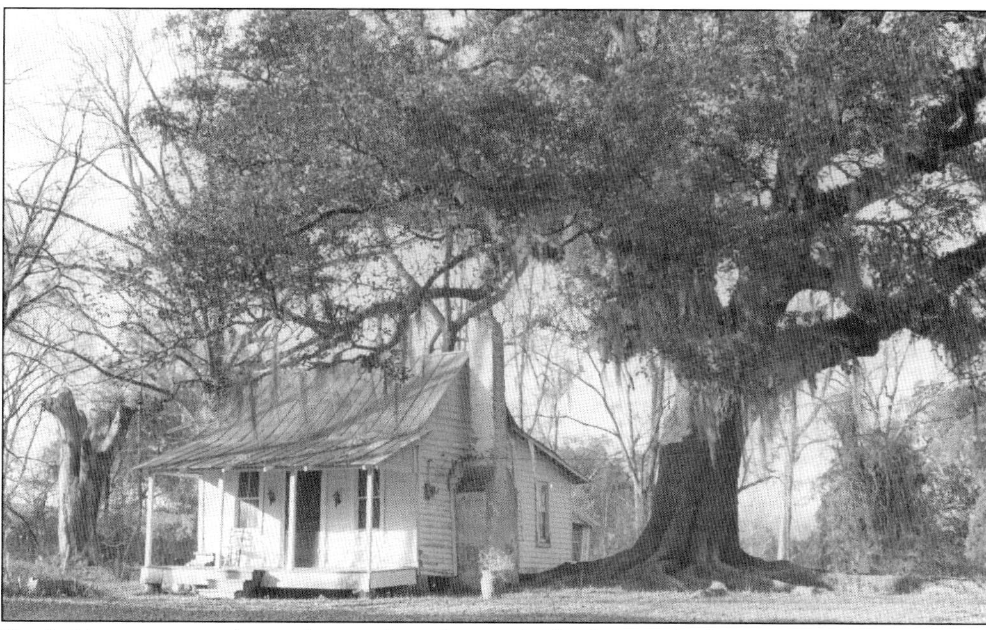

Shaded by a towering live oak tree, this whitewashed cabin on Ambrosia property is typical of the rustic abodes of early plantation workers—simple frame dwellings with covered porches and fireplaces. Some structures were double-pen and could house two separate families. Its proximity to the main house indicates that this was the home of house servants, while field hands would have had cabins closer to the farm fields. (WFHS.)

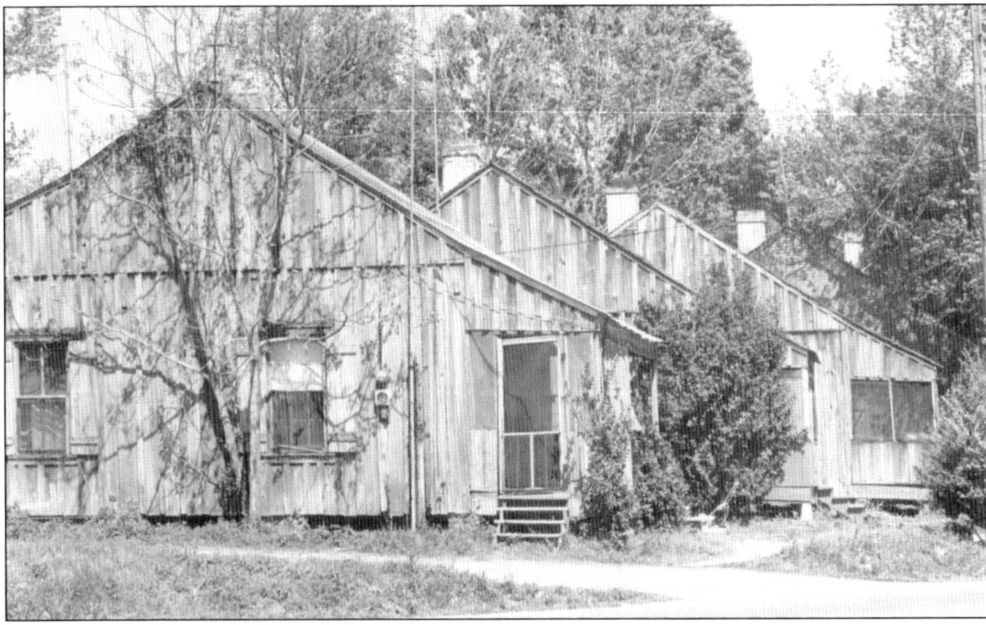

Quarters-type housing in the essentially black corner of St. Francisville called Red Horse, these cabins were located on Commerce Street near the two-story structure that for years housed the Boll Weevil Café. In the 1920s, it was the Faithful Workers Lodge, but it had originally been located in Bayou Sara and was dismantled and moved up the hill to a location safe from flooding. (Collection of Grady Smart.)

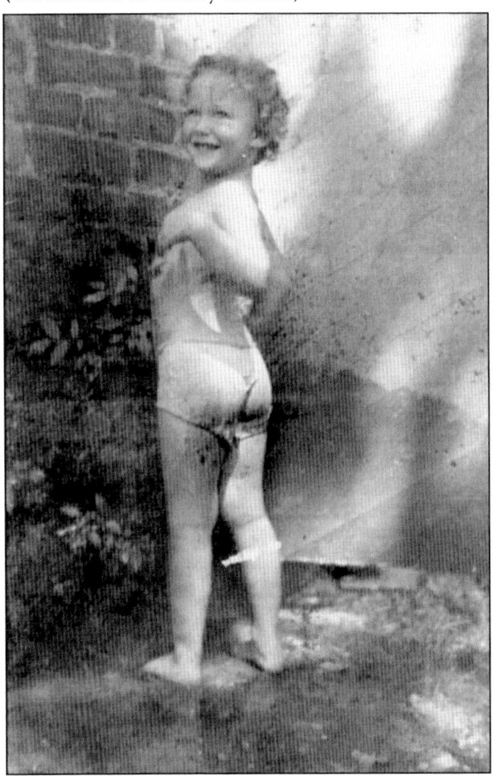

Every old house, both large and small, had its outdoor cistern designed to catch and hold rainwater from the roof. These were large barrels of cypress perched high atop a rounded brick base. Every country child knew that the drip from the cistern was the prime place to cool off on hot summer days. (Collection of Anne Butler.)

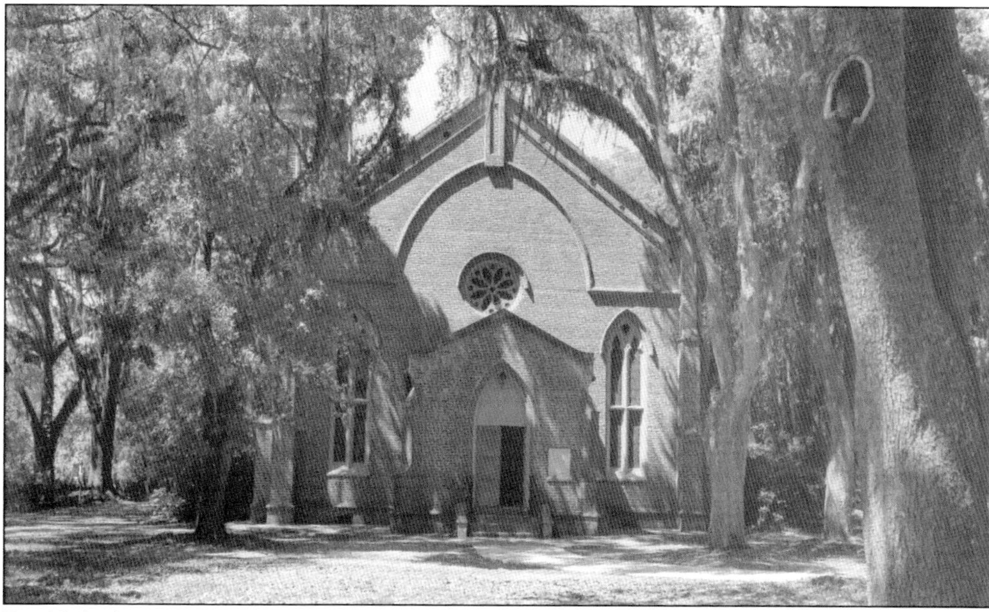

Established in 1827 as the state's second-oldest Episcopal congregation, Grace Church in 1838 recorded 3 marriages, 14 funerals, 21 white baptisms, and 56 black ones. Since 1858, the congregation has worshipped in this picturesque English Gothic–style structure surrounded by moss-draped live oaks, and its peaceful cemetery is filled with fine 19th-century monuments as well as the grave of Union commander John E. Hart, interred during an 1863 ceasefire. (WFHS.)

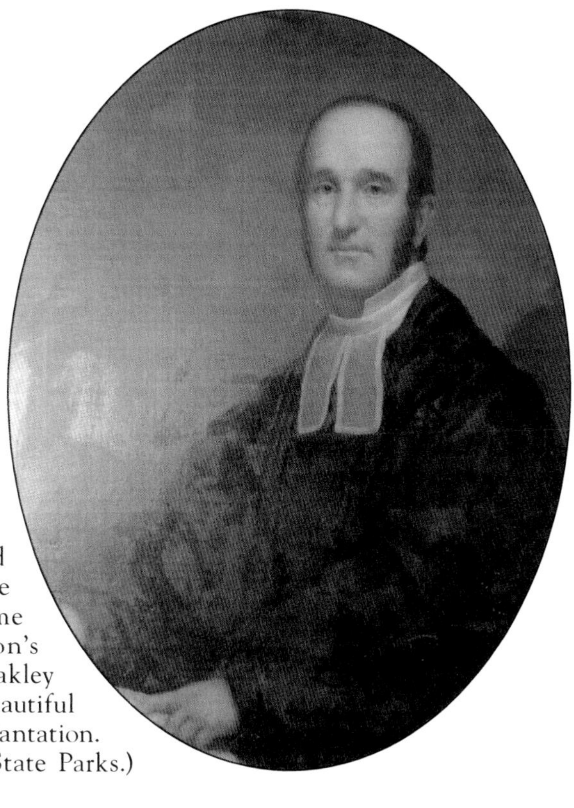

Rev. William R. Bowman was called to serve as the first rector of Grace Episcopal Church. He would become the second husband of Audubon's pupil, the widowed Eliza Pirrie of Oakley Plantation, and their son married beautiful belle Sarah Turnbull of Rosedown Plantation. (Collection of Louisiana Office of State Parks.)

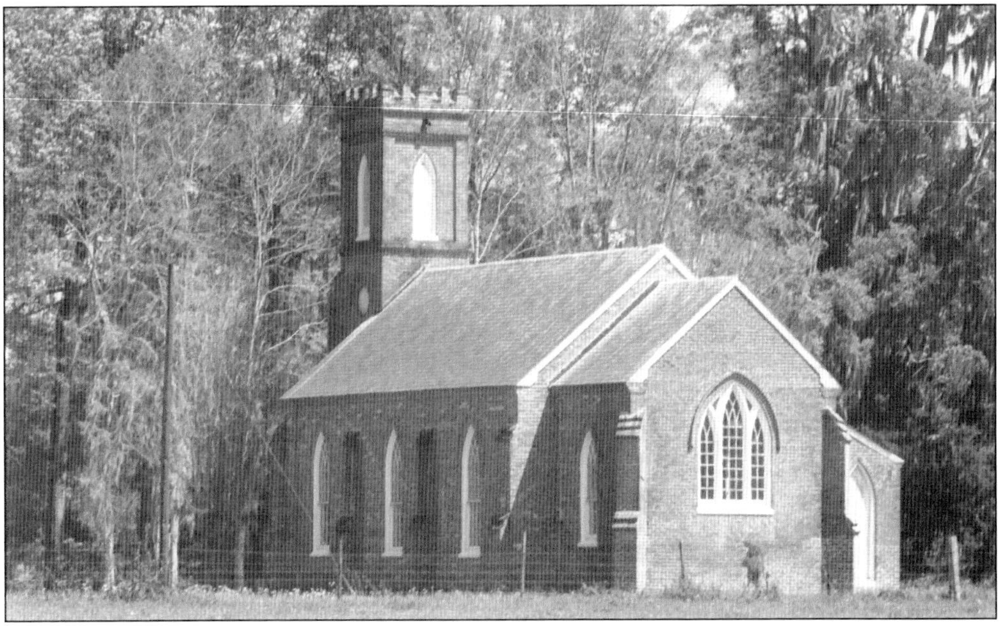

Gothic Revival St. Mary's Episcopal Church was built of brick in 1857 on five acres of land donated by Sarah Mulford of Retreat Plantation. It served plantation families of the Weyanoke community until it was deconsecrated in 1947. Now empty but still hauntingly beautiful, the structure is used for occasional weddings and an annual service for the congregation of Grace Episcopal Church. (WFHS.)

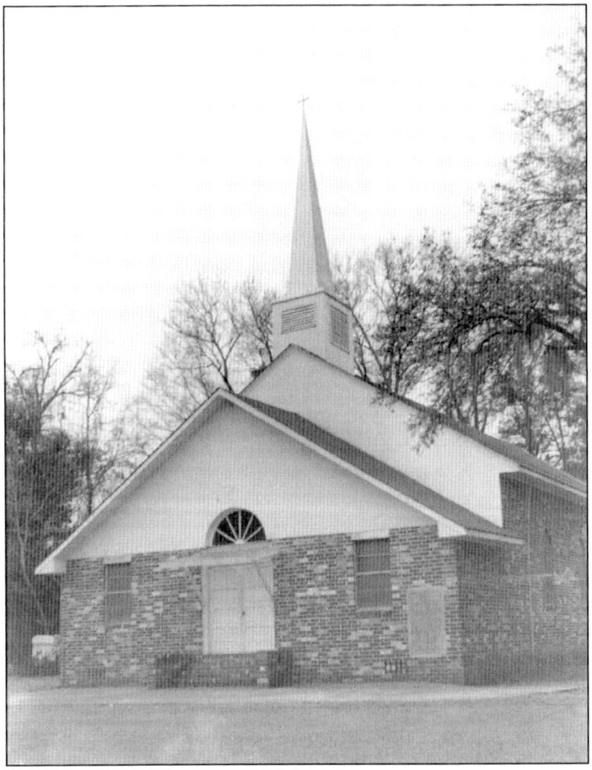

The oldest black church in West Feliciana, Afton Villa Baptist Church was founded in 1871, when Susan Barrow donated plantation land for a church and school because of her abiding concern for providing formalized religious instruction and education for area residents of color. The original congregation of several hundred freed slaves had been meeting in a hollow in the woods. The present structure was built in 1890 and bricked later. (Collection of Anne Butler.)

On part of a Spanish land grant sold to the congregation for $1 when the church parish was organized in 1873, St. John's Episcopal Church in Laurel Hill is one of only two parochial country missions in the Louisiana Diocese. Most of the construction costs were borne by a faithful parishioner in memory of his daughter, whose grave in the surrounding cemetery was visible through the window from the family pew. (WFHS.)

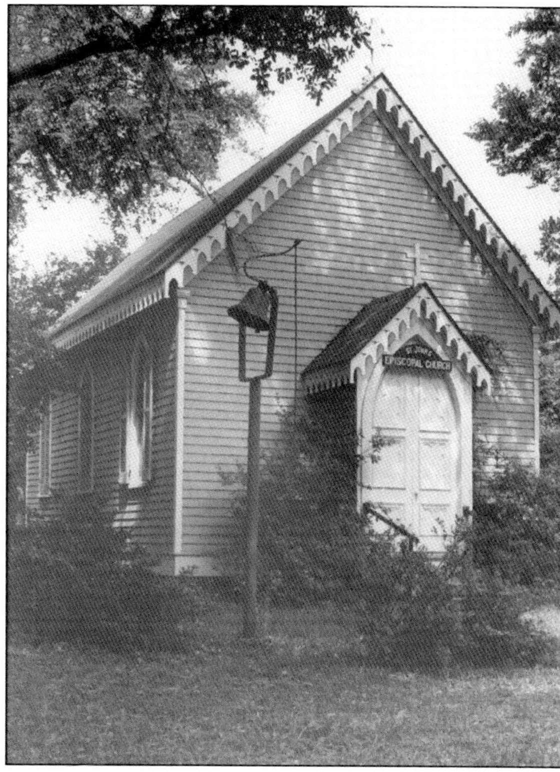

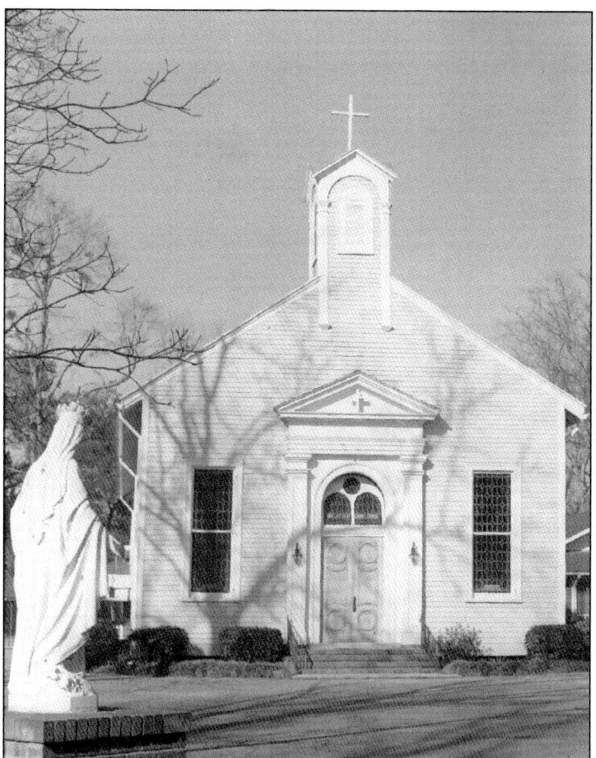

Our Lady of Mount Carmel Catholic Church was completed in 1893 from plans reportedly drawn by Confederate general Pierre Gustave Toutant Beauregard. Magnificent views of Bayou Sara and the Mississippi River are afforded from its site atop the high bluff at St. Francisville. It was to this spot in the late 1700s that Catholic monks from across the river ferried their dead for burial safe from the floodwaters. (WFHS.)

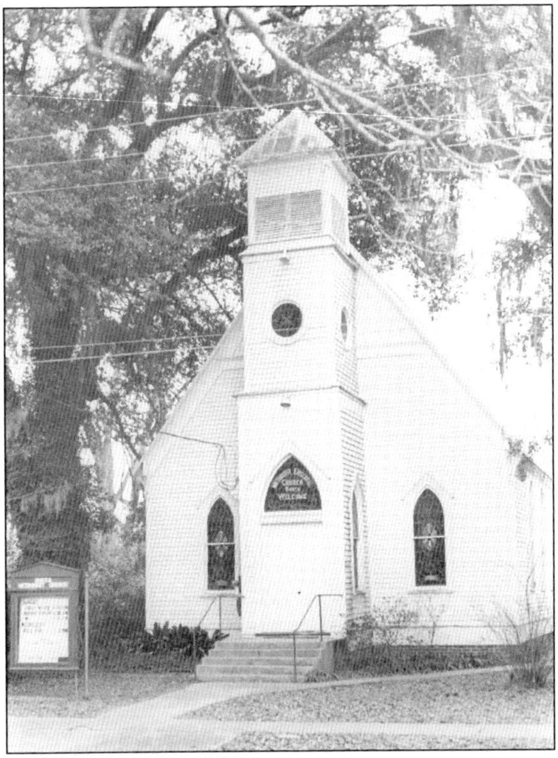

United Methodist Church, built in 1899 on Royal Street, replaced a larger one in flood-prone Bayou Sara dating from 1844. The old church had upstairs galleries wide enough to accommodate dozens of slaves during services as well as townsfolk seeking safe, dry shelter during floods. This frame structure, with splendid simplicity of style, has the original Bayou Sara bell in its central bell tower. (WFHS.)

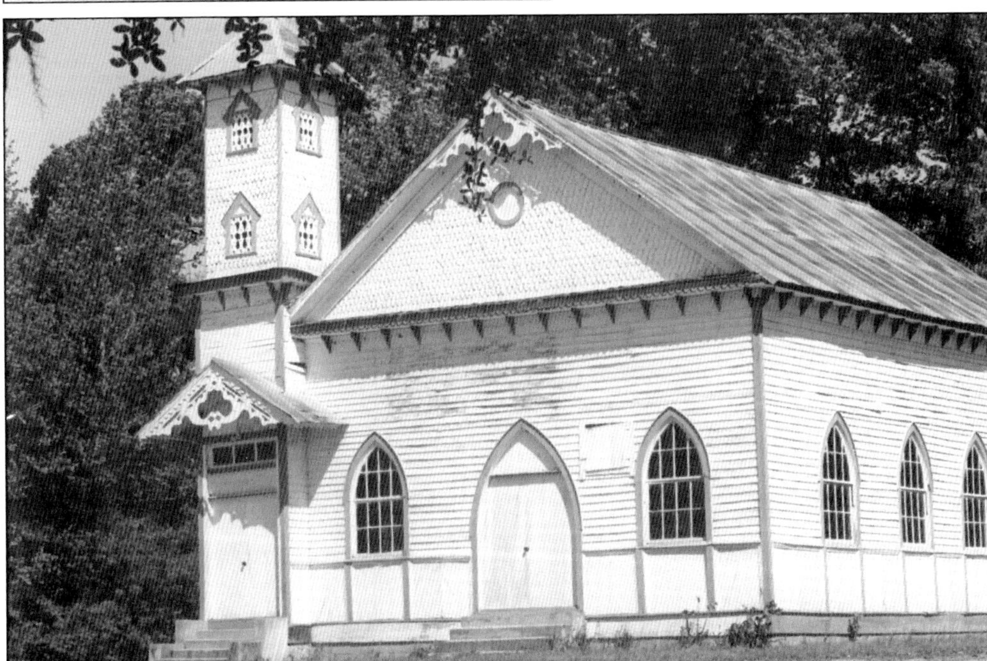

Fish-scaled belfry and Victorian trim have graced Independence Baptist Church since it was built in the early 1900s, though bricks have replaced the wood siding on the lower portion of the structure. Land for church and school for black parishioners was donated by Susan Barrow, mistress of Ambrosia and Independence Plantations. (WFHS.)

Four

COMMERCE

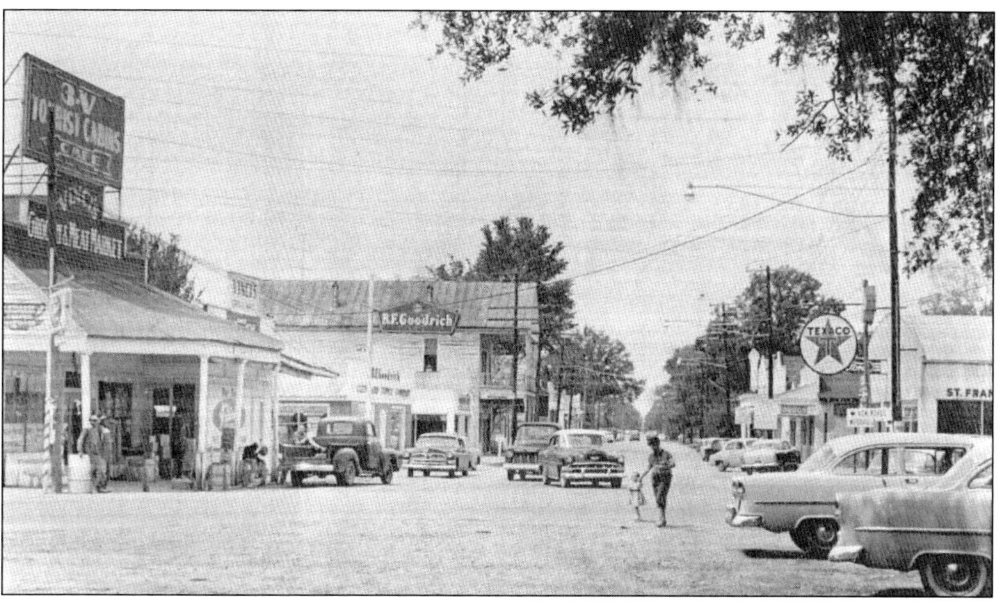

The corner of Ferdinand and Commerce Streets was, and still is, the busiest intersection in St. Francisville. Seen here in the 1950s, it had the only traffic light downtown. It was occupied by the Vinci brothers' businesses, shown on the left: the two-story, double-galleried grocery, a meat market, a gas station, a café, and the 3-V Tourist Courts, throwback 1930s cabins with attached garages. (WFHS.)

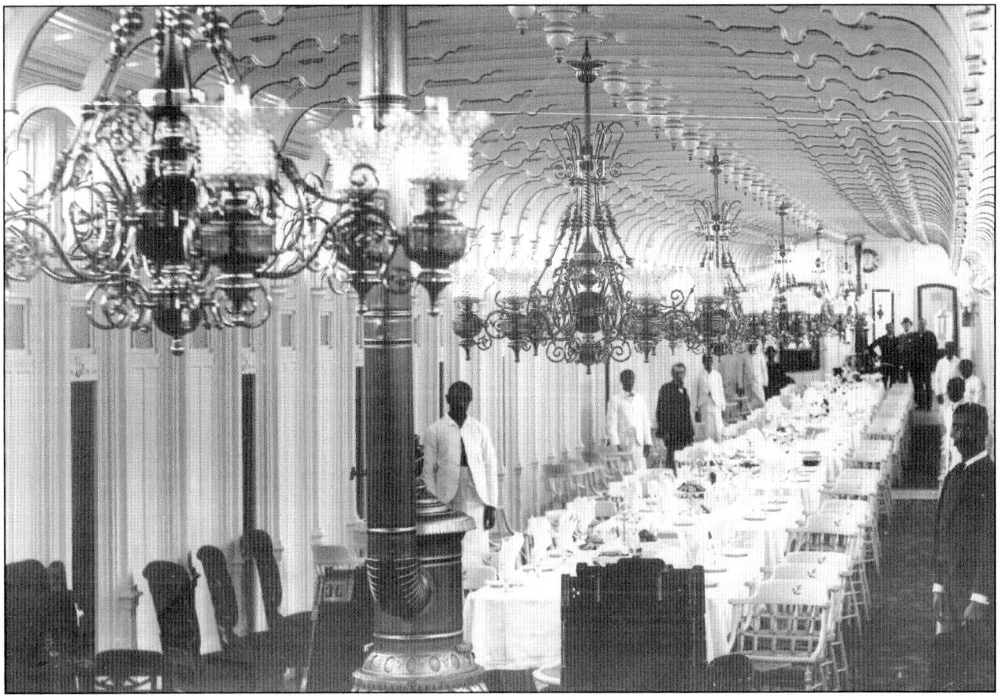

Commerce and travel centered on the Mississippi River in the early years, with dozens of fast packets and steamboats docked at Bayou Sara landing to transport cotton and other goods to market and to carry Feliciana folk to New Orleans and thence around the world. The 19th-century passenger paddle wheelers looked like floating palaces, and their dining salons featured fine multicourse gourmet feasts served by attentive, white-jacketed waiters. (WFHS.)

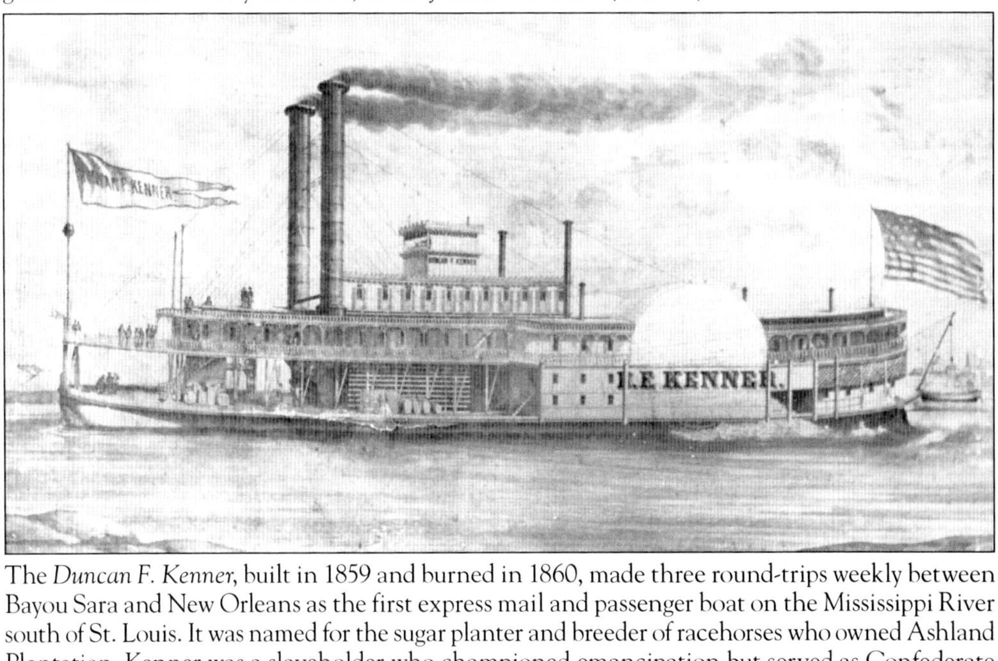

The *Duncan F. Kenner*, built in 1859 and burned in 1860, made three round-trips weekly between Bayou Sara and New Orleans as the first express mail and passenger boat on the Mississippi River south of St. Louis. It was named for the sugar planter and breeder of racehorses who owned Ashland Plantation. Kenner was a slaveholder who championed emancipation but served as Confederate emissary to Europe. (Collection of Anne Butler.)

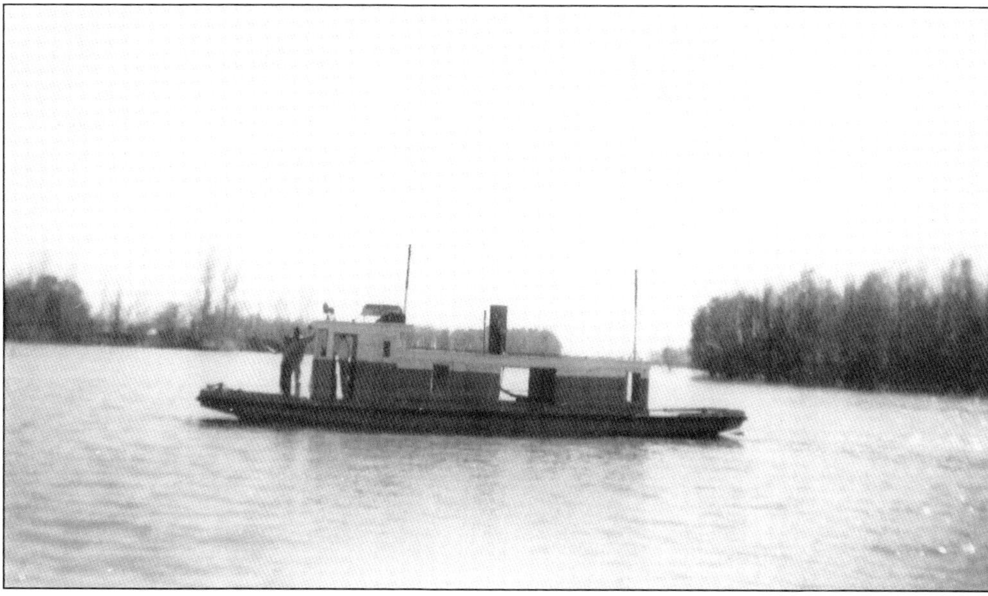

In the early 20th century, transportation across the Mississippi River between St. Francisville and New Roads was via the *Red Cross* ferry. The 30-horsepower cypress boat was operated by several generations of the Bennett family, who were still ferryboat pilots into the early years of the 21st century when the last one, Morris, retired. The *Red Cross* is shown here in the 1930s. (Collection of Bennett family.)

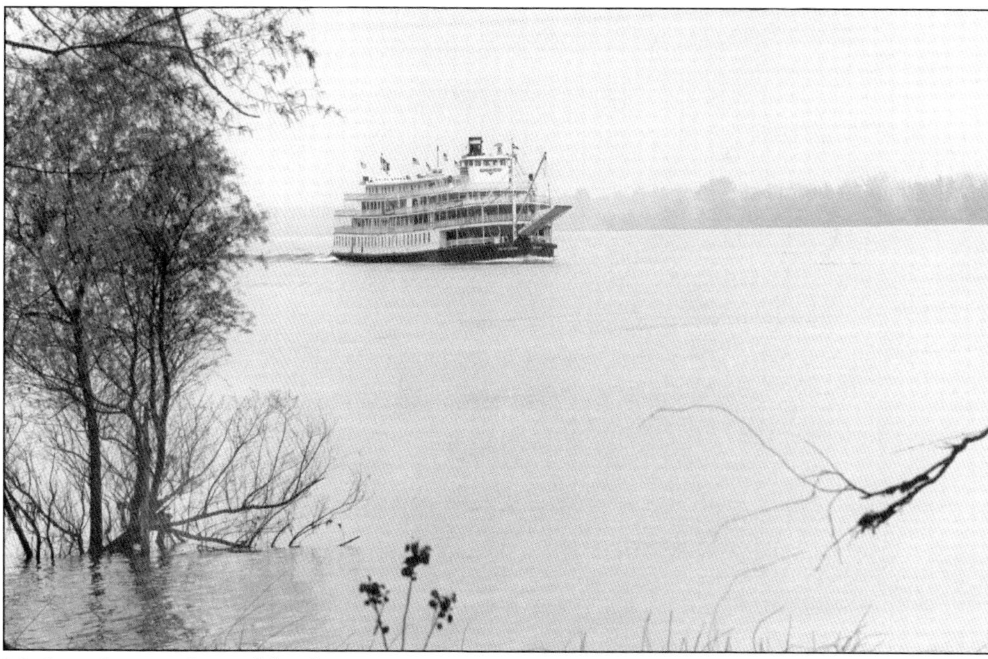

Modern-day riverboats like the steam-powered *American Queen* still stop at Bayou Sara and disembark passengers from around the world to visit St. Francisville, a year-round tourist destination. Tourism is an important driver of the West Feliciana economy today, with plantation homes and gardens to tour, recreational opportunities in the Tunica Hills, bed-and-breakfasts for overnight stays, a historic downtown, and a relaxed lifestyle that appeals to harried urban-dwellers. (WFHS.)

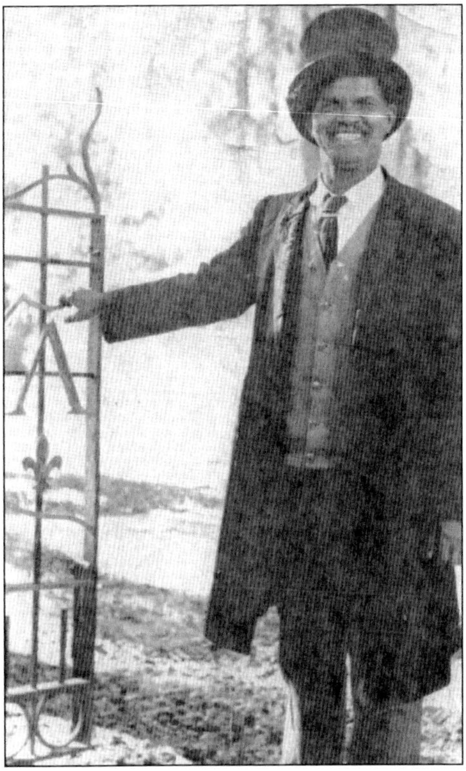

Tourism has changed since the 1940s, when a gatekeeper in top hat and tails stood at the entrance to Afton Villa Plantation and swept a low bow to every passing vehicle. This is John Tilley, whose grandmother Jenny Lind Tilley was brought as a young slave to Afton Villa when her mistress married Bartholomew Barrow. A later gatekeeper, John White, was struck by a car and killed in 1946. (WFHS.)

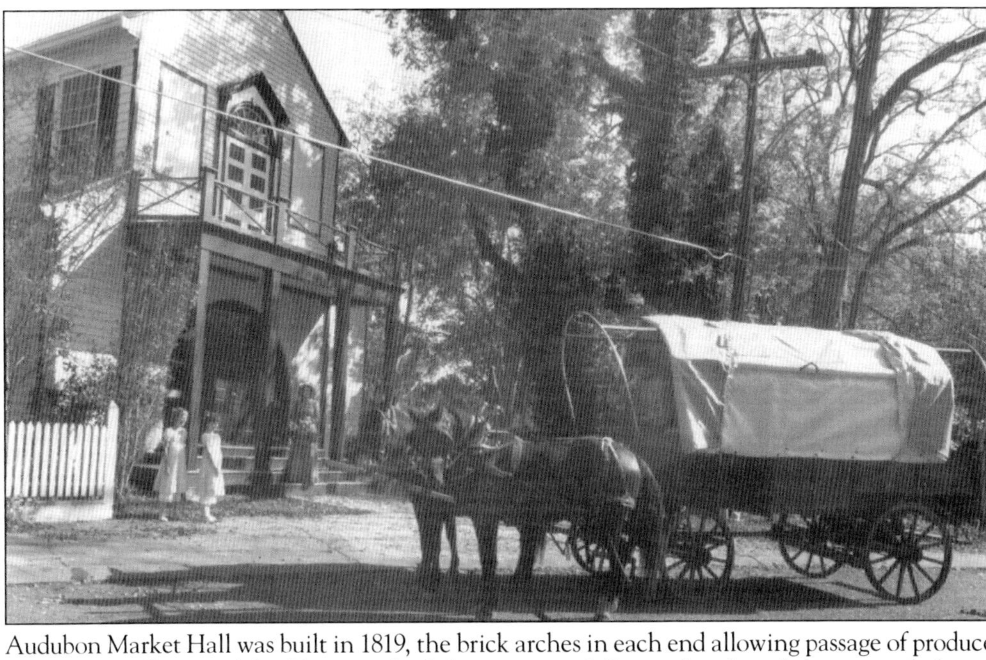

Audubon Market Hall was built in 1819, the brick arches in each end allowing passage of produce wagons to stalls rented for $2 a month. Sales were carefully regulated, and the town clerk was charged with enforcing sanitary regulations, keeping the market "clean and free from all bad and offensive smells." The structure later housed Masons, Confederate veterans, the Drama-Library League, and St. Francisville municipal offices. (WFHS.)

The middle of the 19th century saw an influx of Jewish immigrants escaping persecution in Europe. Julius Freyhan, shown here with his four daughters, arrived in 1851 and built a thriving business empire in Bayou Sara and St. Francisville, making him one of Louisiana's wealthiest men. J. Freyhan & Co. was the principal source of supplies for area plantations, selling an annual $1 million in goods and handling 14,000 bales of cotton. (WFHS.)

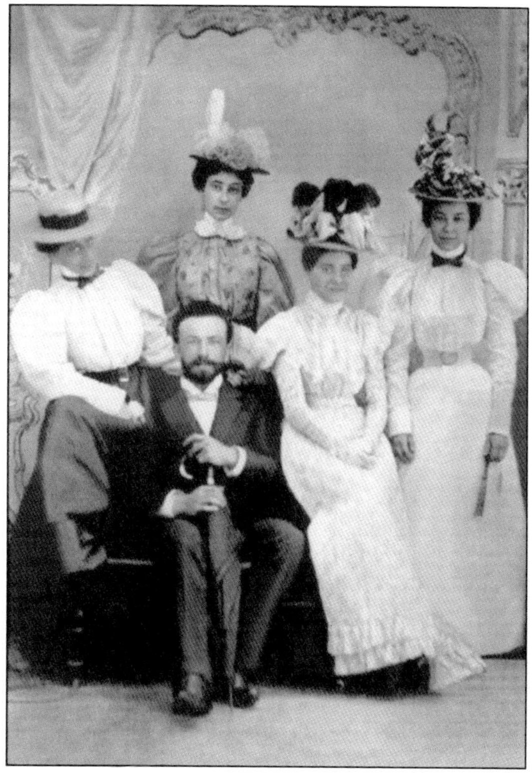

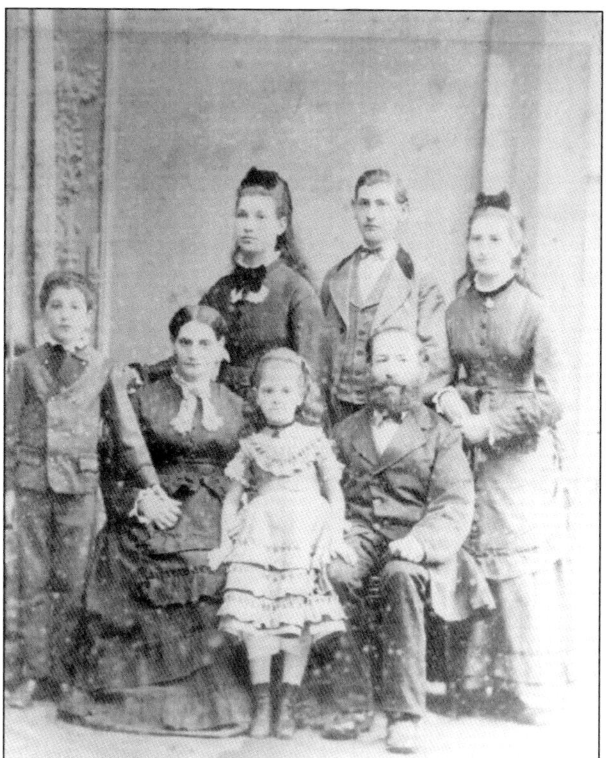

Julius Freyhan brought to this country his nephew Morris Burgas Jr. to keep his books, buy cotton, and manage cotton warehouses and mercantiles. Morris Jr., born in 1862, was a graduate of the University of Berlin and Oxford. Morris Burgas Sr. is shown here in Berlin in 1868 with his wife, Beate Freyhan Burgas. Also shown are, from left to right, their children Herman and Ida in the first row, and Clara, Siegfried, and Emma in the second row. (Collection of Hannah Rosenthal Wood.)

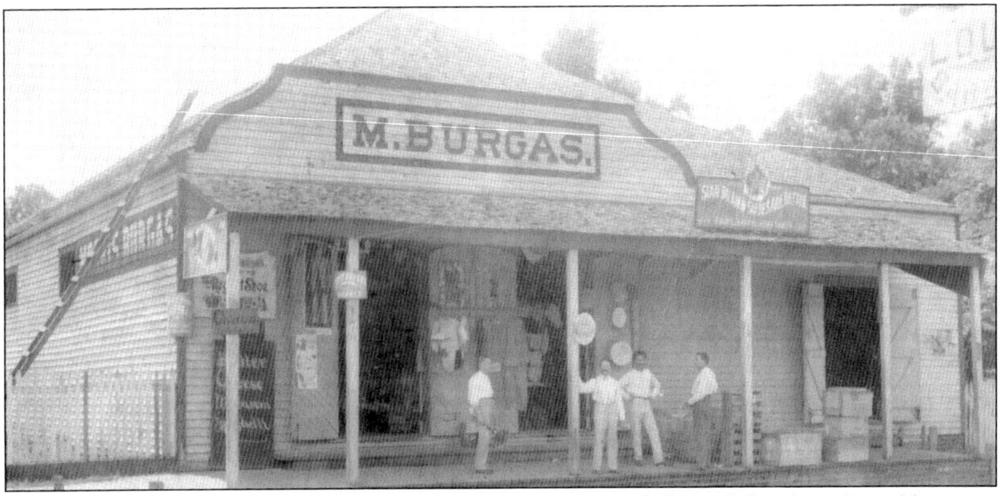

Jewish immigrants, many having arrived penniless, prospered through hard work and business acumen. From peddlers to store clerks to owners of their own mercantiles, they established themselves as contributing community members and encouraged relatives to join them in the South, at one time the center of American Jewish life. Morris Burgas had a fine general merchandise store on Ferdinand Street by the 1890s. (Collection of Hannah Rosenthal Wood.)

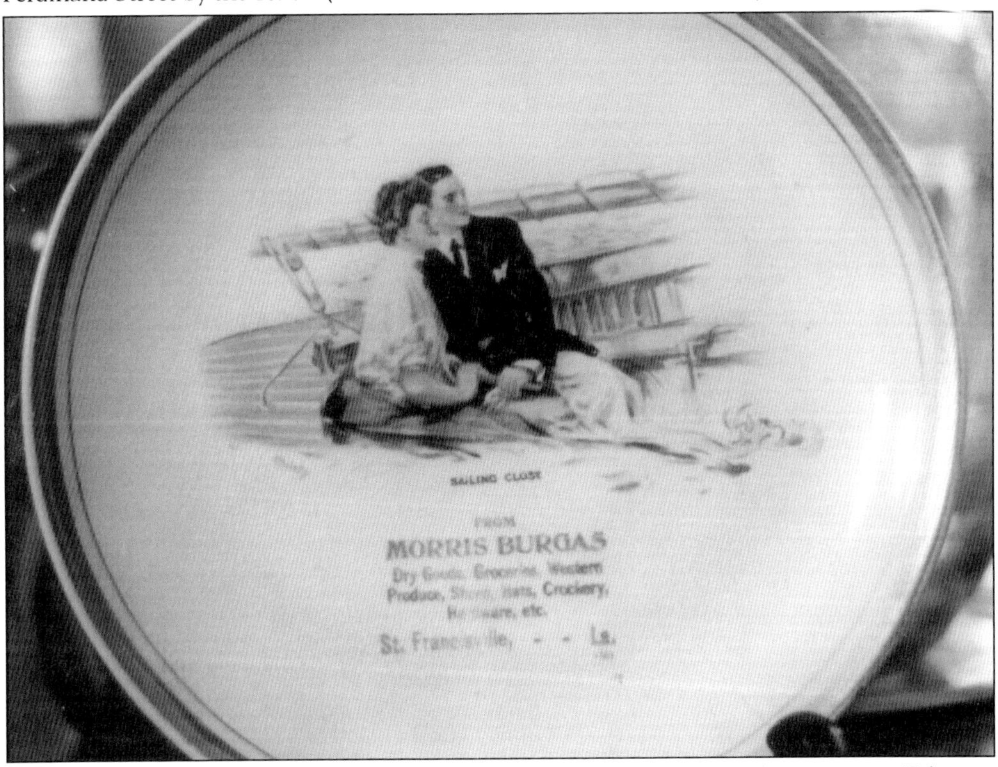

Shopkeepers customarily rewarded loyal customers with special favors. At Christmastime, Feliciana merchants often ordered sacks of oysters and fresh citrus shipped upriver from New Orleans as gifts. Morris Burgas, whose store advertised "dry goods, groceries, western produce, shoes, hats, crockery and hardware" while promising "highest price paid for cotton, moss, and all produce," gave away these romantically illustrated Dresden plates in 1894. (Collection of Hannah Rosenthal Wood.)

The marriage of Rena Rosenthal and Sam Burgas united the families that would continue the operation of the mercantile begun by Morris Burgas. The first of the Rosenthals to arrive in the Felicianas were Moritz and his wife, Hannah, who came just after 1870 in a wagon pulled by oxen. Moritz Rosenthal was an expert shoemaker. (Collection of Hannah Rosenthal Wood.)

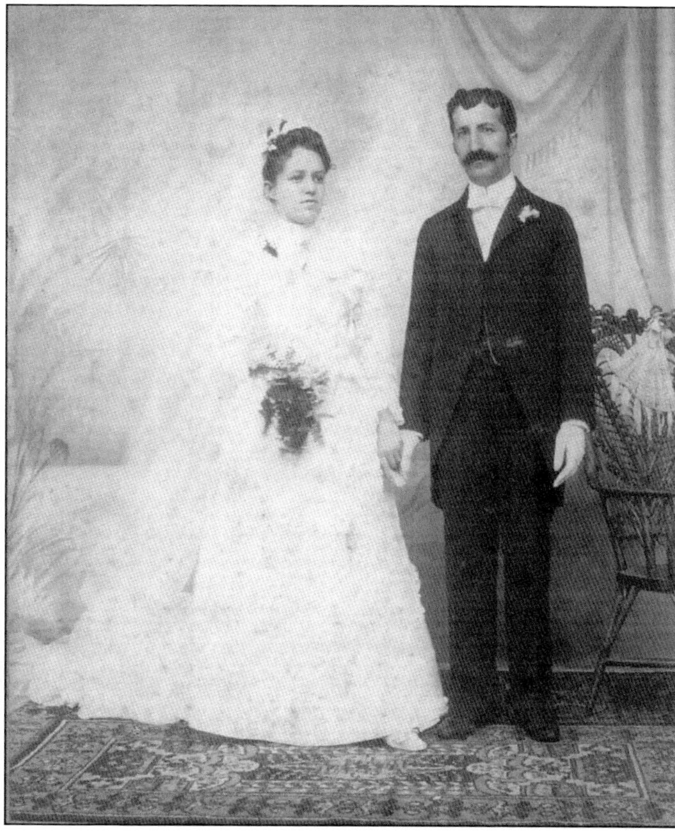

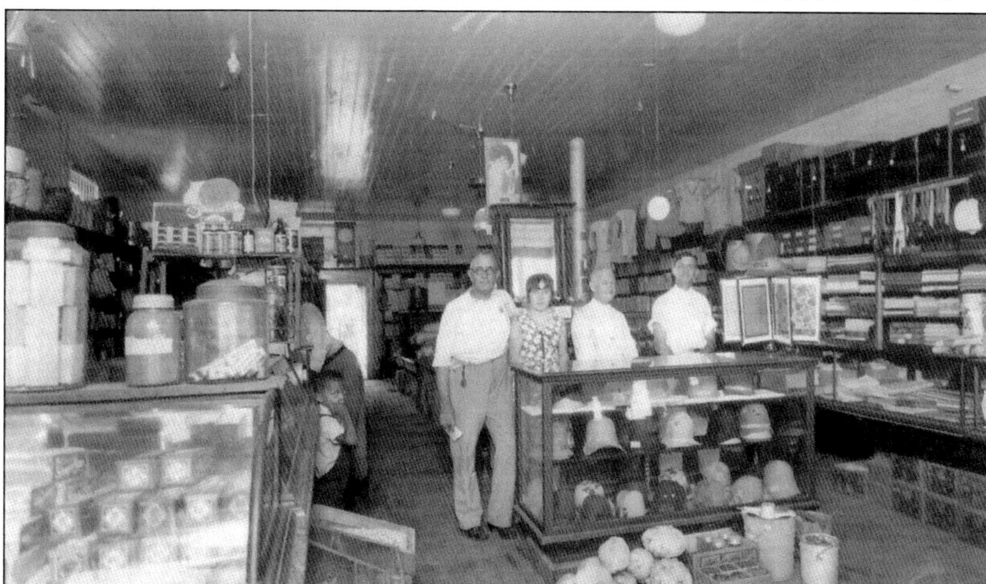

In May 1929, the interior of the frame Morris Burgas Store, then and now on St. Francisville's busy Ferdinand Street, shows dry-goods inventory neatly piled to the ceiling. Waiting to help customers are, from left to right, Adolph Rosenthal, May McCartney, Sam Rosenthal, and Joe Rosenthal. (Collection of Hannah Wood Rosenthal.)

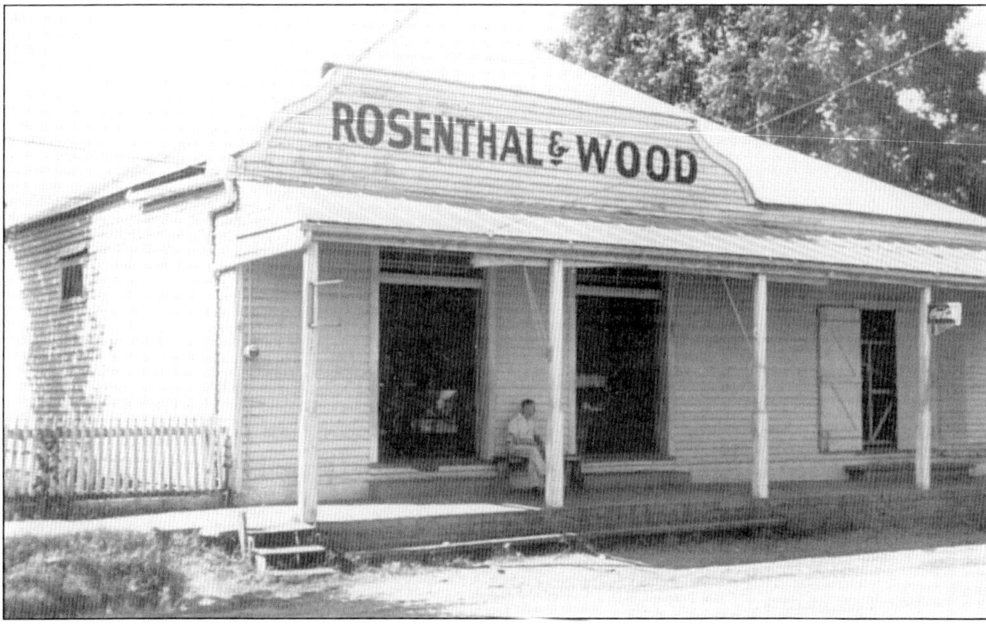

Hannah Rosenthal, granddaughter of Moritz Rosenthal, married J. Kenneth Wood, and the old Burgas Store became Rosenthal & Wood, later just J. Kenneth Wood Store. The rambling store building stands today, occupied by an arts/antiques co-op. Hannah, though she became a Catholic in 1947, meticulously cared for the oak-shaded Hebrew Rest Cemetery, established in 1891, throughout her life. (Collection of Hannah Rosenthal Wood.)

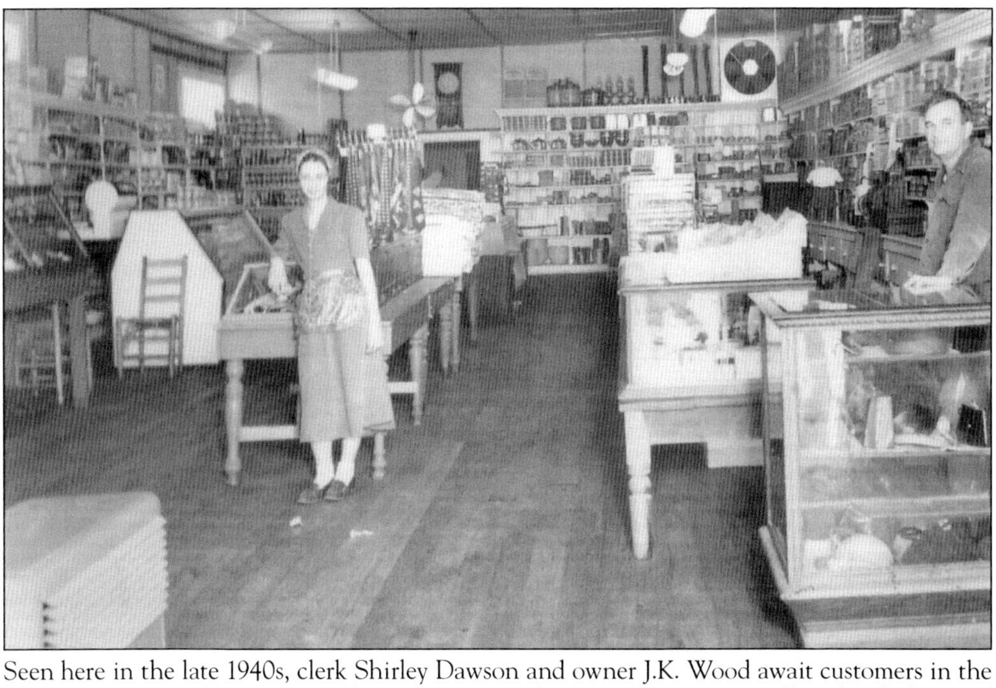

Seen here in the late 1940s, clerk Shirley Dawson and owner J.K. Wood await customers in the Rosenthal & Wood Store on Ferdinand Street in downtown St. Francisville. The shelves and display cases are neatly stocked with everything from clocks and teakettles to children's clothes and men's ties. (Collection of Hannah Rosenthal Wood.)

Adolph Teutsch came to America in 1880 and operated a dry-goods emporium selling everything from buggies to coffins. He built a fine house, Evergreenzine. Teutsch oversaw construction of Temple Sinai. It was dedicated in 1903, after he had been laid to rest in the Jewish cemetery. His widow, Justine, wed the nephew her late husband had brought over from Bavaria to help in his business. His name was Rudolph Teutsch (pictured). (WFHS.)

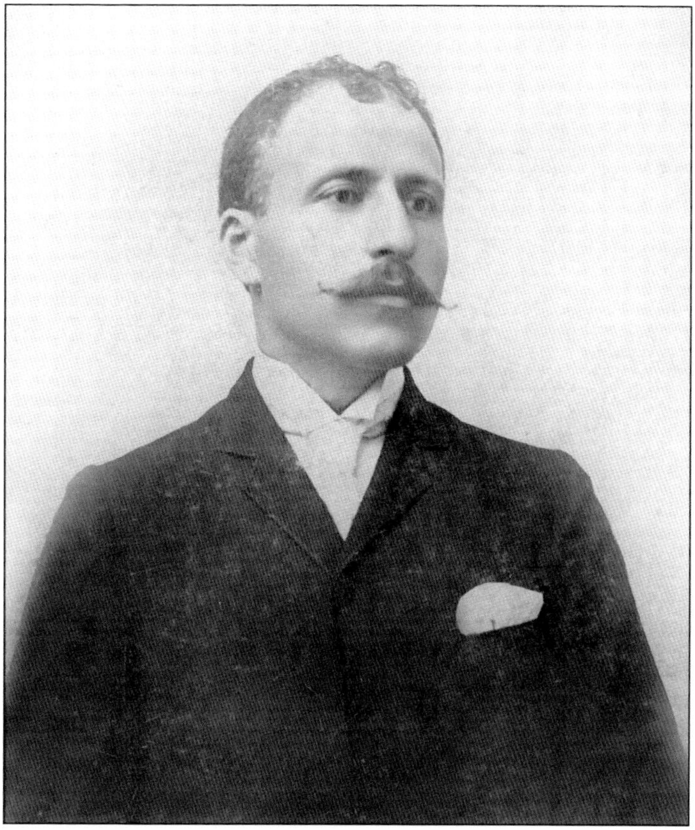

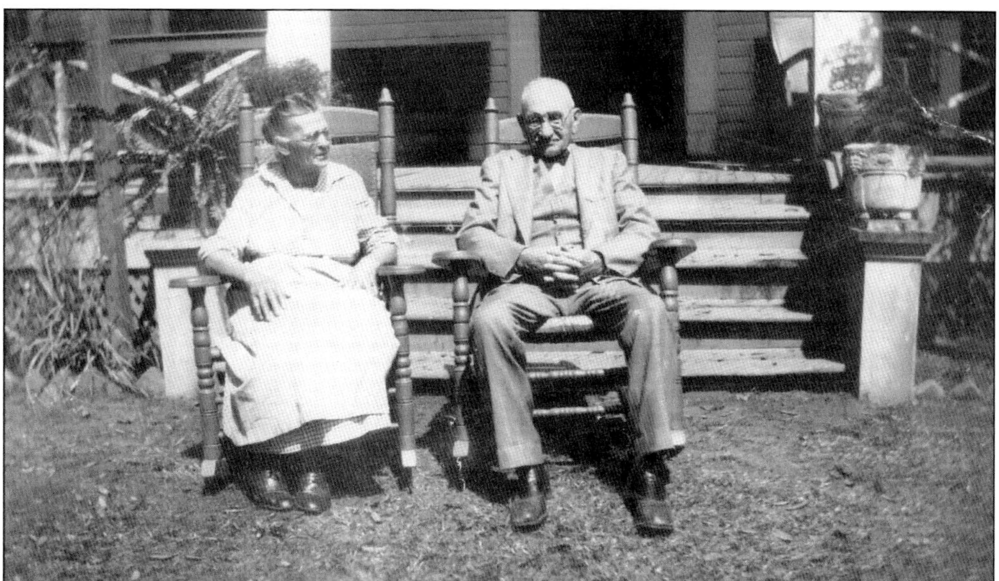

By 1916, Evergreenzine was owned by Charles Weydert, like the Teutsch family of German descent. Bespectacled and bow-tied, still wearing his three-piece suit after a lifetime in business, Weydert rocks contentedly before the front steps of Evergreenzine with his wife in her apron and gingham dress. (Collection of Weydert family.)

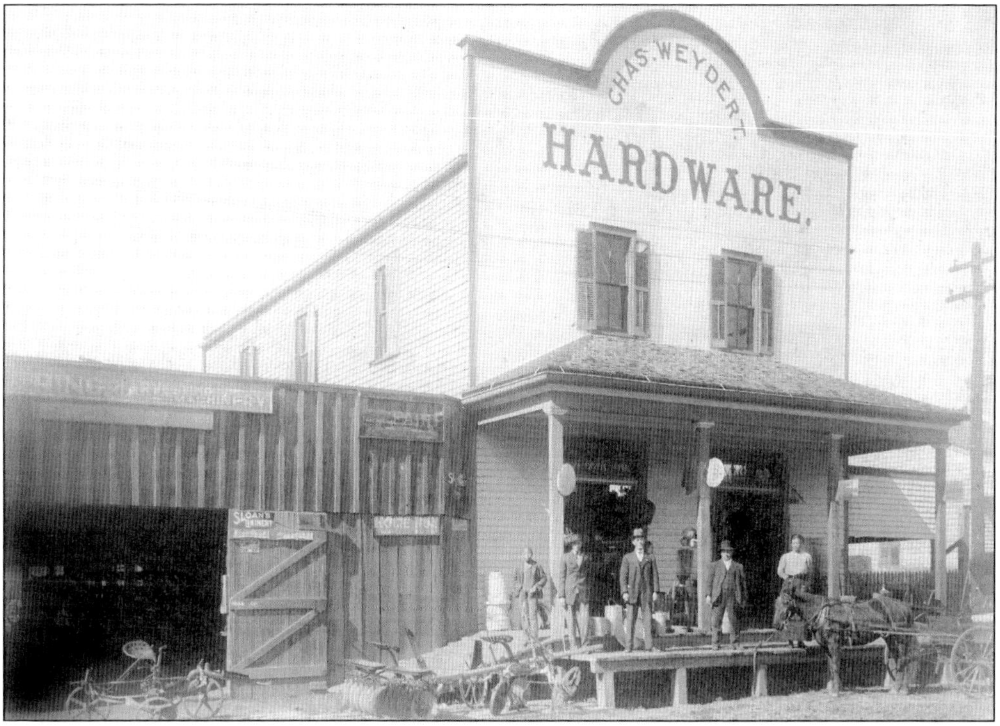

Charles Weydert's first business enterprises were in Bayou Sara. He operated a large hardware store, selling farm equipment, machinery, tools, seed, and everything else under the sun; and a blacksmith shop, busy in the days of iron wheels and horse-drawn conveyances. Below, Weydert poses in the open doorway of the blacksmith shop with his wife and baby daughters. The long leather aprons protected the legs of the workers from the heat of the flames. Frequent flooding caused Weydert to eventually move his business and family up the hill into St. Francisville, where they occupied Evergreenzine on Ferdinand Street. Its entrance walkway is still embellished by an iron gate decorated with the family name. (Both, collection of the Weydert family.)

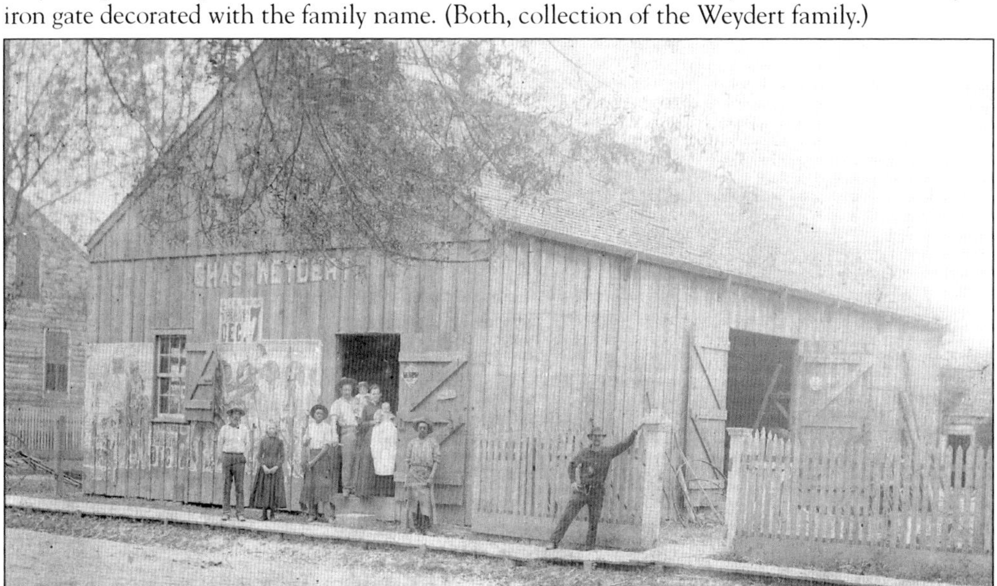

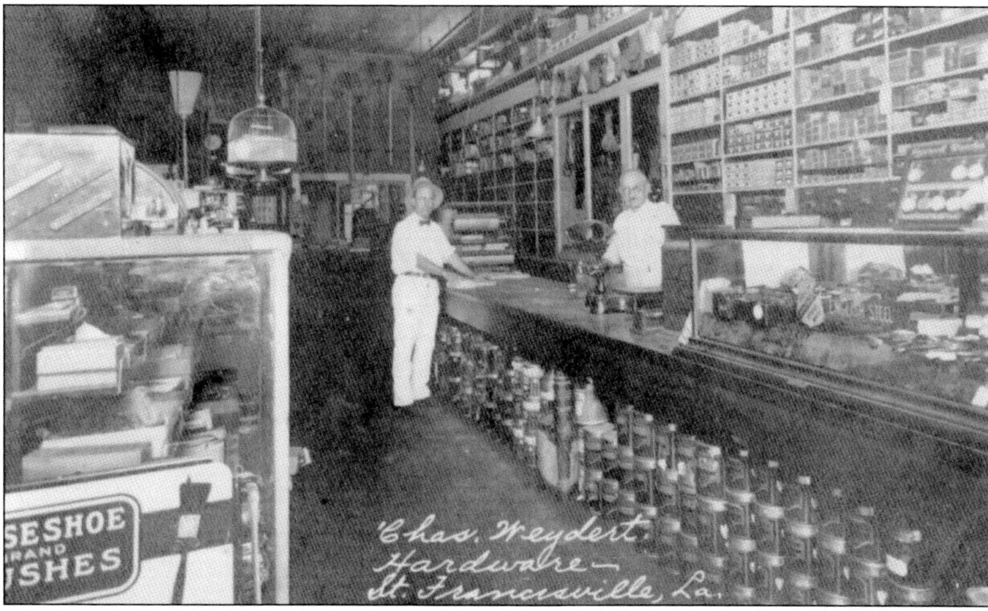

Charles Weydert moved his hardware store into an 1880s structure near his home at Evergreenzine in St. Francisville and stocked it with necessities like paint and brushes, gentlemen's pocket watches, brooms and garden tools, even birdcages. Today the building is the headquarters and museum of the West Feliciana Historical Society. The beautifully restored building is open daily, with exhibits and tourist information. (Collection of Weydert family.)

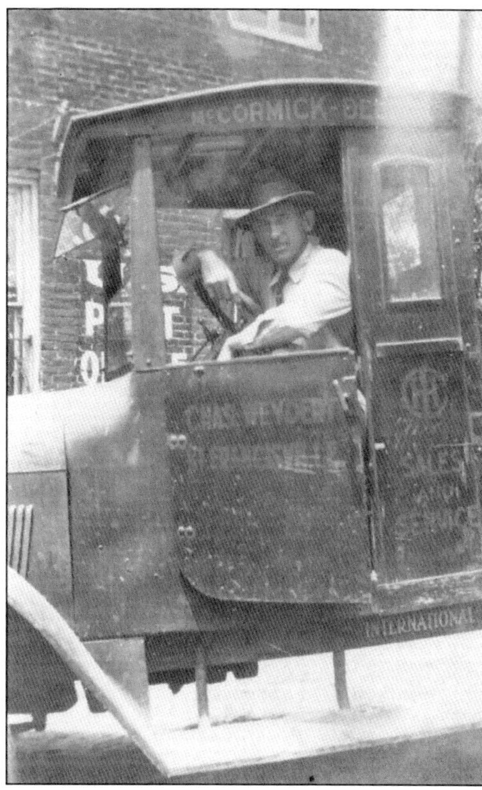

Driving the Charles Weydert hardware store company truck is Bennie Weydert, Charles's son. The vehicle, an International Harvester truck from around 1920 with a continental engine, huge running board, and pop-out front windshield, was a moving billboard advertising the store's sales and services. The brick post office building is seen in the background. (Collection of Weydert family.)

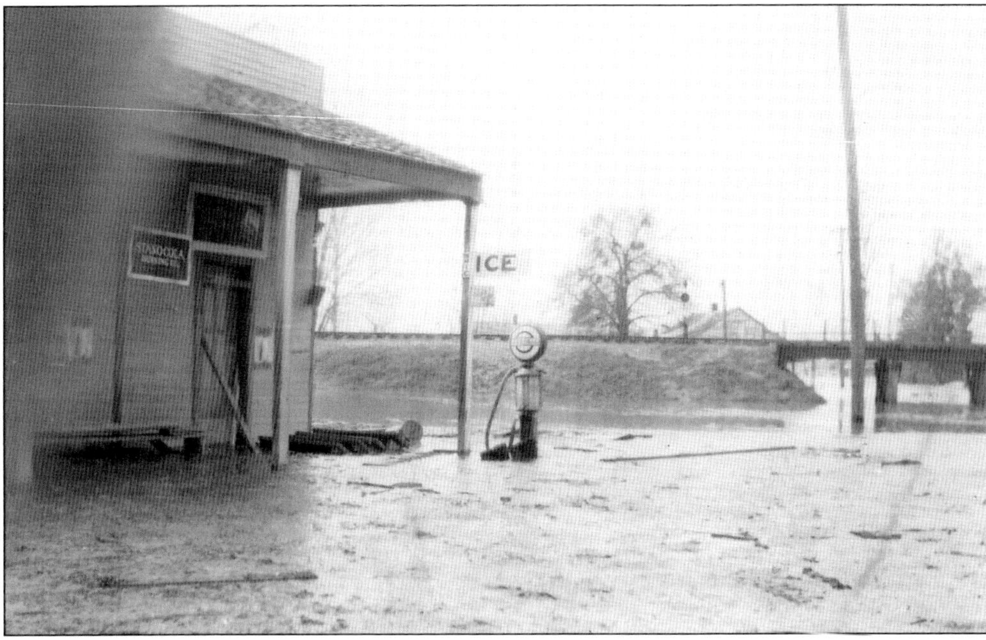

The Sansoni grocery, shown when the levee broke, moved into St. Francisville by 1910 and was operated by Frank Sansoni, of Italian descent. He is remembered as relishing raw oysters dipped in egg, then using the wall-mounted store phone to have long conversations with May Aubic, an elderly spinster and expert at camellia grafting who lived behind the Catholic church. They eventually married, late in life. (Collection of Russell Daniel.)

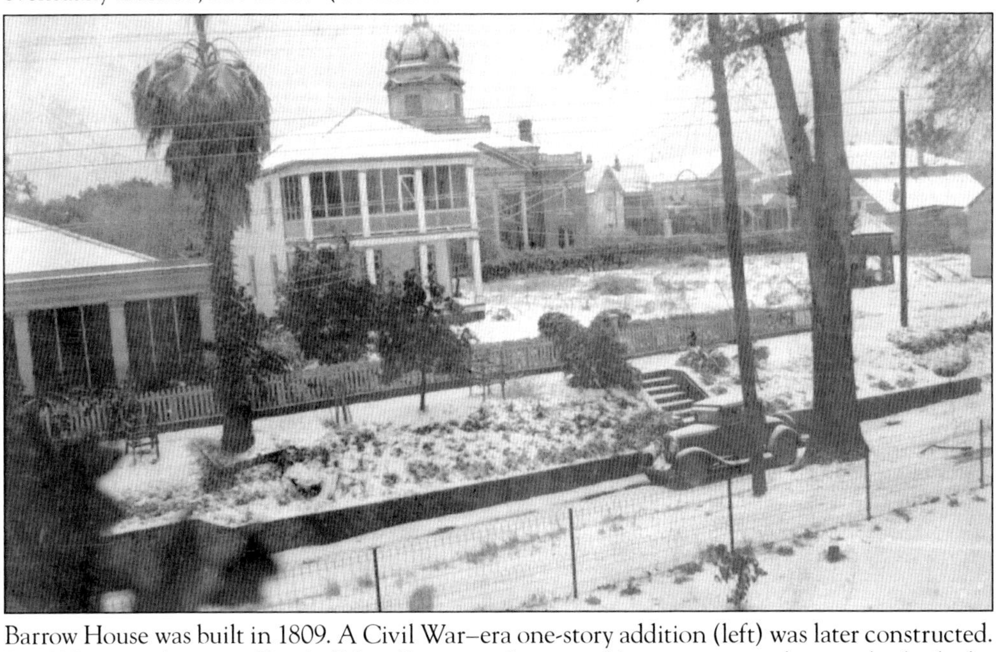

Barrow House was built in 1809. A Civil War–era one-story addition (left) was later constructed. In 1892, it was home to Dr. A. Feltus Barrow, a horse-and-buggy country doctor who built the two-story sanitarium seen here (in front of the courthouse dome) so that expectant mothers from isolated reaches of the parish and other patients needing quarantined quarters could be confined closer to medical care. (Collection of Virginia Dipple Reames.)

Robert Brasseaux had the area's first service station and gasoline distributorship, in 1910, selling kerosene to isolated country stores that kept hand-cranked drums on their porches in the days before electricity. The kerosene was shipped from the Esso refinery by the Louisiana Railway and Navigation Company railroad, and Brasseaux unloaded the tank cars into barrels hauled by a mule-drawn wagon. Here, two unidentified boys stand before an early gas pump. (Collection of Myrtle A. Brasseaux.)

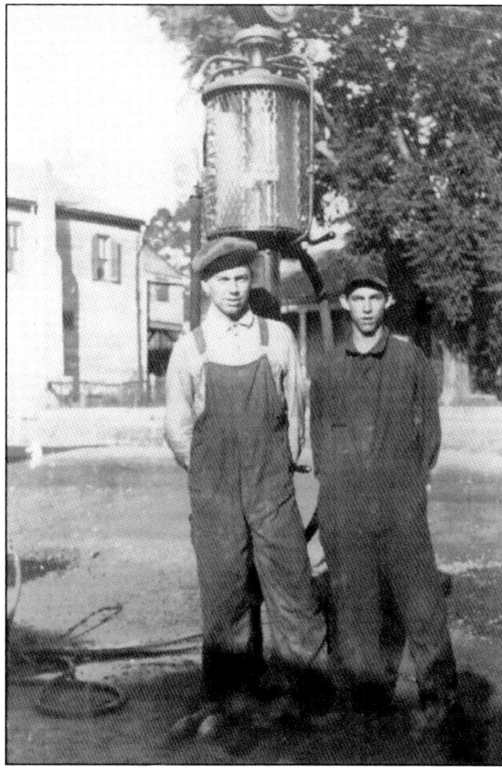

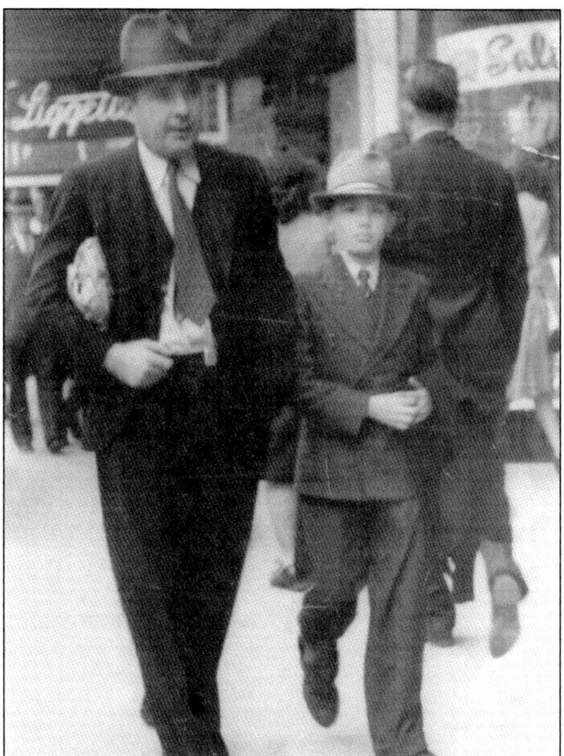

Robert C. Brasseaux's grandson J. Russell Daniel today runs the family gas distributorship, officially recognized for over a century of service. Shown here with his father in downtown Baton Rouge, he was lucky to survive to continue the business. As a toddler, he made the newspapers when he "stepped into the arc of an axe being wielded by his grandfather. R.C. Brasseaux, chopping on a tree." (Collection of Russell Daniel.)

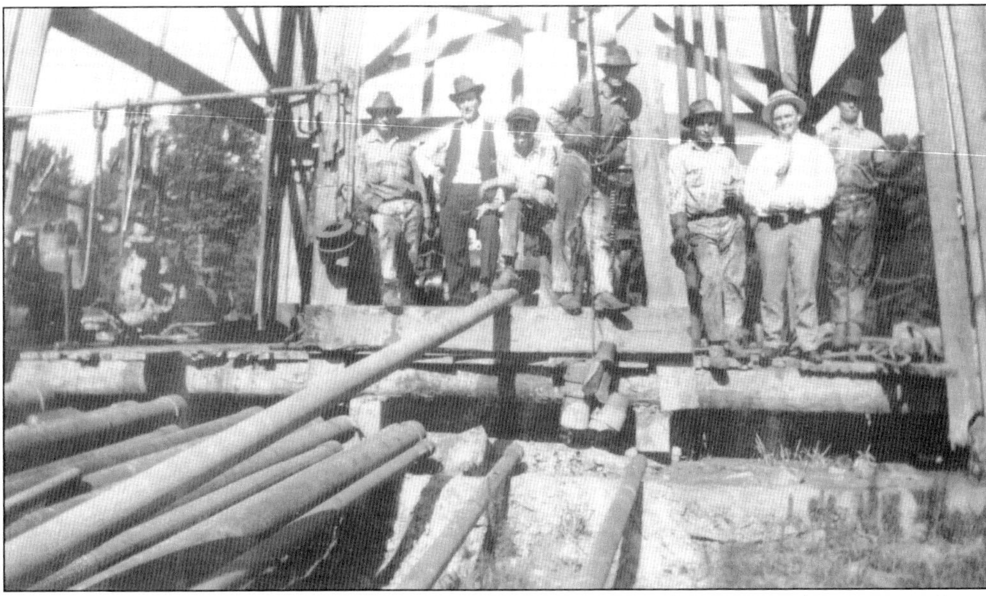

In 1917, V.M. Jackson of Rosemound Plantation had a famous geologist assess the prospects for oil and gas and received a discouraging report. There was, however, sporadic interest over the years, as seen in this early well image showing a wooden derrick, casings, and shale bit. Today, with improved exploration techniques and advancements like horizontal drilling, the parish's inclusion in the Tuscaloosa Marine Shale seems promising. (Collection of Myrtle A. Brasseaux.)

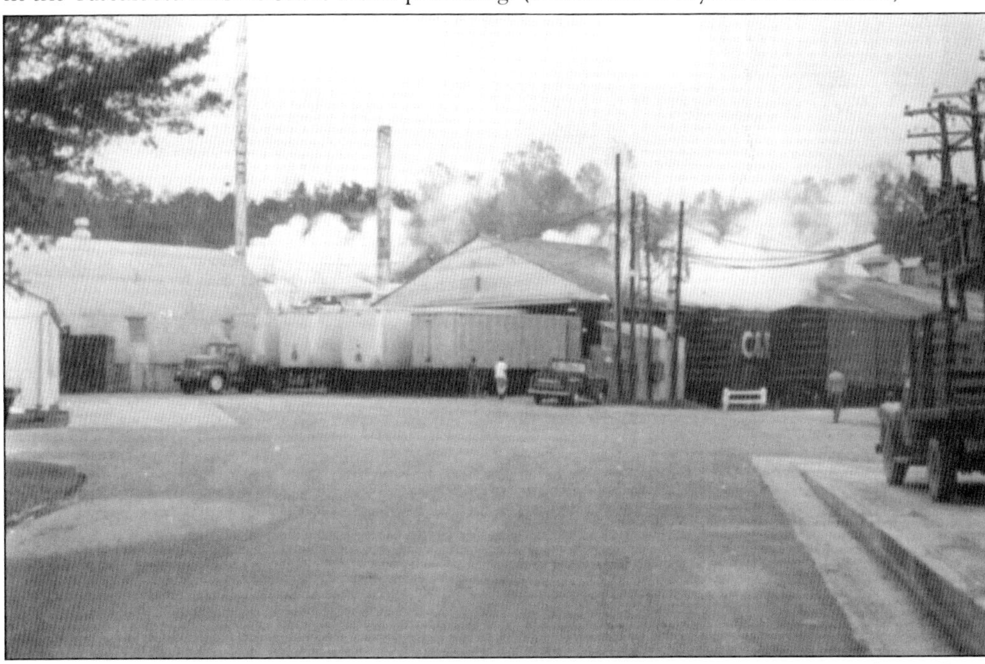

As seen here, Princeville Canning Company is going full steam in 1966. It was located just down the hill from St. Francisville's historic district. Dr. Julian Miller of the LSU horticulture department helped Harry Daniel initiate big-time commercial sweet potato production in West Feliciana in the 1940s. For years, all the small farmers grew potatoes to sell to the cannery, and all the farmers' wives worked seasonally in the canning plant. (WFHS.)

Harry Daniel's son Ed, with partner Jordan Truitt, planted more than 1,000 acres of sweet potatoes and employed 100 or so farmworkers. While it was the big player in the mid-1900s sweet potato era in the Felicianas, Princeville Canning Company was eventually sold to Joan of Arc and finally to Pillsbury. The local canning plant was closed, and area potato production dropped sharply. (WHFS.)

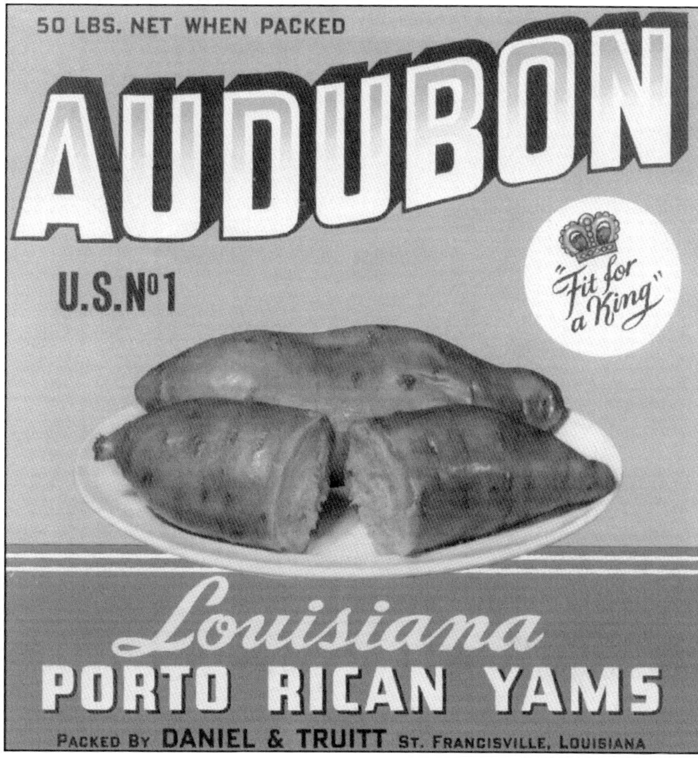

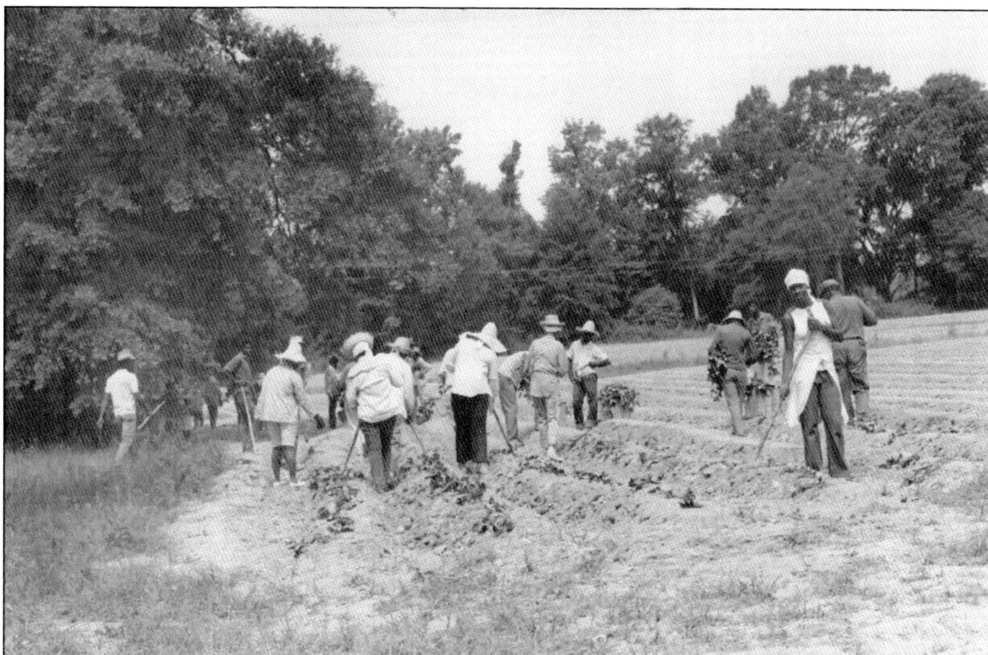

When the packinghouses and cannery were in operation in St. Francisville, some 2,500 acres of potatoes were planted. Seed potatoes were bedded until they sprouted the slips to be transplanted into fields, 12,500 to an acre. They were planted in June and harvested in late summer after 120 days of growing season. Both men and women cultivated the crop. (WFHS.)

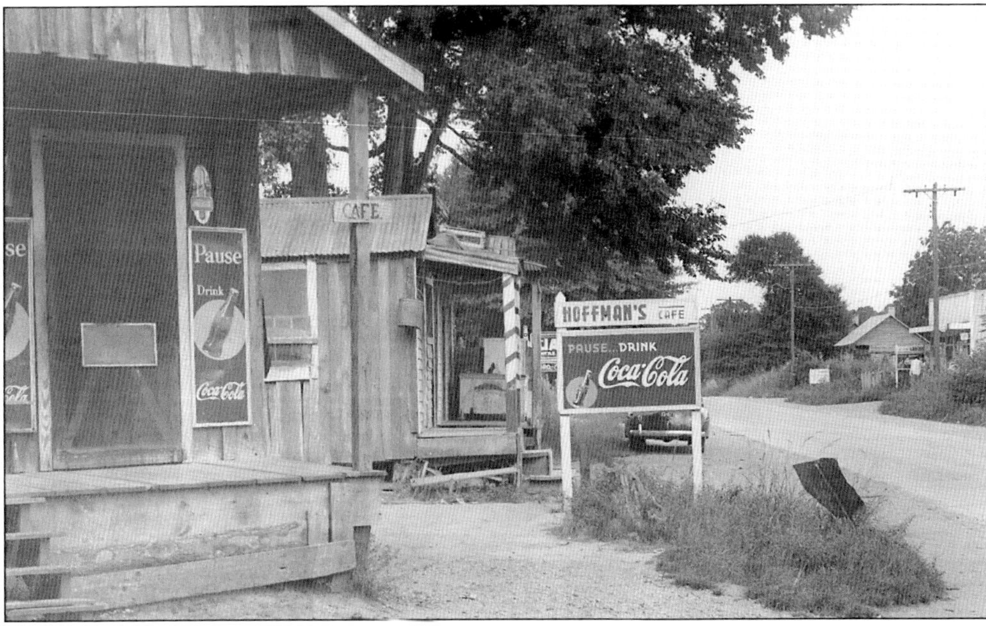

Besides rustic cabins housing families, Commerce Street in St. Francisville through the mid-1900s was lined with small, frame structures containing businesses. The buildings had roofs of tin and were cobbled together with mismatched boards. These establishments served mostly black customers. Hoffman's Café advertised Coca-Cola, and that refreshing pause must have been welcome on hot, dusty summer days. (WFHS.)

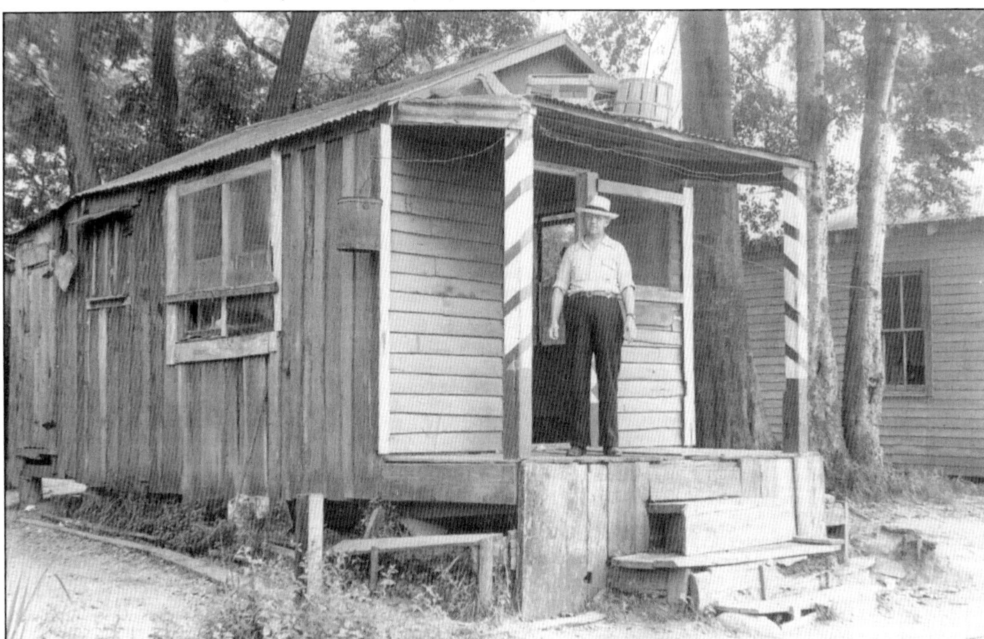

This small wooden cabin on Commerce Street was the barbershop. Stripes are painted on the two front columns. Note that its windows are barred, its steps are dangerously askew, and a produce basket is perched atop its porch roof for some unknown reason. Fearsome Sheriff Teddy Martin stands on the porch. He is probably not there to get a haircut. (WFHS.)

Every isolated rural community had its country store, the center of social life and the repository of community memories. Hardwood began as a lumber camp for Dinkman Lumber Company in the 1930s. By 1946, King Lumber Industries took over and employed over 150 men. King Lumber built a sawmill and dry kiln, erected some 100 houses in the sawmill quarters for employee families, and operated a large company store. In the store building were commissary, meat market with a real butcher, pharmacy, and doctor's office—all for the benefit of King employees and their families. The Hardwood Post Office occupied the north end of the building. King sold the lumberyard in the early 1970s, the store folded, and the dry kiln and sawmill burned down. Some of the quarters housing was torn down to make way for subsidized housing. (Both, collection of Anne Butler.)

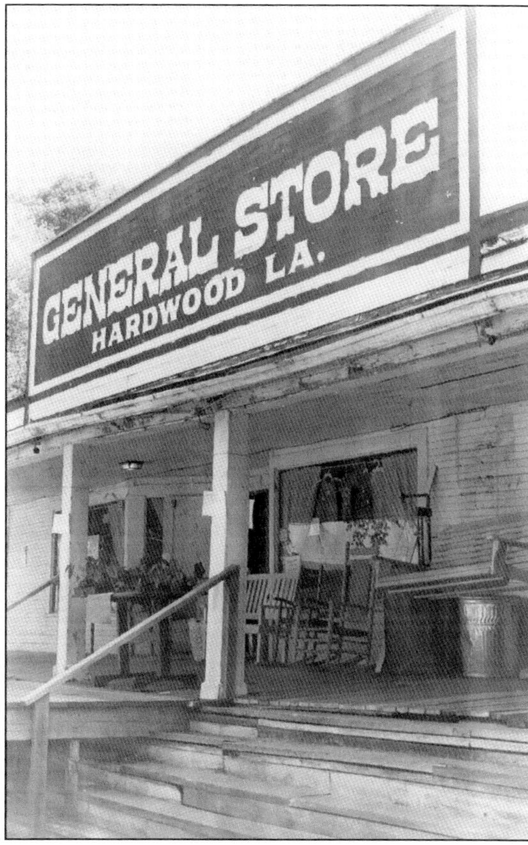

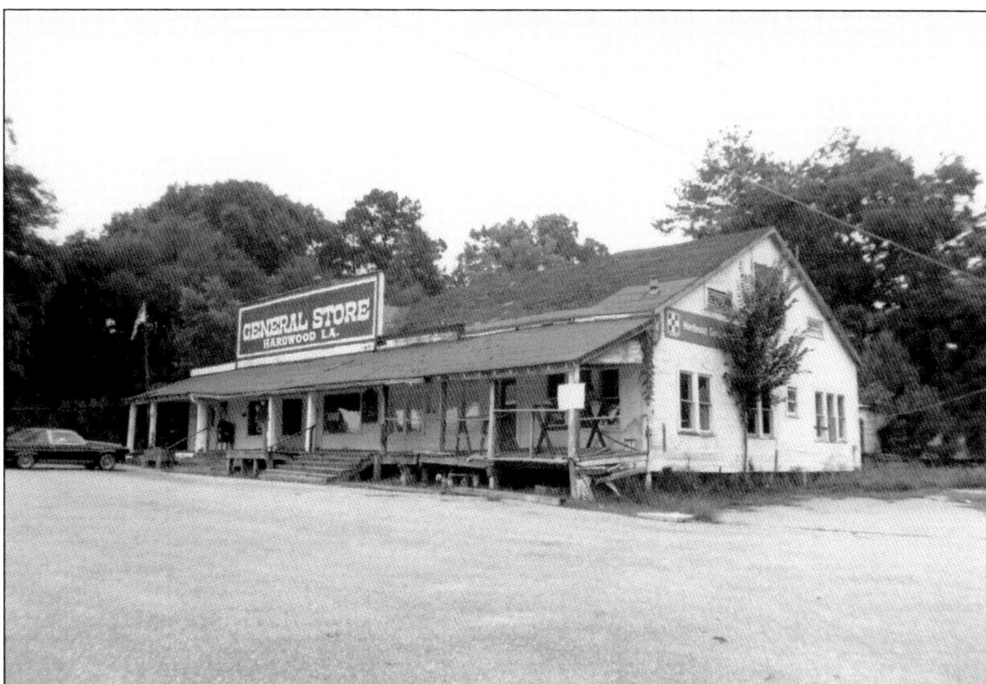

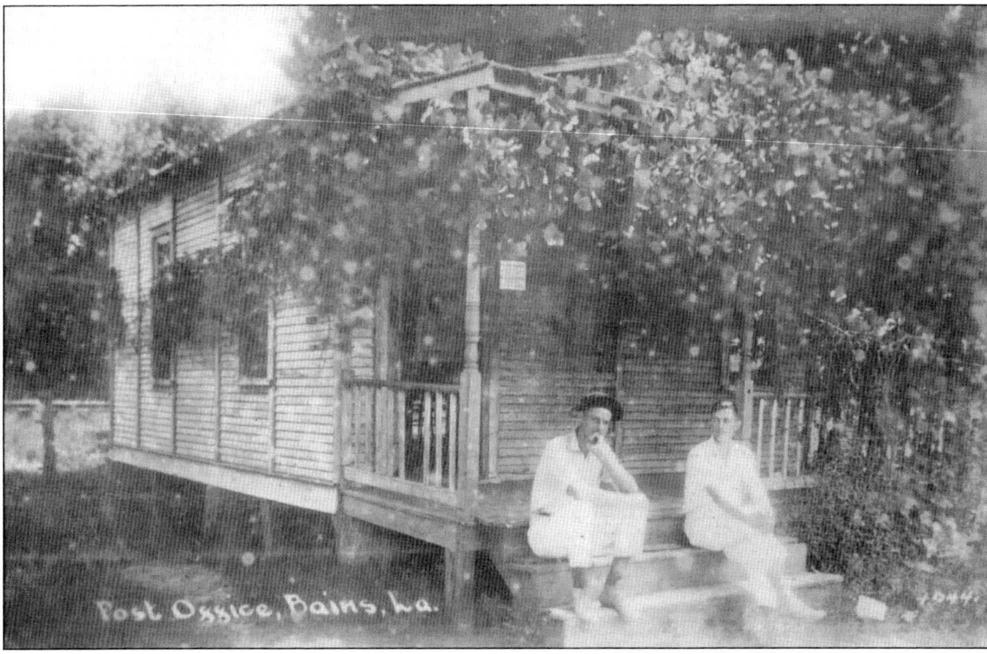

At the time of this postcard image, the Bains, Louisiana, postmistress was Elizabeth Douglas, daughter of the Reverend William Kirtland Douglas. The responsibility was a family affair, handed down through several generations. Shown here seated on the vine-covered gallery are John T. Douglas (left) and an unidentified friend. The mail came in on the morning train, and outgoing posts were picked up by the evening train. (Collection of Mary Thompson.)

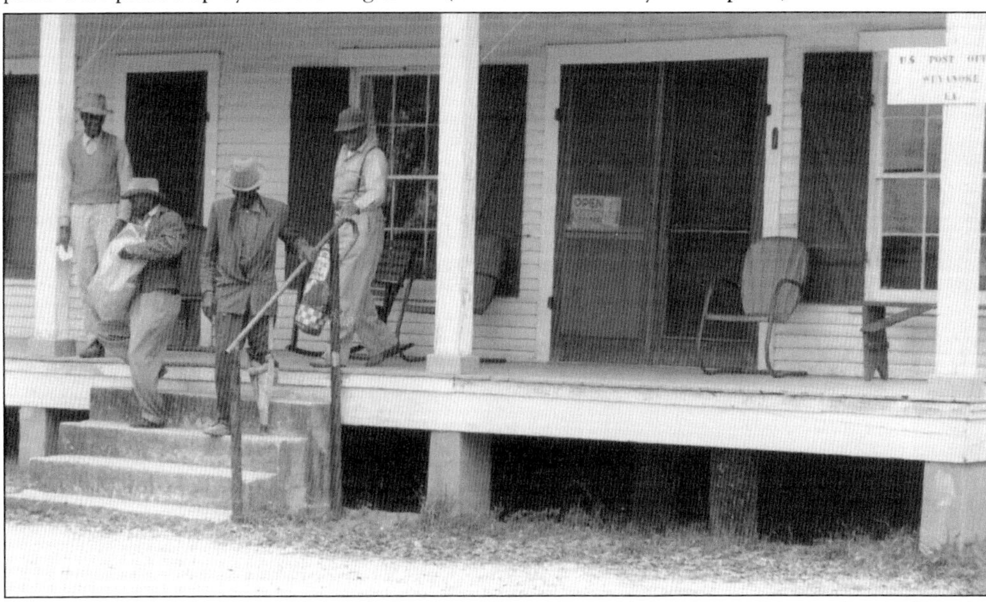

In the 1920s, the post office for the surrounding Weyanoke community was located in the historic plantation house called Live Oak. In 1934, Leona Plettinger, the third generation of her family to serve as postmaster, moved it to the little country store in her neat, frame home on the Tunica Trace. Note the rough peg leg on the gentleman descending the steps (possibly Nathaniel Ford). (WFHS.)

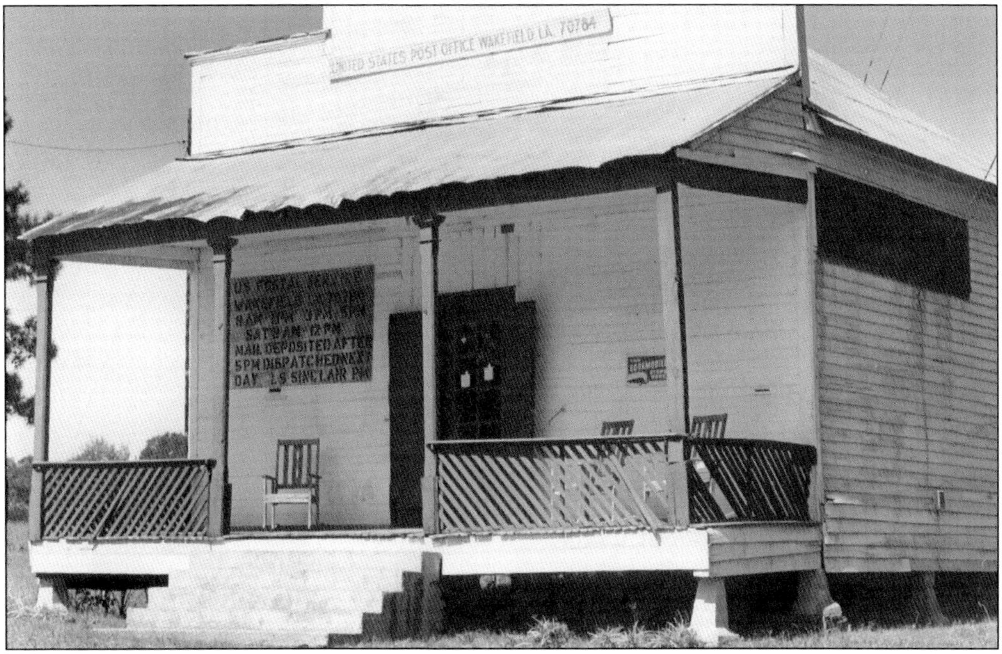

The little Wakefield Post Office, with its stepped parapet facade, provided rockers on its front porch. This was the community gathering spot as patrons collected mail and visited with neighbors. It was located on Wakefield Plantation, part of an immense Spanish land grant to early settler Alexander Stirling. The last of his descendants to live in the Wakefield house, Lilie Stirling Sinclair, served as postmistress here. (WFHS.)

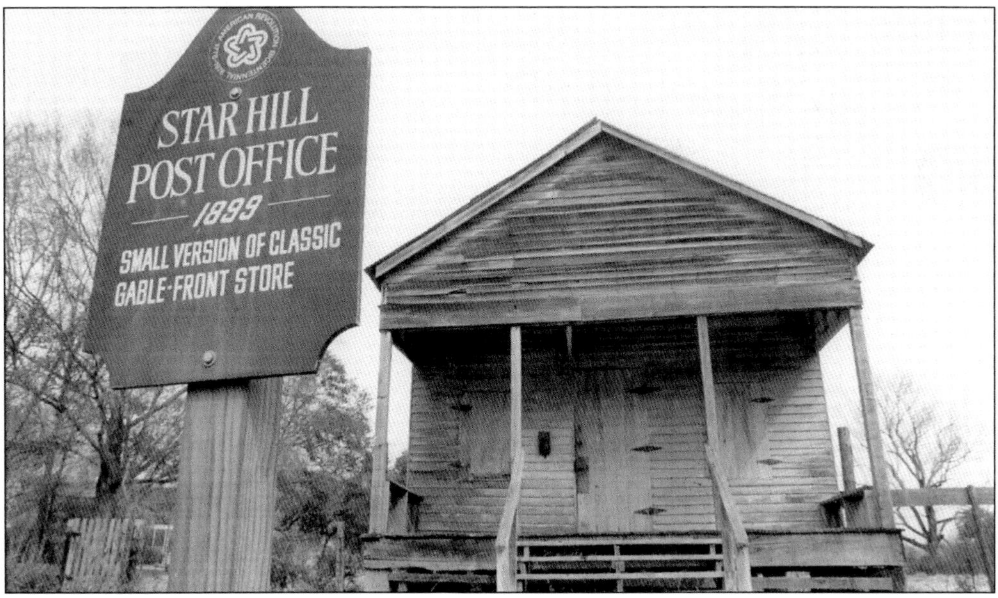

Dating from 1899, the Star Hill Post Office, a "small version of classic gable-front store," had a succession of area farmers as postmasters/storekeepers over the years. The first postmaster was Robert Daniel. Following him were J.W. McQueen (1895–1901), M.O. Daniel (1901–1903), Emmett Curtis Harvey (1903), T.D. Bickham (1904–1940), and, lastly, Leslie O. Bickham (1940–1955). (Collection of Beryl Bickham Eisworth.)

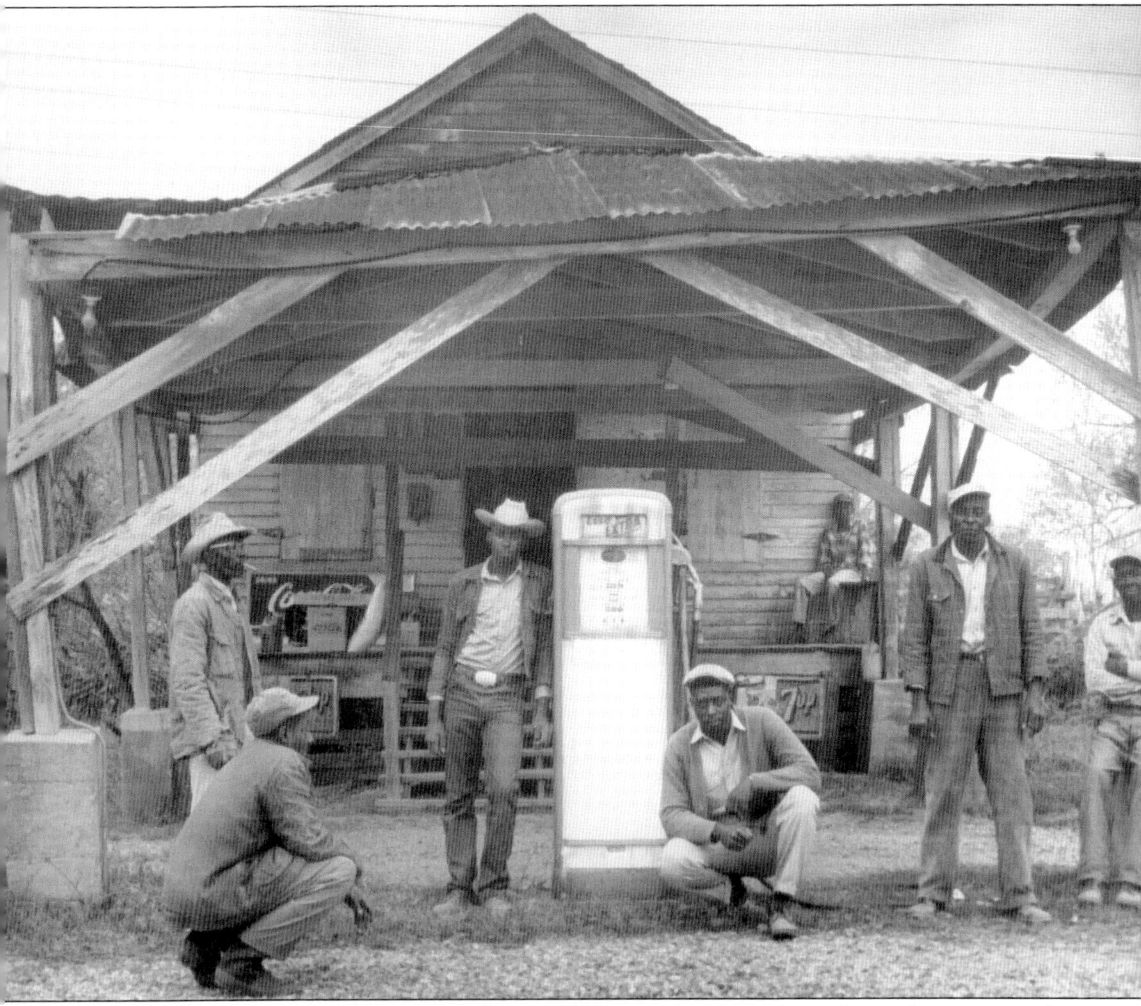

This mid-1900s image of the Star Hill Post Office and Bickham Store shows that a tin roof was added at some point to cover the gas pump. The last cancellation stamp for postal service there was June 30, 1955, but Leslie Bickham ran the store until his death in 1966, and the building is still standing. The store carried feed and seed, nails, groceries, fabrics and clothes, hoop cheese, cold drinks, salami, and other staples. When the school bus dropped off neighborhood children, there was a big run on RC Colas and Stage Planks. This was obviously a favorite gathering place. Shown here are area workers, from left to right, Governor Thomas (with cigar), Lev White (squatting), Bully London Jr., Roosevelt London, Bully London Sr., and Buddy White. Bully was a gifted blacksmith, barber, and butcher. Thomas was a hardworking cattleman, farmer, and father of about a dozen children. (Collection of Beryl Bickham Eisworth.)

Five

Notable Folks

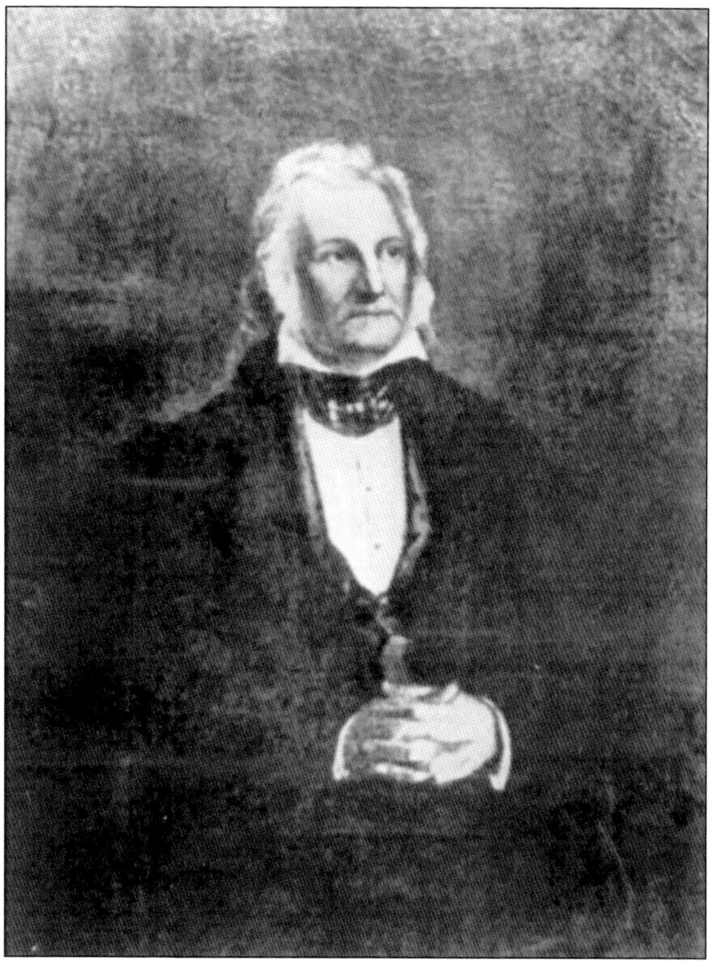

Artist John James Audubon, who painted dozens of his famous bird studies while in West Feliciana, is shown in an 1849 portrait by his son John Woodhouse Audubon at Minnie's Land, New York City. This was painted about the time the elder Audubon entered his decline. He is only 64 years old, but looks considerably older. (Collection of Louisiana Office of State Parks.)

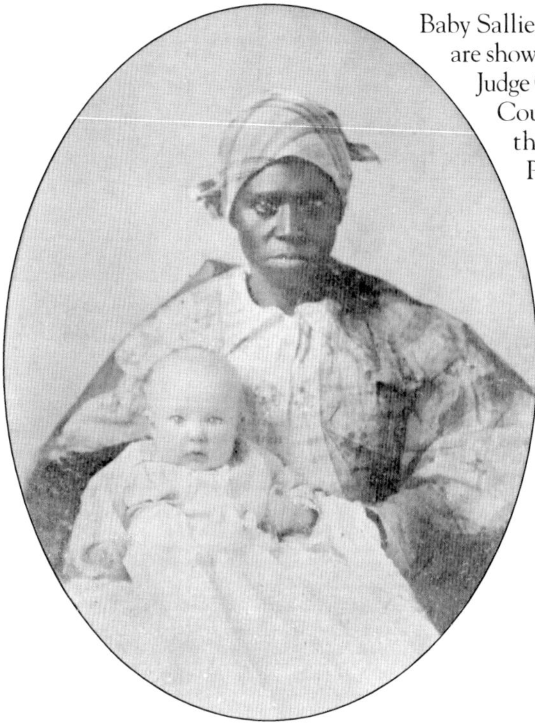

Baby Sallie Mathews and her beloved nurse Aunt Dicey are shown in 1859. Late in life, Sallie, granddaughter of Judge George Mathews of the first Louisiana Supreme Court, married James Alexander Ventress, and they made their home at Butler Greenwood Plantation, her family property dating from the late 1700s. (Collection of Anne Butler.)

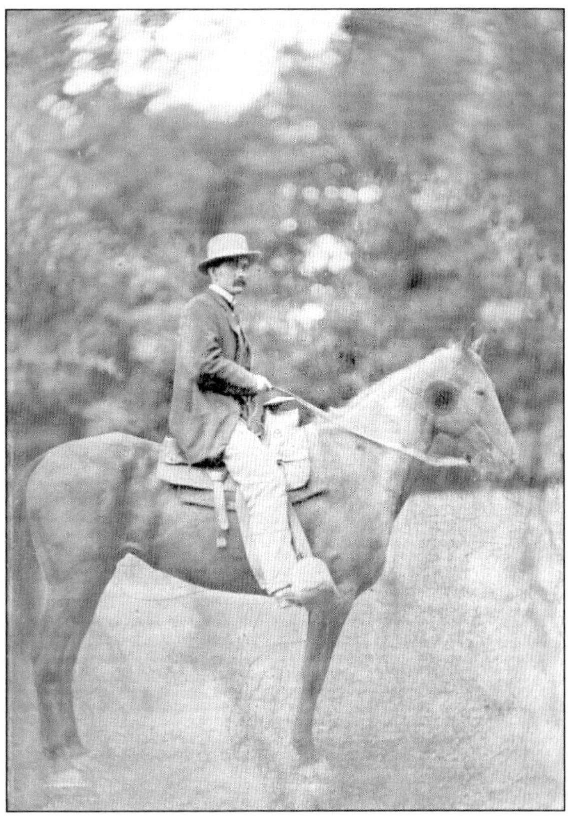

Vincent Micajah Jackson (1857–1918) built Rosemound Plantation near Laurel Hill. The St. Francisville newspaper in 1917 called it one of the most beautiful plantations in the parish, with its rolling hillsides and fertile valleys. His grandfather arrived in West Feliciana in the late 1700s. (Collection of Mary Anne Stevens.)

Beautiful Sara Anne Lemon, seen here with a treasured cameo at the neck of her high-collared dress, was born in 1857 at Laurel Hill in the northern reaches of West Feliciana Parish. She married Vincent Micajah Jackson; their daughter Lucille married Bertram F. Babers in 1903. Direct descendants of the couple still live in their old house on Rosemound Plantation, built in 1894. (Collection of Mary Anne Stevens.)

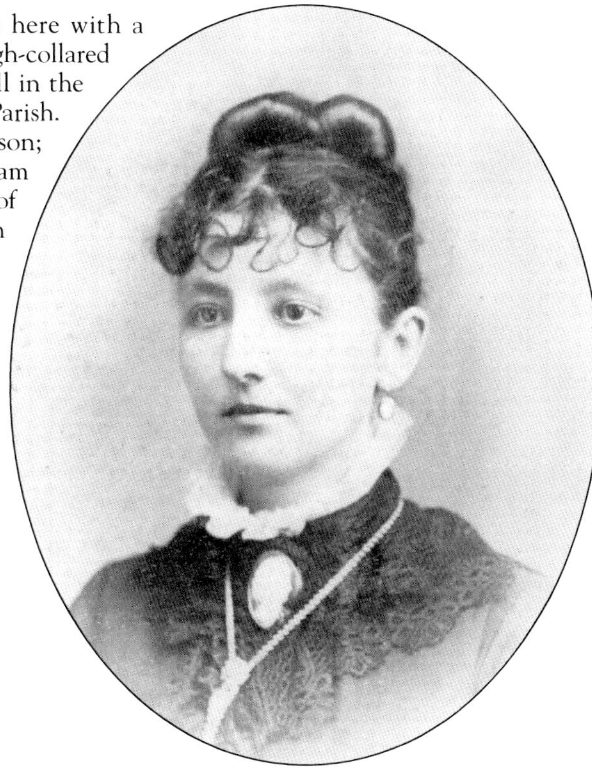

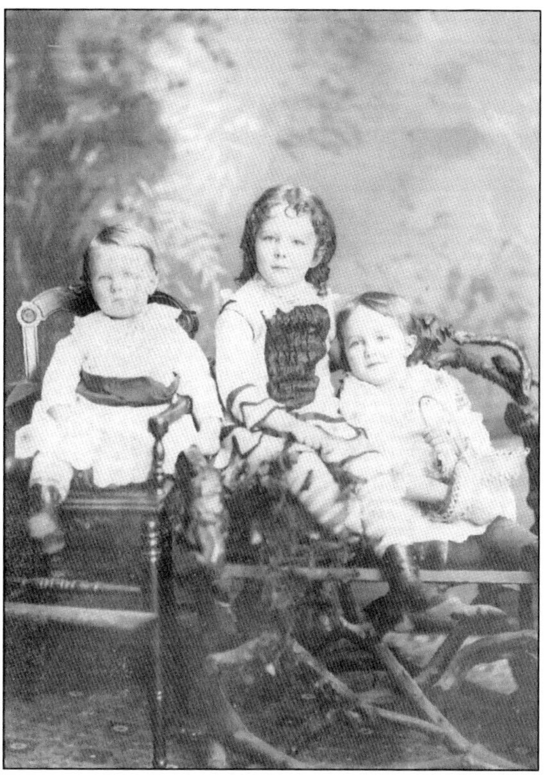

Traveling to New Orleans via steamboat in the 1880s to have professional photographs made on Canal Street was de rigueur for West Feliciana's plantation families. Shown here are the children of Judge George Lawrason: Zelia (center), born in 1876; Annie (right), born in 1878; and baby George. Judge Lawrason authored the Lawrason Act, which still governs state municipalities. (Collection of Anne Butler.)

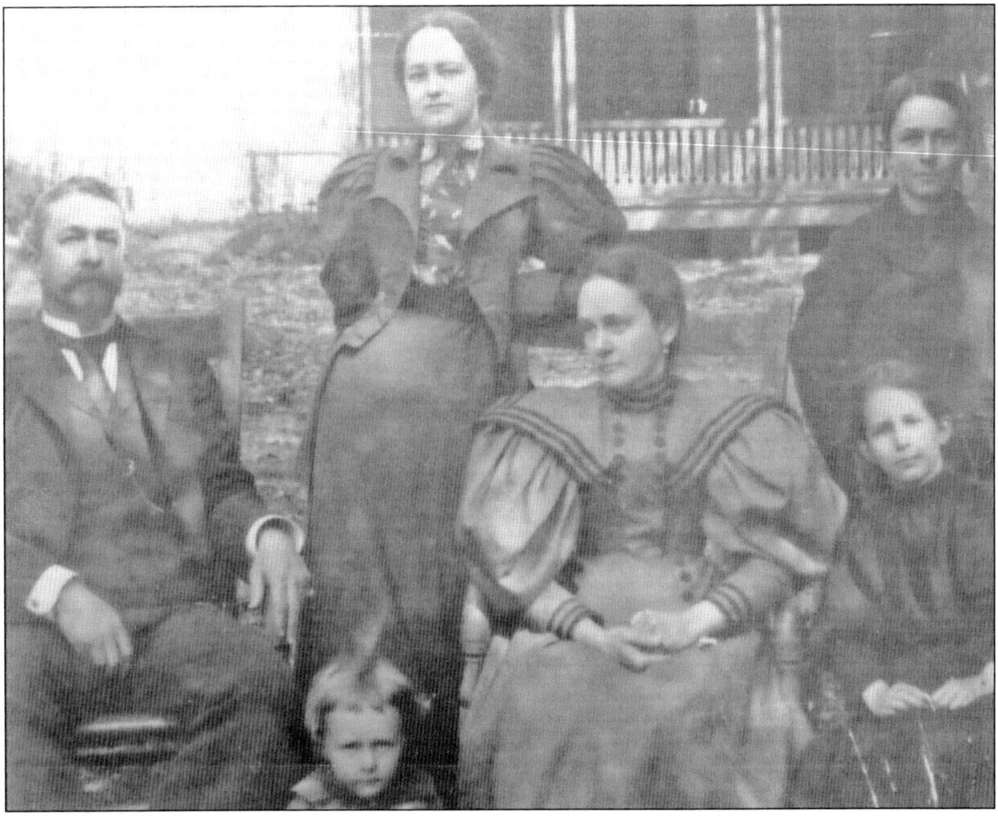

The family of Judge Samuel Lawrason and his wife, Harriet Mathews, were photographed in front of the old house at Clover Hill Plantation, where they lived until building Hillcroft in St. Francisville in 1905. Clover Hill Plantation became Girl Scout Camp Marydale. The house burned down in the 1950s. Daughter Annie is standing at center. (Collection of Anne Butler.)

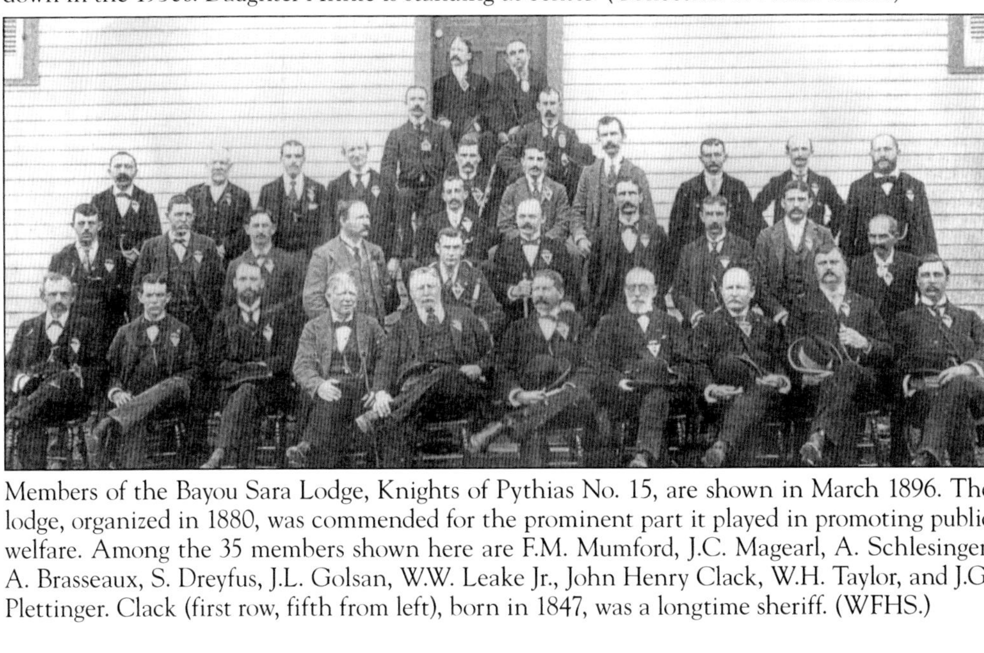

Members of the Bayou Sara Lodge, Knights of Pythias No. 15, are shown in March 1896. The lodge, organized in 1880, was commended for the prominent part it played in promoting public welfare. Among the 35 members shown here are F.M. Mumford, J.C. Magearl, A. Schlesinger, A. Brasseaux, S. Dreyfus, J.L. Golsan, W.W. Leake Jr., John Henry Clack, W.H. Taylor, and J.G. Plettinger. Clack (first row, fifth from left), born in 1847, was a longtime sheriff. (WFHS.)

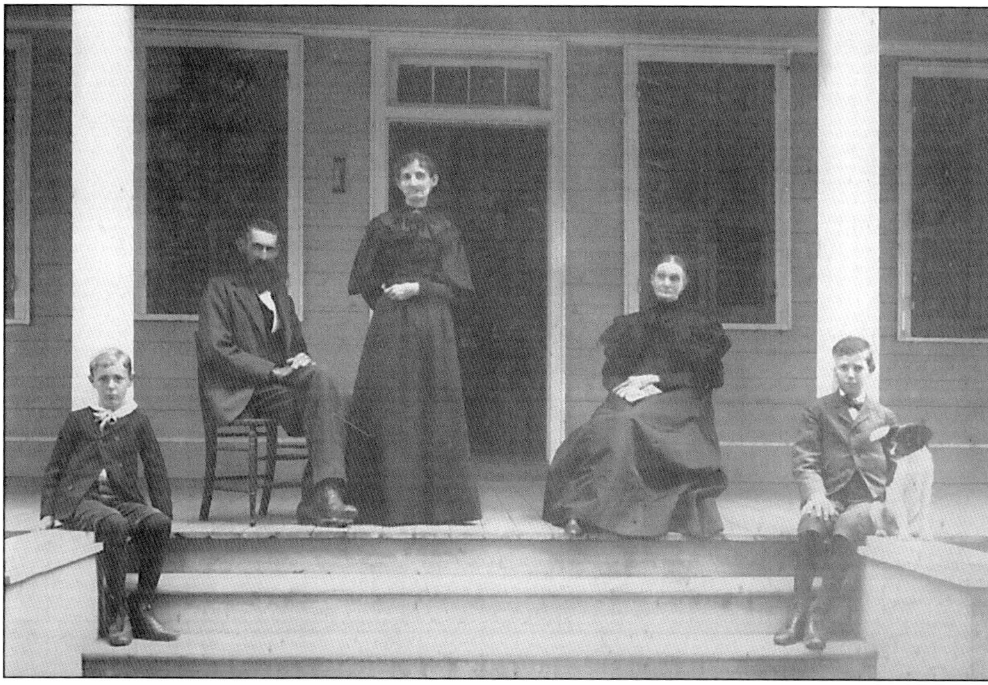

The family of George Henderson Wilcox is shown around 1900. Pictured are, from left to right, Alfred Wilcox, George H. Wilcox, his wife, Mollie Thompson Wilcox, her mother, Isabella Thompson, and Fred Wilcox. (Collection of Frances Cutting.)

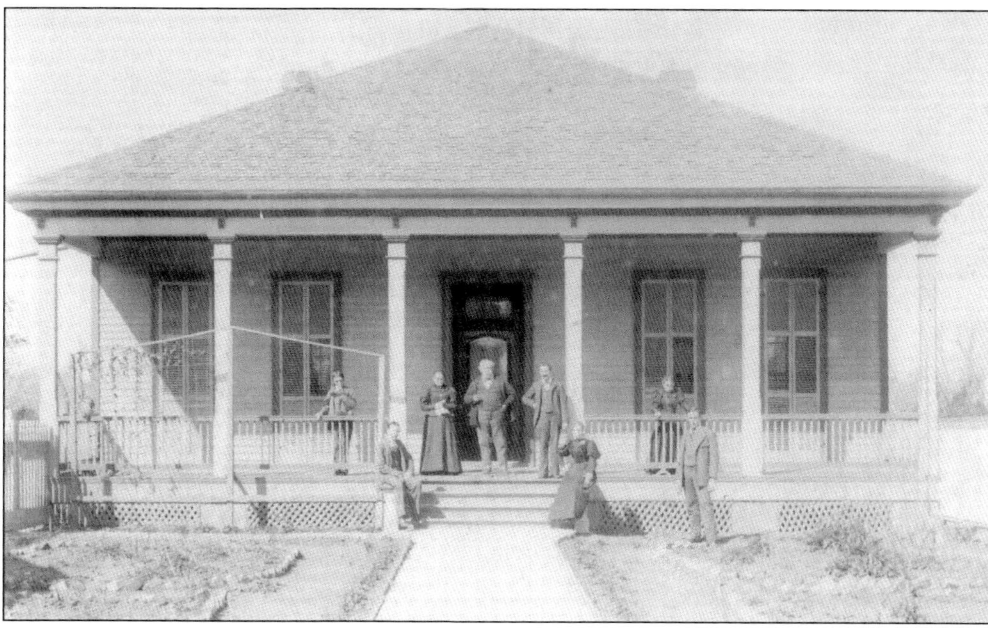

Moritz Rosenthal (center) and his wife, Hannah (center, left), stand in satisfaction on the porch of the fine house on Ferdinand Street. It is occupied by Moritz's descendants to this day. Also shown here are Joseph Max (far left) and Sam Rosenthal (second from left), Morris and Rena Rosenthal Burgas (right of center), Fannie Meyers (second from right), and Adolph Rosenthal. (Collection of Hannah Rosenthal Wood.)

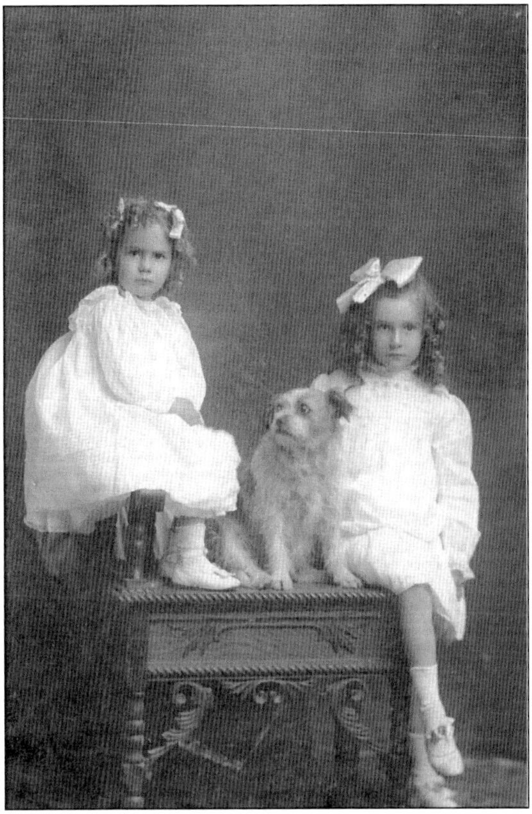

Mamie (right) and Sadie Fort lived at Catalpa Plantation, established in the early 1800s by William J. Fort. His grandson through marriage united the Forts with other early plantation families. Oakley's Eliza Pirrie's son with Rev. William Bowman married Sarah Turnbull, daughter of Rosedown's builders, and William J. Fort III (father of Mamie and Sadie) would marry not one but two beautiful Bowman daughters. (Collection of Mary Fort Thompson.)

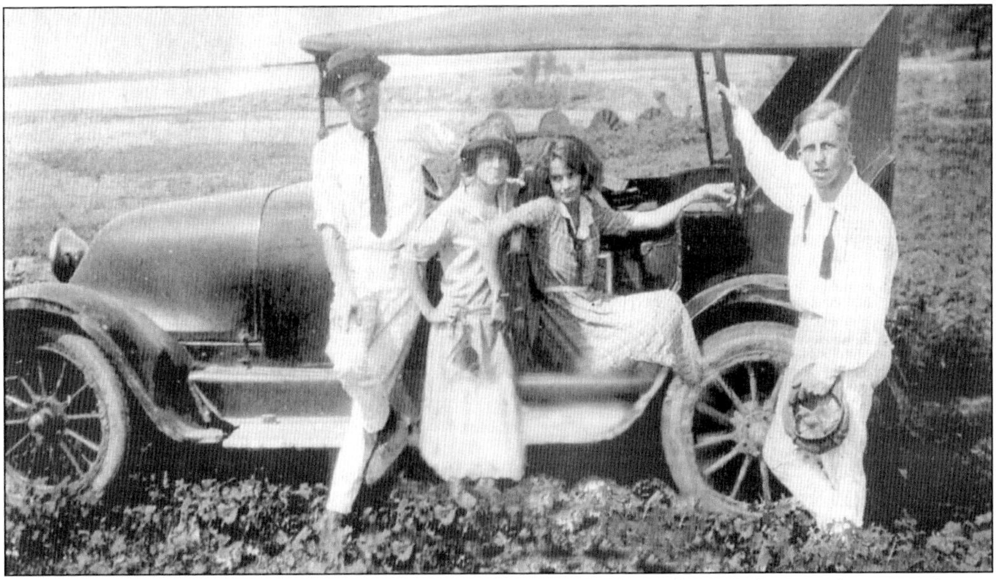

Seen here in the early 1920s, Mamie Fort (seated) and friend Sarah Brandon are shown with two handsome gentlemen. A fearless adventurer with a delicious wit, Fort was descended from the founding families of Rosedown and Oakley Plantations. At home at Catalpa Plantation, she toasted paying guests with sherry into her nineties and reveled in pointing out the Civil War bullet hole in the cast-iron greyhounds guarding the entrance. (Collection of Mary Fort Thompson.)

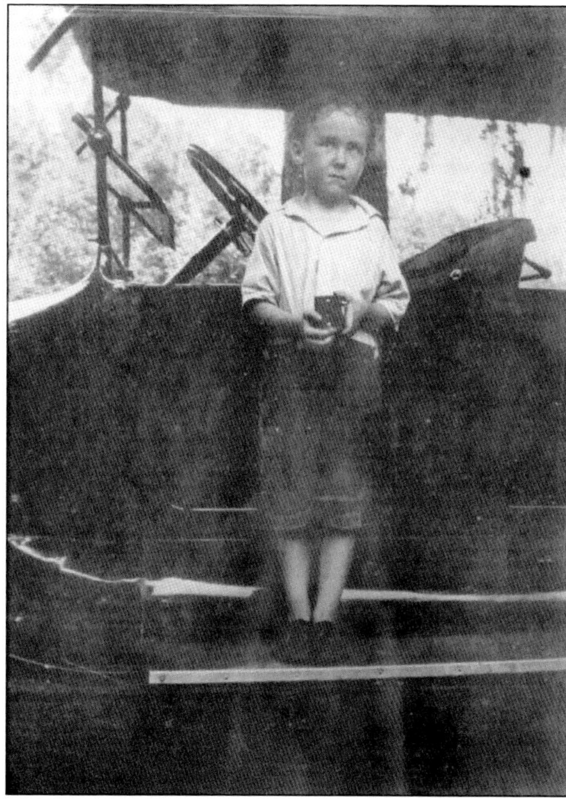

Charlie Butler, shown around 1913 in short pants on the running board of an early-model Dodge, was the last of the Butlers born at the Cottage Plantation, which was purchased by his great-grandfather in 1811. It was sold out of the family in the 1950s when the last two elderly residents, unmarried brother and sister, passed away. It is now a popular bed-and-breakfast. (Collection of Anne Butler.)

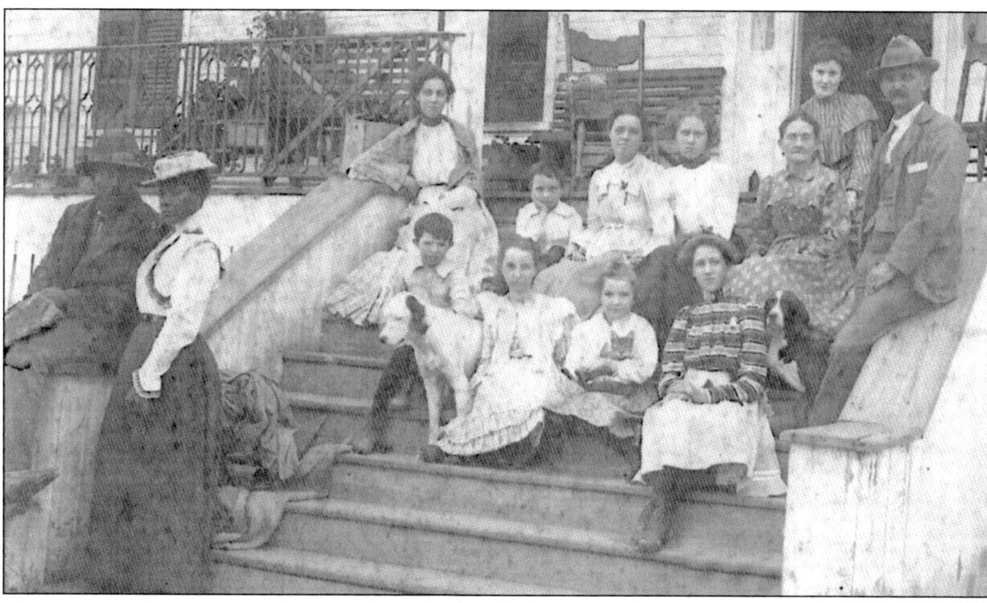

This turn-of-the-century photograph of the Reilly family at the big house on Angola Plantation shows Wesley Reilly, seated at right, with his wife, Annie, seated next to him. Also posing here are a number of their children, a few Barrows, a governess named Nettie Hayes, the mailman and cook (far left), and even a couple of dogs and cats. The plantation would soon become the state prison farm. (Collection of Anne W. Shoemake.)

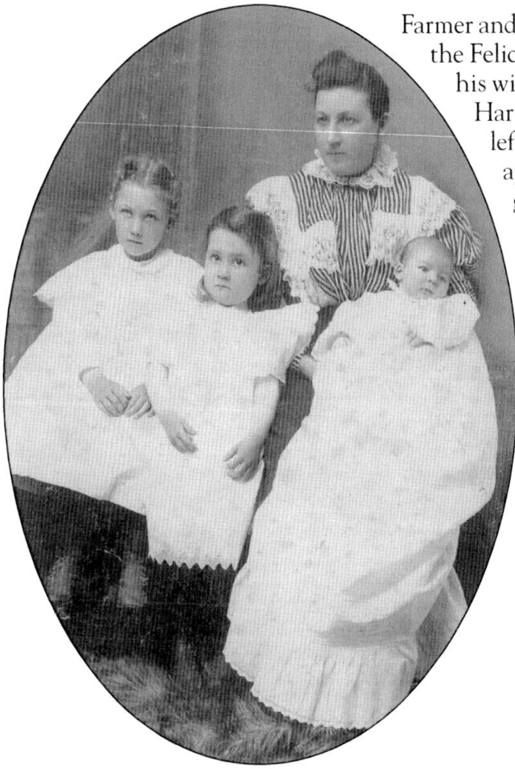

Farmer and cattleman Thomas DeWitt Bickham arrived in the Felicianas in the 1880s and had eight children with his wife, Sallie Belle Harvey, daughter of Nancy Ford Harvey. Here, she is shown with daughters Edith (far left) and Effie. Sallie is holding baby Ewell in what appears to be a long, lace-trimmed christening gown. (Collection of Beryl Bickham Eisworth.)

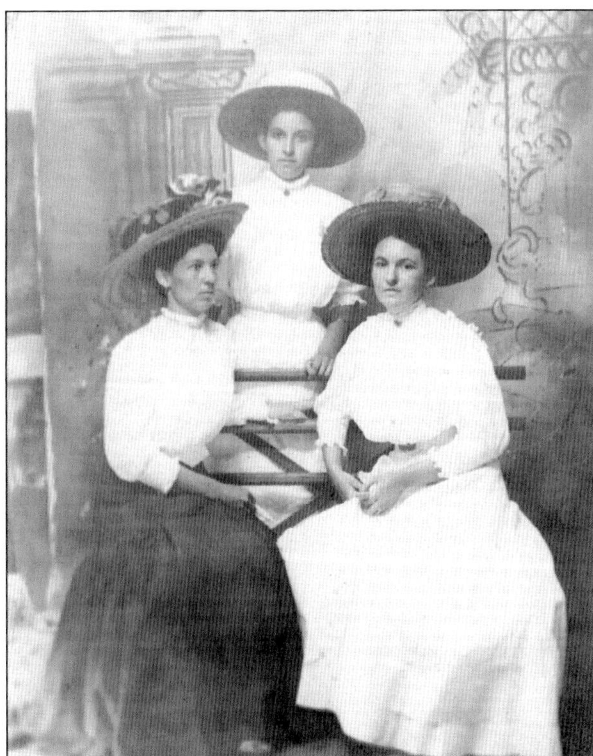

Seen here probably around the turn of the century are the sisters of Sallie Belle Harvey Bickham—Hattie Harvey (left), Lettie Harvey (center), and Dora Harvey Foxworth. They are wearing broad-brimmed hats resplendent with ribbons and flowers, high-necked blouses, and long skirts, which is typical attire of the times. (Collection of Beryl Bickham Eisworth.)

Edith Bickham, daughter of Thomas DeWitt and Sallie Belle Harvey Bickham, is shown here in her garden in 1895. She has a sorrowful look on her face, and it was no wonder: Edith had recently been widowed. Her husband, Claude Daniel, had served the parish as sheriff. (Collection of Beryl Bickham Eisworth.)

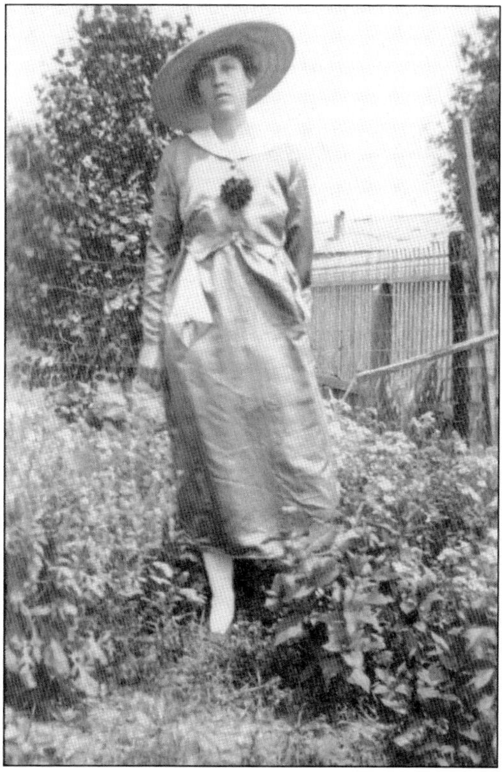

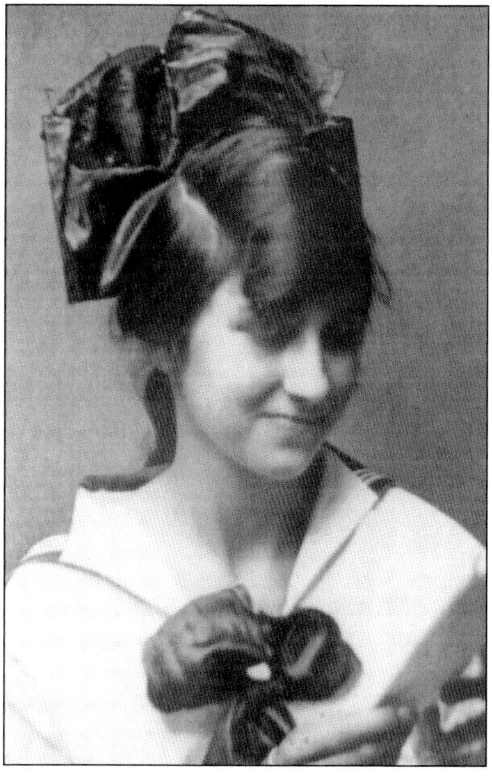

Beautiful young Thelma Bickham, one of eight children born to Thomas D. and Sallie Belle Bickham, would marry into the Terrebonne Parish family of US senator Allen Ellender. Her husband was the senator's brother Claude Ellender. She often served as the widowed congressman's hostess for social and political functions. (Collection of Beryl Bickham Eisworth.)

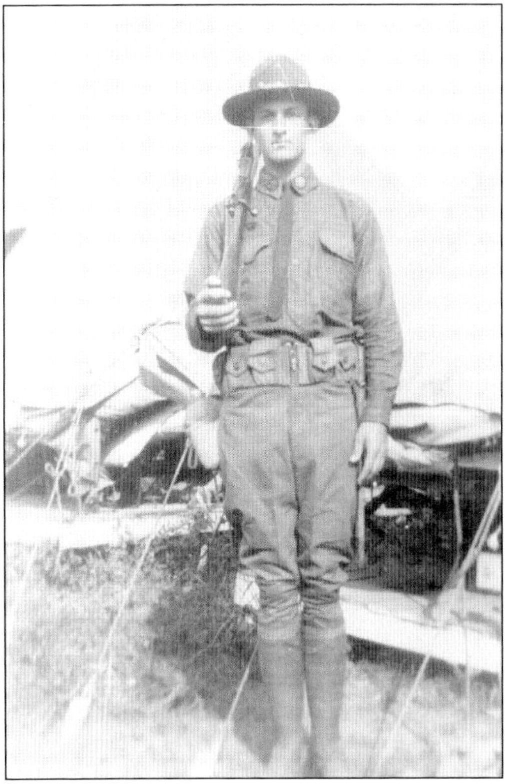

Leslie Bickham, seen here in uniform, participated in the 1920s in a national program called Citizens Military Training Camp, which consisted of part-time, four-year training and drills under the auspices of the US War Department at various military bases. He and his hometown friend Jim Leake attended training sessions in Florida and at Camp McClellan in Alabama. (Collection of Beryl Bickham Eisworth.)

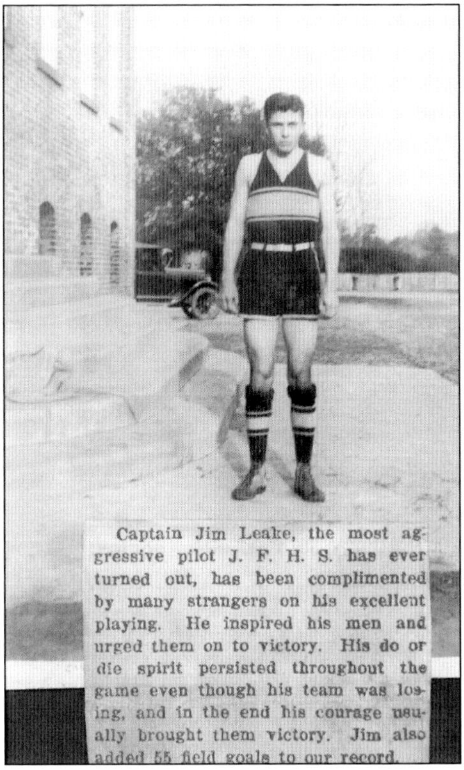

Jim Leake is shown at the entrance to Julius Freyhan School, the parish's first public school, constructed of brick in 1905. It burned down in 1907 and was rebuilt by 1909. Leake was captain of the basketball team and a star player. He was called "the most aggressive pilot JFHS has ever turned out, inspiring his men on to victory and making 55 field goals in a season." (Collection of Myrtle A. Brasseaux.)

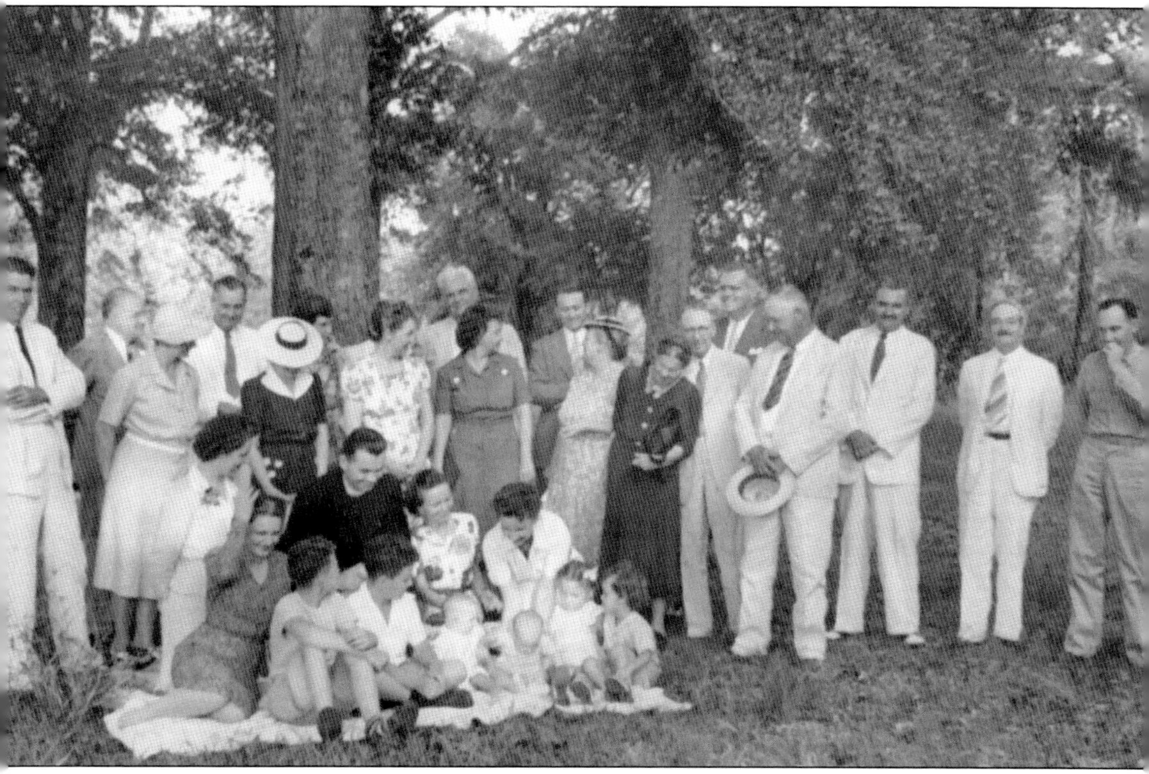

The Laurel Hill gentry, the men in their white linen or seersucker suits, are gathered under shade trees to preserve memories of a baptism in the summertime in the mid-1940s. Shown here are, from left to right, (seated) children Hamilton Willis, Bertram Babers III, William Ruffin Barrow, Douglas Barrow, Mary Barrow and McConnell Barrow; (kneeling) adults JoAnne Savage, Ruth Babers, unidentified priest, May Bolling Cross (Mrs. Holloway), and El Barrow; (standing) Jackson Babers, Bolling Cross and his wife Nell Cross, Ruffin Hamilton, Bella Buchanan (future Mrs. Ruffin Hamilton), Mary Hamilton Willis, Lucille Jackson, Natalie Barrow, Bertram Babers Sr., Estelle McConnell Barrow, Fred Holloway, Mrs. Pelayo, Jane Argue, Warren Seymour, Bertram Babers Jr., Douglas Montrose Hamilton, Montrose Hamilton Barrow, Mr. Pelayo, and Lt. Col. Ruffin Calhoun Barrow. Area plantations represented by these families included Tanglewild, Rosemound, Hazelwood, Laurel Hill, Independence, Ambrosia, and Inheritance. The close relationships of these families may be seen by the repetition of family names in various combinations. (Collection of Mary Anne Stevens.)

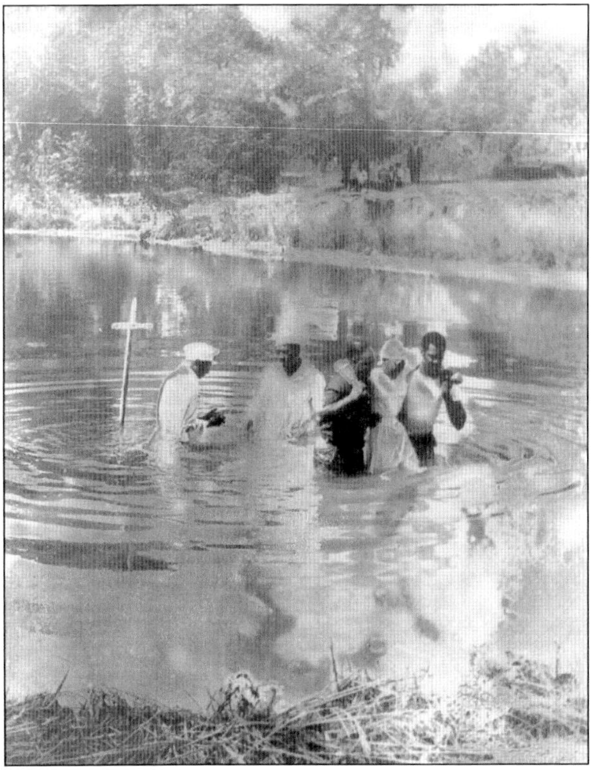

Into the mid-1900s, Rosedown Baptist Church still baptized the time-honored way, with full immersion in pond waters to literally and figuratively wash away sins. Plantation owners had given an acre of land for church and cemetery. Here, Rev. Lafayette Veal (left) has just baptized a young church member, shown being helped from the water by deacons, including Nolan Veal (center). (Collection of Anne Butler.)

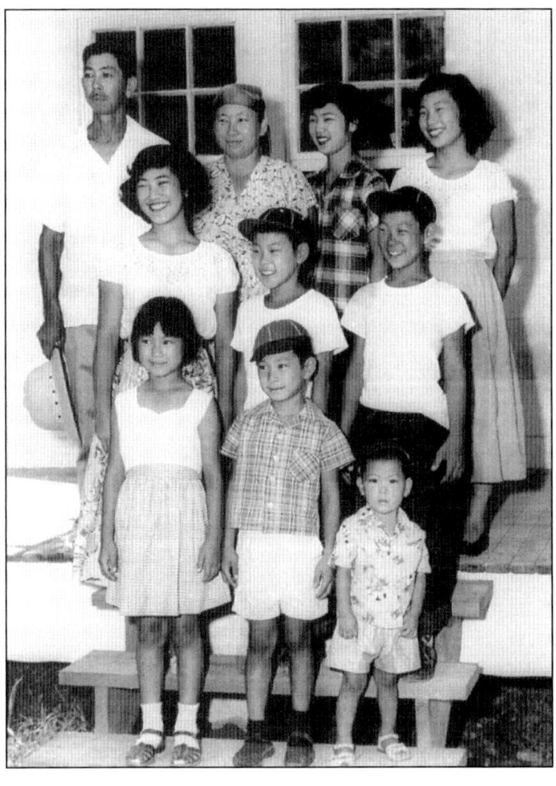

After enduring being interned during World War II, the Imahara family left California and moved to St. Francisville to restore the 19th-century gardens of Afton Villa Plantation. Parents James and Haruka are in the third row, far left. Recently, son Walter (second row, right), a retired nurseryman and world champion weightlifter, has developed an incredible contemporary garden called Imahara's Botanical Garden to honor his family's horticultural legacy. (Collection of Metz/Imahara family.)

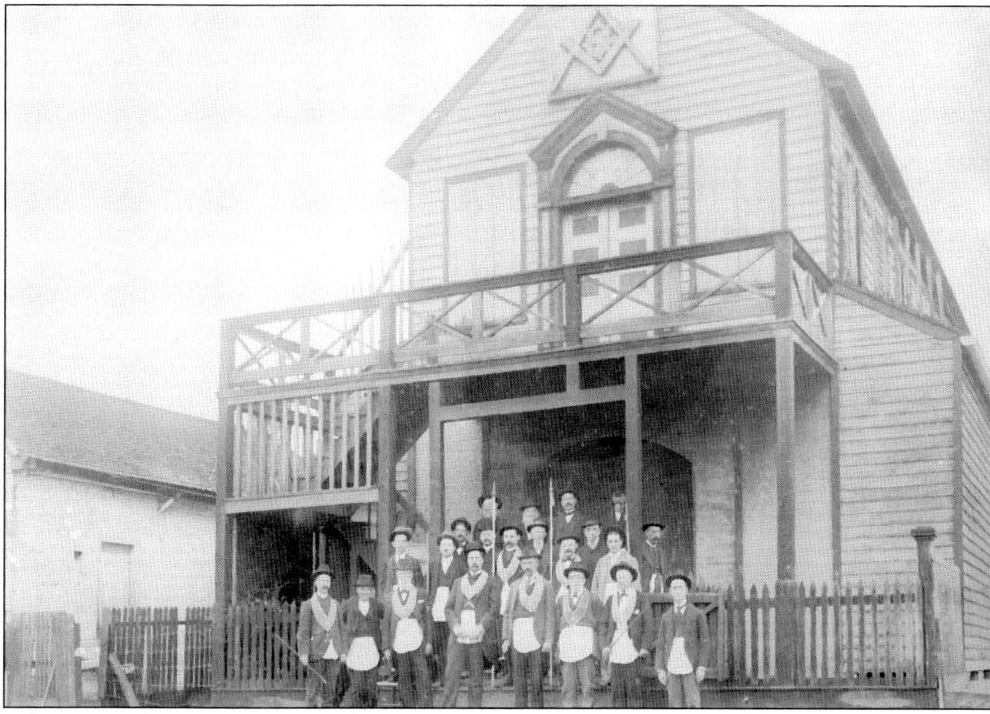

Feliciana Lodge No. 31, Free and Accepted Masons, officially chartered on March 25, 1828, was organized as early as 1817. The second-oldest lodge in the state, its members met for years in Audubon Market Hall (pictured). The powerful ties of this brotherhood were demonstrated in 1863, when Confederate Masons literally stopped the Civil War to respectfully bury a Union gunboat commander, a brother Mason from Schenectady, New York. (WFHS.)

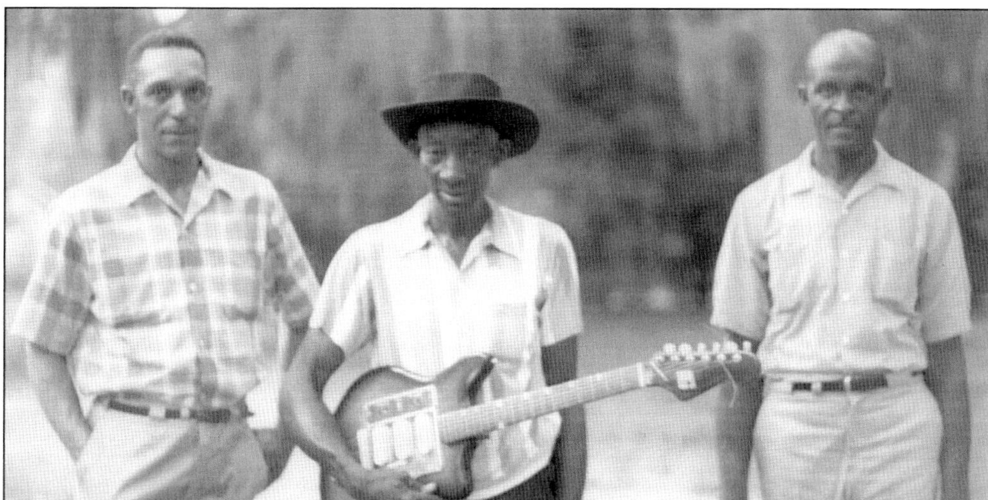

Blues musician Scott Dunbar (center) is shown here with Sam Davis (left) and John Richardson. Dunbar made his first guitar at eight from a cigar box and left school to support his family, working for 50¢ a day. A popular fishing guide, he wired his lakeside cabin to overhanging branches; when the Mississippi floodwaters pushed into Lake Mary, the house shifted, but it would not be washed away. (Collection of Mary Fort Thompson.)

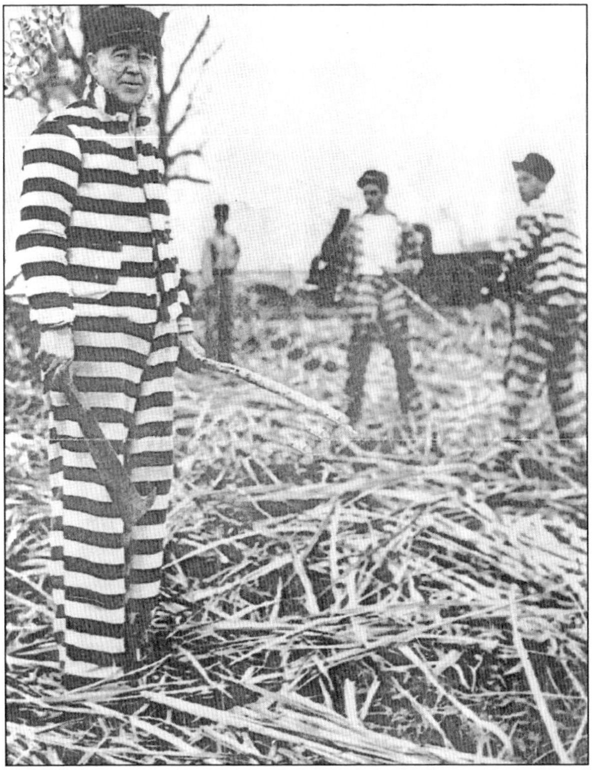

Caught up in what was known as the Louisiana Hayride scandals of the Huey Long era of politics in Louisiana, Dr. James Monroe Smith (left) was president of Louisiana State University. He was considered "politically pliable" and an "academic puppet" for Governor Long. Dr. Smith was convicted of forgery, embezzlement, mail fraud, and tax evasion and was sentenced to Louisiana State Penitentiary at Angola. (Collection of Louisiana State Penitentiary.)

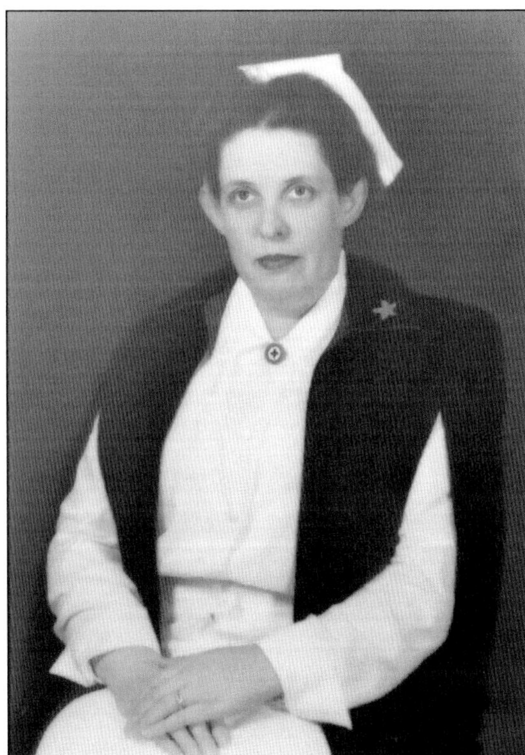

The first nurse at the state prison at a time when there were no resident physicians, Irish-born Mary Margaret Daugherty was considered by inmates their angel of mercy. She bravely became an outspoken witness before the Citizens' Committee appointed by Gov. Earl Long to look into allegations of brutality and mistreatment at Angola. She resigned in 1951 after nearly eight years of treating victims of rampant violence. (Collection of Louisiana State Penitentiary.)

Mattie Carter is shown in July 1948 beside the old cypress barrel cistern used to catch rainwater at Oakley Plantation. She was one of the early staff members who worked so hard to restore the historic home when the state purchased the property after the last of the Matthews family, elderly descendants of Audubon's pupil Eliza Pirrie, died or went into nursing homes. (Collection of Louisiana Office of State Parks.)

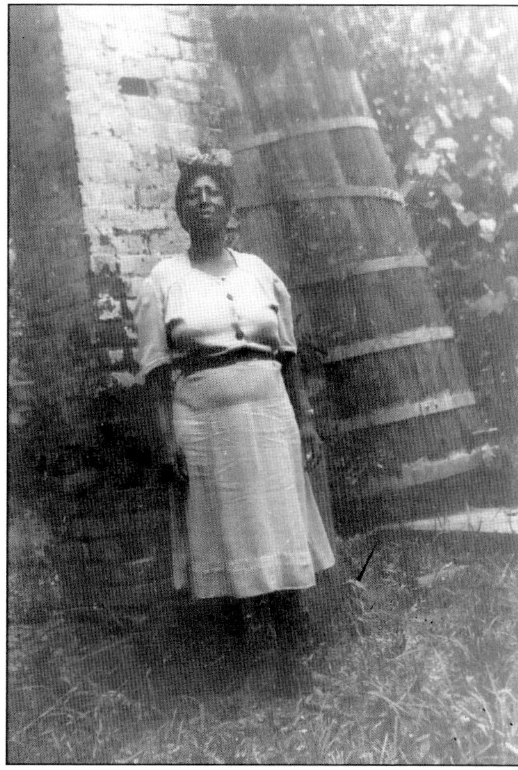

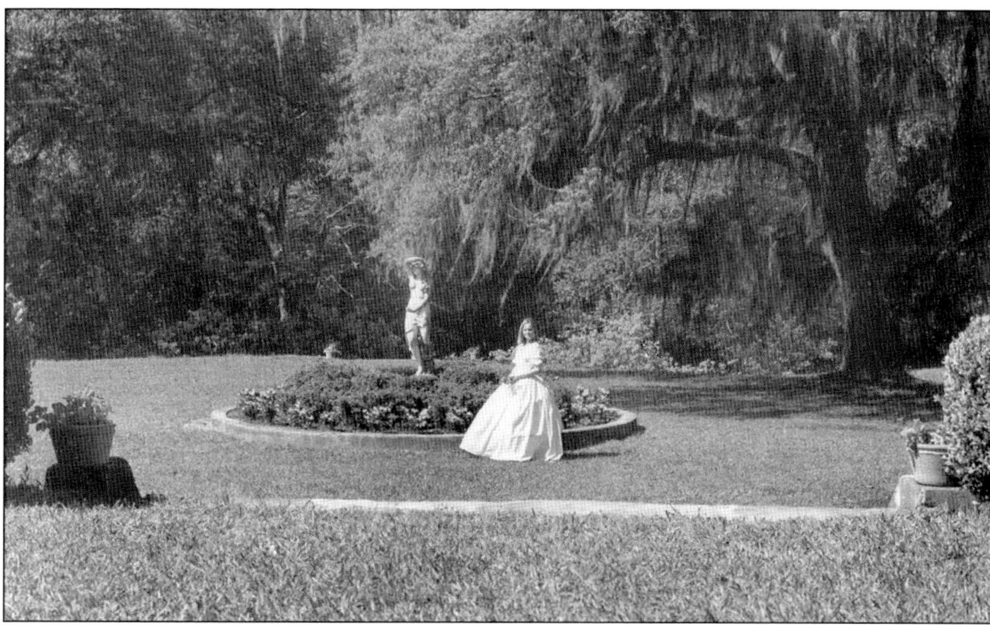

The remarkable 19th-century gardens saved many an old plantation when they touched the hearts of preservationists, including Rosedown and Afton Villa (shown here). Even after the house had burned down in the 1960s, the magnificent oak avenue and hardy plantings at Afton inspired the Morrell Trimbles to restore the landscaping and turn what could have been a desolate site into an inspiring thing of real beauty. (WFHS.)

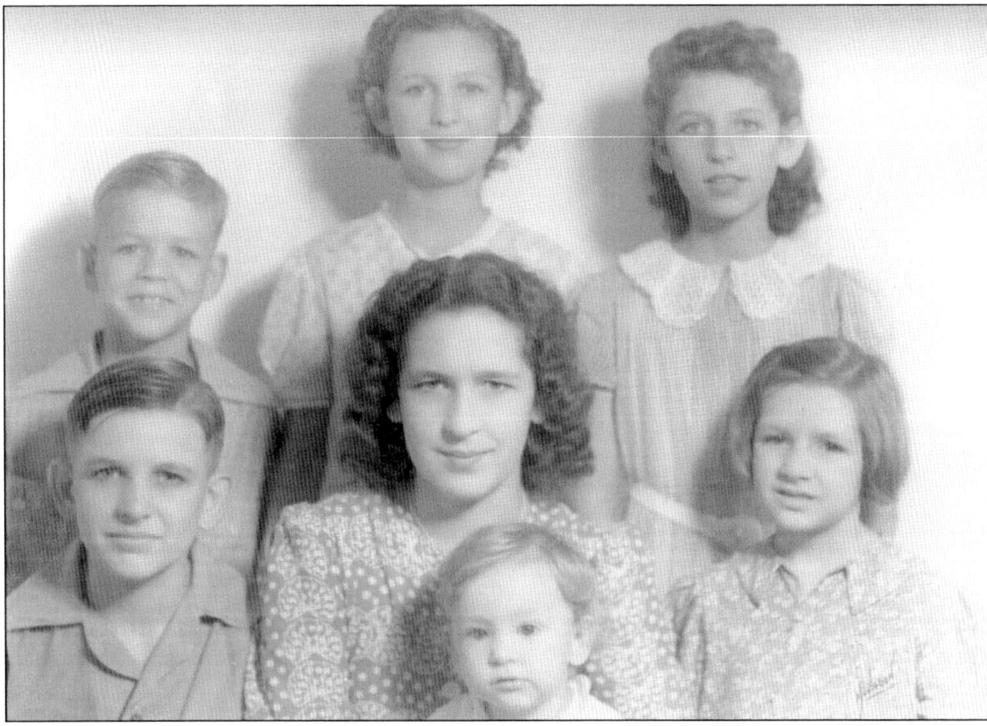

In 1938, Phillip Morris Bennett Sr. moved his family to St. Francisville in an old Model A. There were six children at the time; seven are shown in this photograph, and there would eventually be nine. They all helped operate the ferry system across the Mississippi River, consisting of two old tugs, the *Melville* and the *Red Cross*, and a wooden barge to hold a few cars. (Collection of Bennett family.)

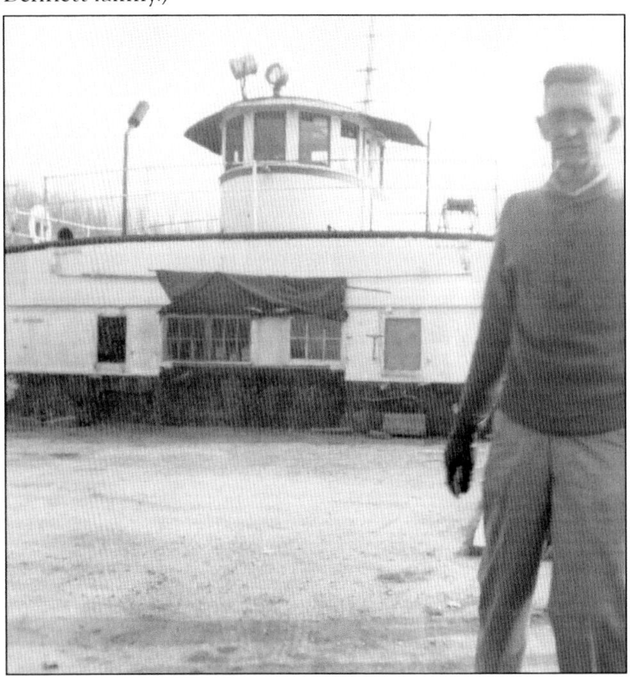

P. Morris Bennett Jr. was five years old when he first took to the water, helping his father operate the ferry across the Mississippi River. He would make his career as a licensed ferry pilot, transporting everything from elephants and monkeys, moonshiners and revenuers, motorcycle weddings and runaway boars. In the 1950s, the state took over ownership of the ferries. Morris Bennett Sr. is shown here. (Collection of Bennett family.)

Six

Community Life

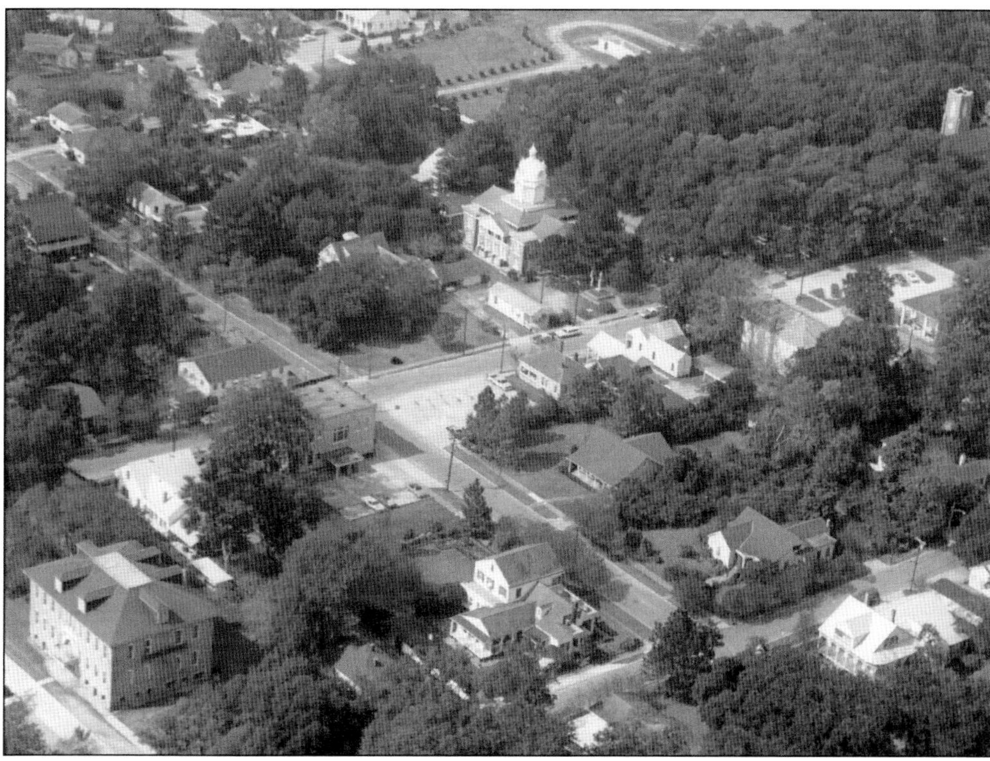

This aerial photograph shows the West Feliciana Parish Courthouse (center), and, beyond it, Our Lady of Mount Carmel Catholic Church's cemetery. Just peeping above the tree line on the right is the bell tower of Grace Episcopal Church. In the foreground at left is Julius Freyhan School, which was built, burned down, and rebuilt in the first decade of the 20th century as St. Francisville's first public school. (WFHS.)

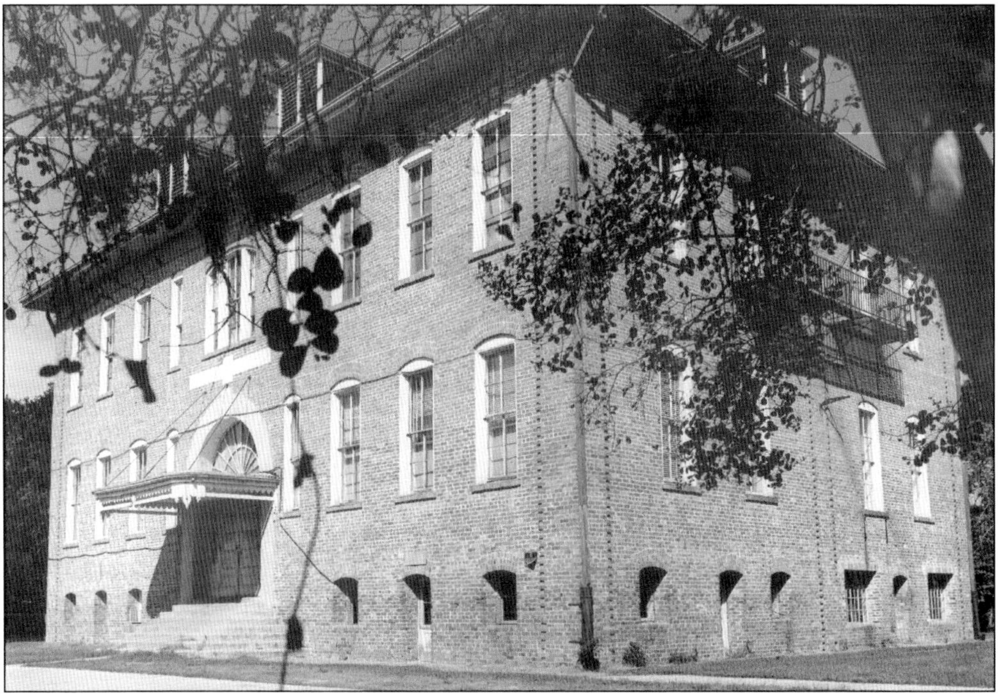

Built in 1905 with primary funding from wealthy merchant Julius Freyhan, the eight-room brick school overlooked the river. It featured handsome decoration and an upper auditorium with a ceiling of pressed tin. In February 1907, the local paper had horrifying news: "The Julius Freyhan High School burned to the ground last night," despite the efforts of hose companies and local citizens. Freyhan's widow donated toward its rebuilding, which was completed in 1909. (WFHS.)

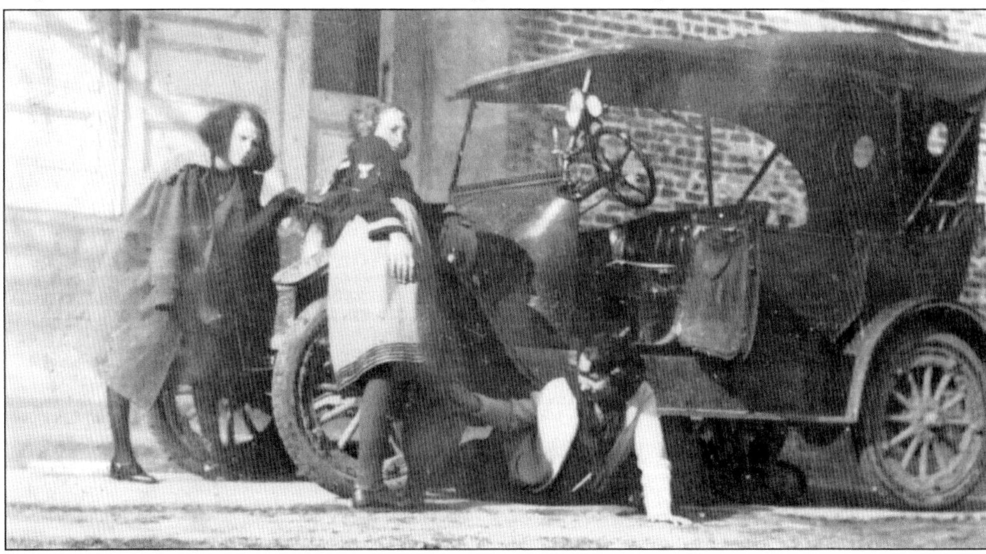

These girls clowning in front of Julius Freyhan School had a car, but when the school first opened, many students rode horseback from country plantations or caught the train into St. Francisville. There was a row of stalls behind the school, and students fed and watered their own horses. During rainy weather, horse-riding students were dismissed early, as some had 25 miles to ride home. (Collection of Myrtle A. Brasseaux.)

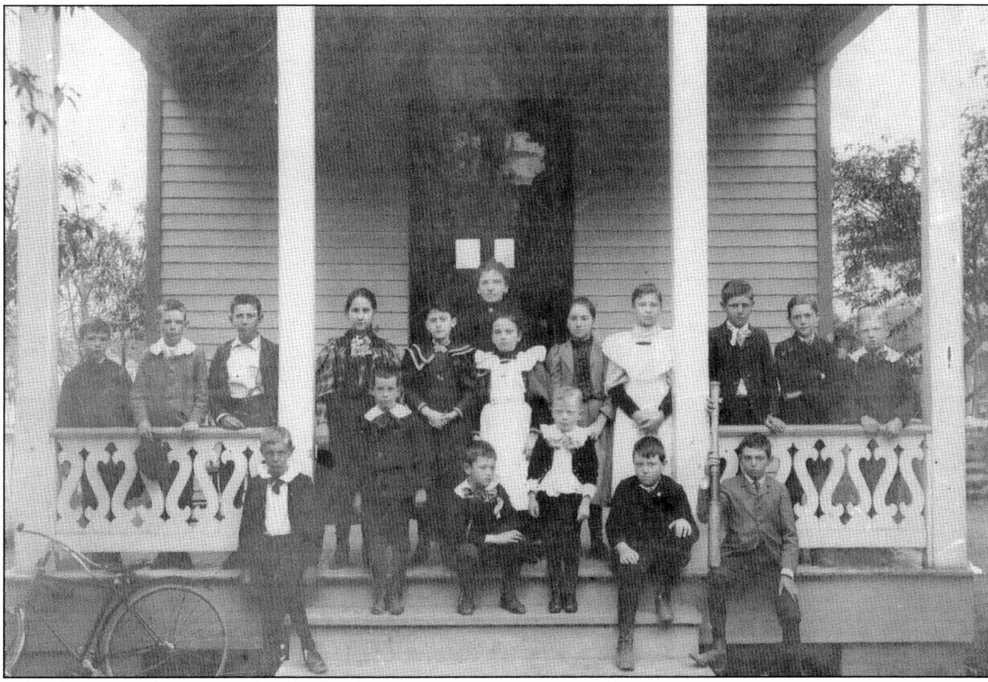

Small private academies like Miss Raynham's on Royal Street preceded the opening of Freyhan High. By 1916, there were also ten rural white schools, one black school in town, and 13 rural black schools, all struggling to exist on a tax millage of 3 percent, aggregating $5,230.58 for the year. In addition, poll taxes brought in $935.25, the Police Jury donated $600, and the St. Francisville Town Council gave $643.98. (WFHS.)

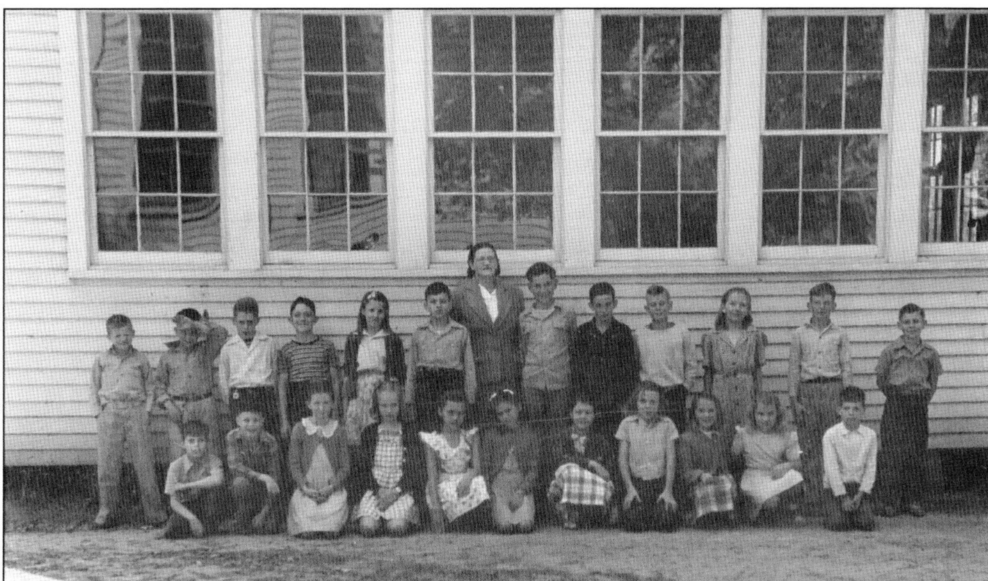

Anybody who grew up in St. Francisville will say that his or her favorite teacher was Gretchen Weydert. She lived in the family home now called Evergreenzine, on Ferdinand Street, just a block away from her father's business, the Charles Weydert Hardware Store and blacksmith shop. (Collection of Weydert family.)

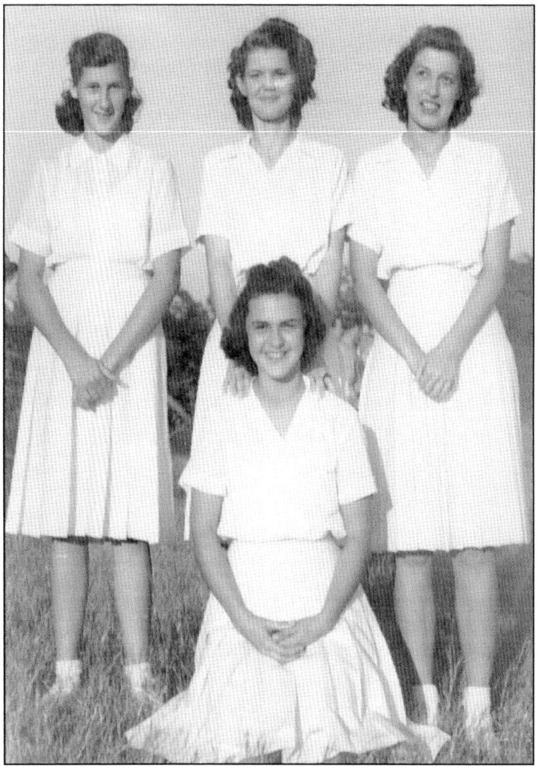

Cheerleaders for Julius Freyhan School in 1941 wear outfits considerably more modest than the scintillating suits of today. Shown here are, standing from left to right, Lucy Percy, Mary Walker, and Rose Butler; kneeling in front, Billie Morris. The school overlooks the river from its hilltop location. The football field down the hill also served as an amphitheater for graduation exercises and other community gatherings. (Collection of Bennett family.)

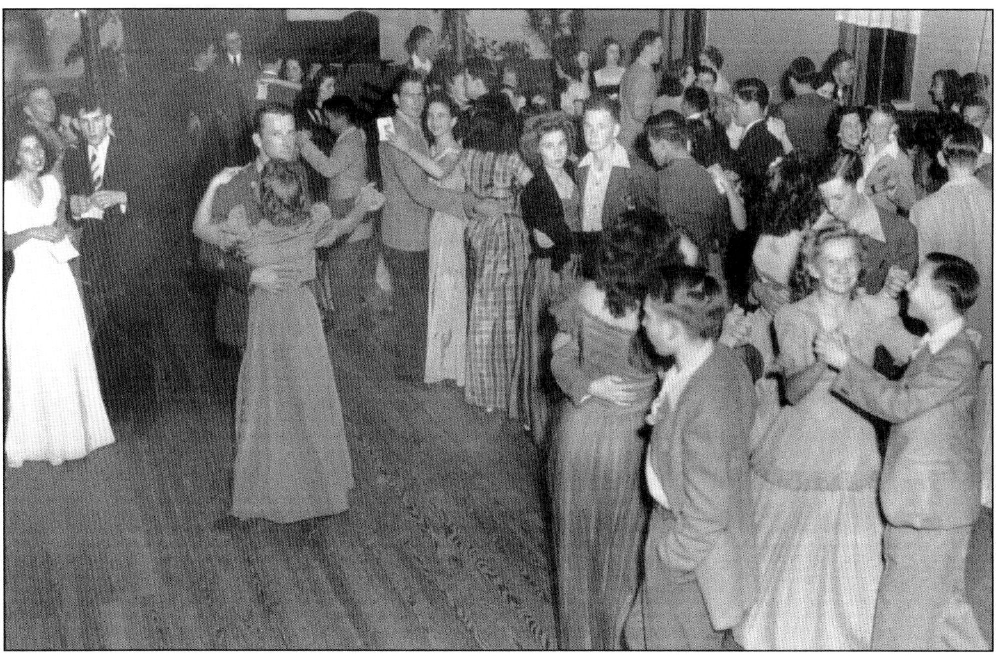

Holiday dances, like this one with smilax Christmas vine twined up the posts for decoration, permitted everyone to dress up in finery. These were highly anticipated events, as evidenced by the excitement shown by the smiling young couple at bottom right. Dances were held in church parish halls or in the social halls of various organizations. (WFHS.)

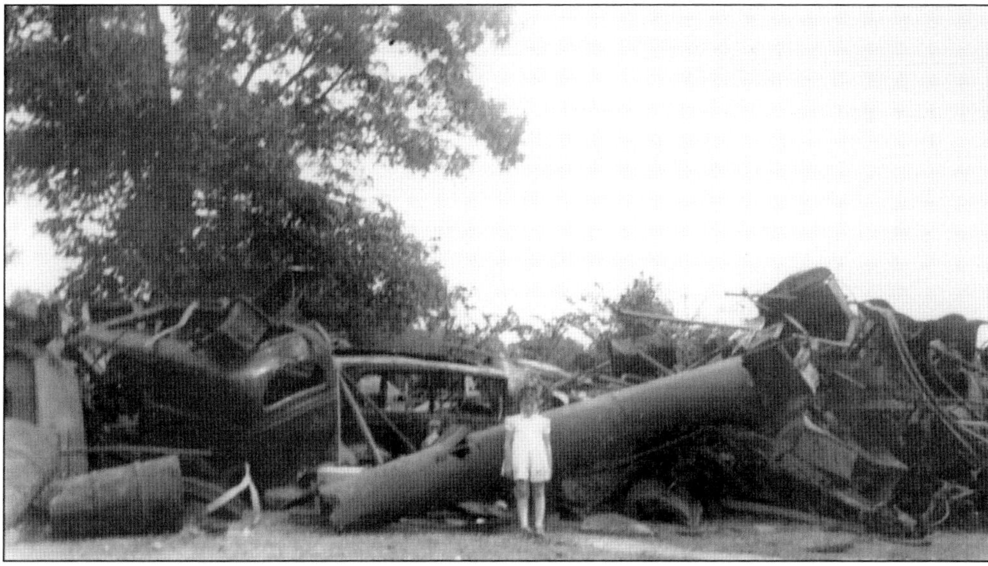

Helen Kendrick poses in front of the massive pile of scrap iron collected for the war effort in the 1940s. Everything was useful, from old cars or truck cabs to gigantic smokestacks and farm machinery. The brave boys of the parish enlisted in huge numbers. A war memorial in St. Francisville's downtown Parker Park celebrates their wartime service. (Collection of Helen Kendrick Williams.)

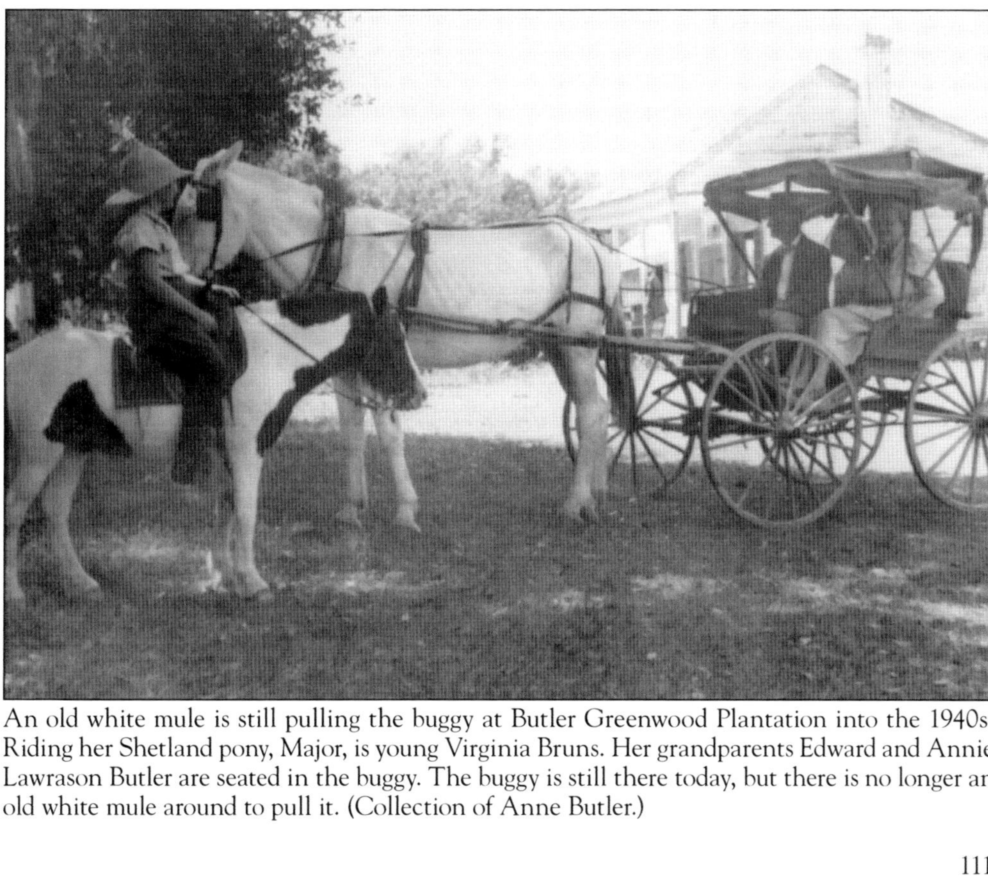

An old white mule is still pulling the buggy at Butler Greenwood Plantation into the 1940s. Riding her Shetland pony, Major, is young Virginia Bruns. Her grandparents Edward and Annie Lawrason Butler are seated in the buggy. The buggy is still there today, but there is no longer an old white mule around to pull it. (Collection of Anne Butler.)

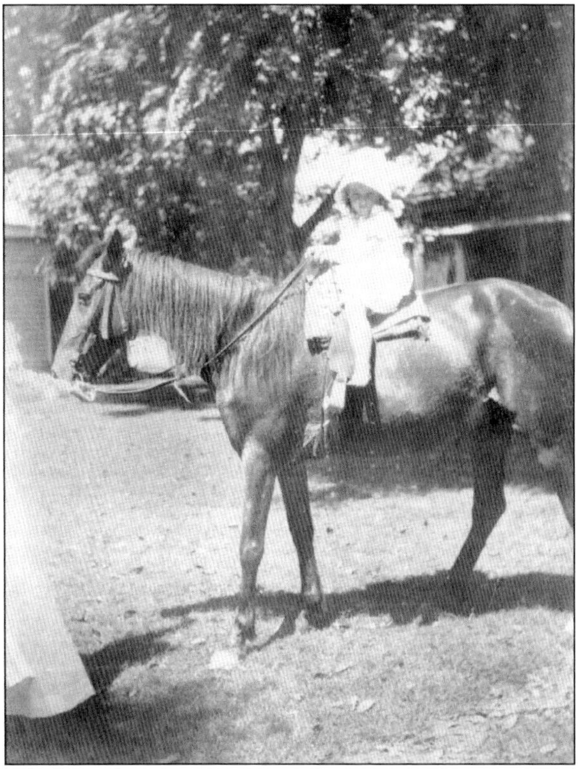

This little miss with her bare feet and big sunbonnet enjoys a horseback ride on the grounds of the Cottage Plantation. Every country place had its riding horses, as well as draft horses and carriage horses. The Cottage barn still houses the old state carriage purchased in Philadelphia in 1820 for Capt. Richard Butler, complete with silver handles, silk curtains, and velvet lining. (Collection of Anne Butler.)

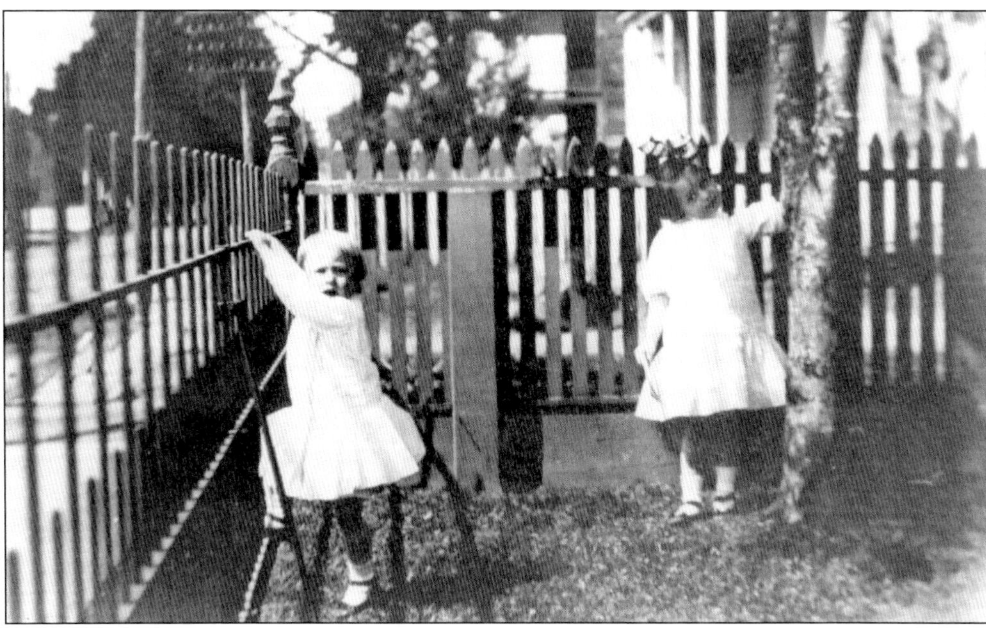

The little daughters of Cap'n Johnny Irvine, by his 1904 marriage to the widowed niece of his stepmother, had a pampered life, romping in the front yard of their fancy house in Bayou Sara. The home was enclosed by iron fencing, with stylish galleried houses for neighbors. The children were not so carefree when floods wiped out the Irvine empire in Bayou Sara and they moved up the hill into St. Francisville. (WFHS.)

In little country towns like St. Francisville in the early to mid-1900s, entertainment was where one could find it. Sometimes, being silly was just plain fun. This photograph from an old scrapbook is labeled "The Bees Knees." It shows a couple of girls, stockings rolled down below their knees and skirts hiked up, having a good time. (Collection of Myrtle A. Brasseaux.)

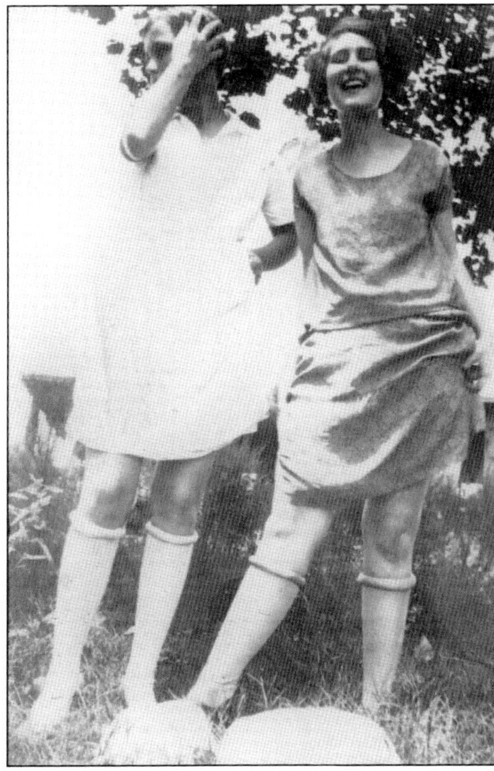

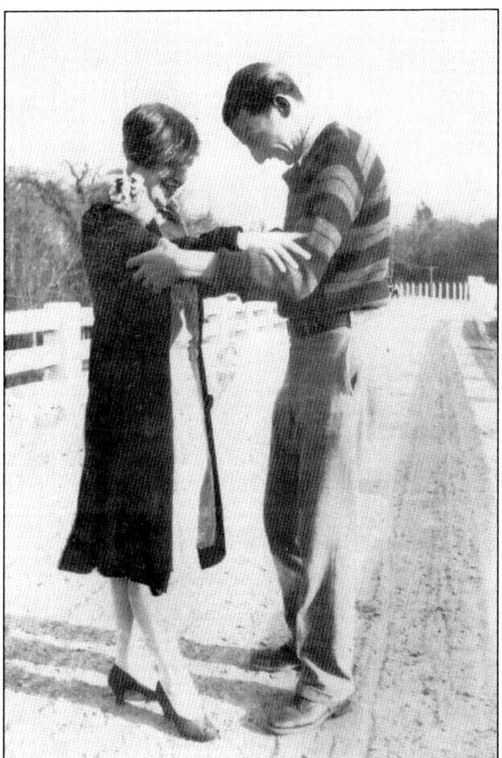

All dressed up and nowhere to go? This stylish couple, her coat collar of fur and his sweater carefully tucked into his trousers, was captured doing the Charleston on an old wood-railed bridge, its surface apparently still dirt. This photograph is from the familiar black pages of an old scrapbook. (Collection of Myrtle A. Brasseaux.)

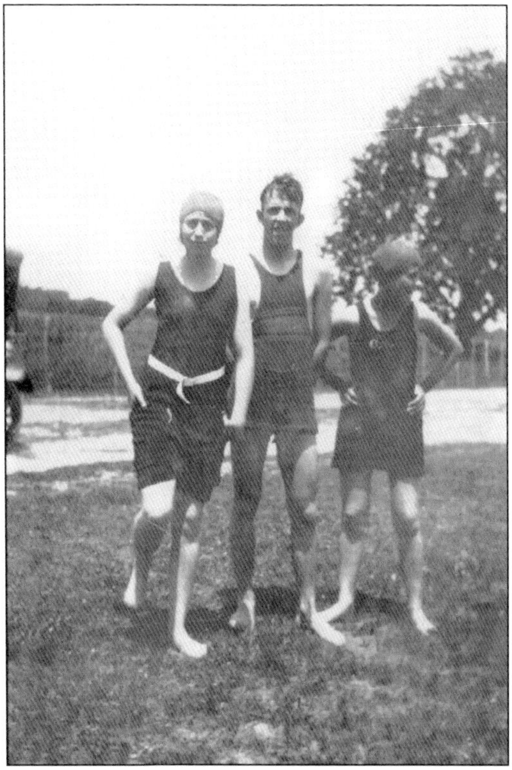

It was not until 1947 that St. Francisville mayor Mumford Leake spearheaded a volunteer effort to build a swimming pool in town. His athletic wife, Lucille, served for years as head of the Red Cross swimming and water safety courses there. Before that, the many creeks with their sandy bottoms provided swimming holes, some more dangerous than others. (Collection of Myrtle A. Brasseaux.)

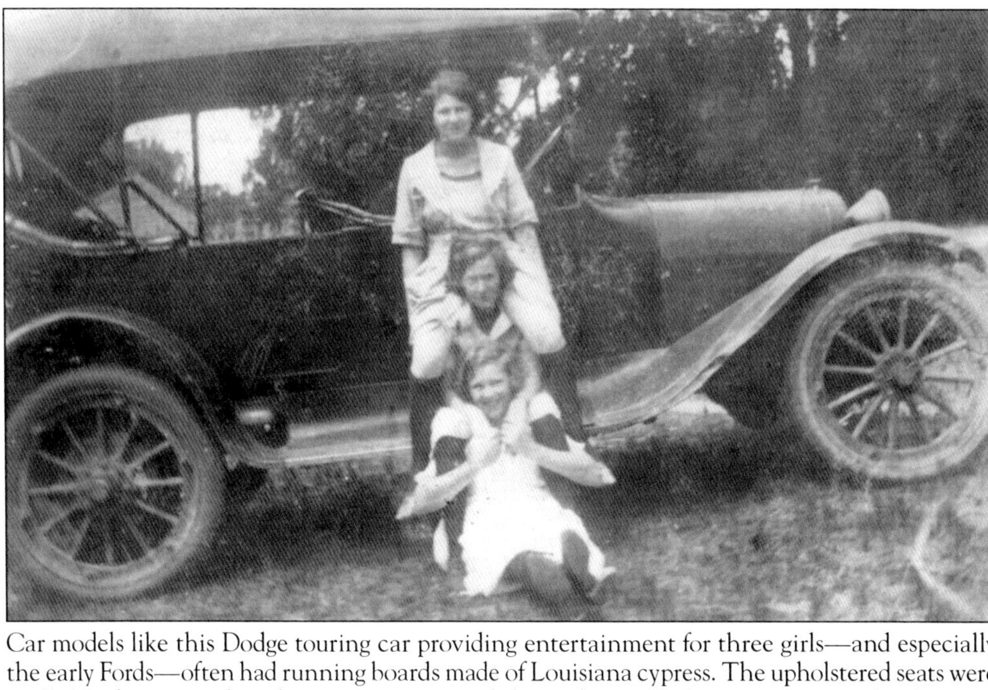

Car models like this Dodge touring car providing entertainment for three girls—and especially the early Fords—often had running boards made of Louisiana cypress. The upholstered seats were stuffed with moss gathered in area swamps and shipped to carmakers in crates made of cypress boards. It was not long before the cypress itself was more prized than the dried moss. (Collection of Myrtle A. Brasseaux.)

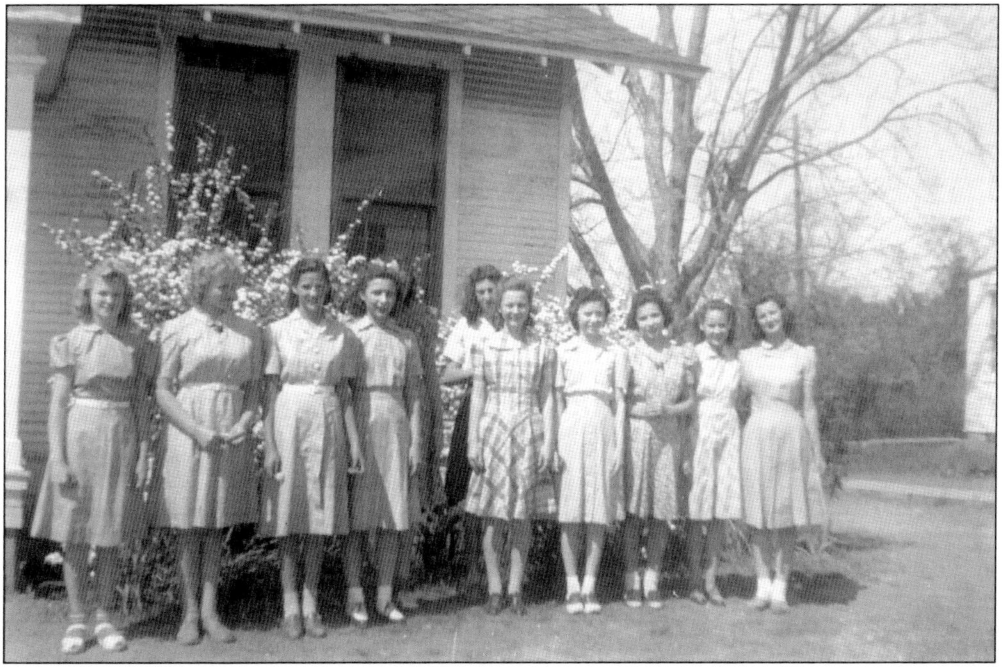

Organizations like the Junior Homemakers Club, shown in these 1941 photographs, kept the students at Julius Freyhan School entertained and occupied. The girls shown here proudly wear dresses they made in class. Organized sports, 4-H and animal husbandry groups, Camp Fire Girls, and other clubs hosted dances and social get-togethers. Dramatic performances were held in the magnificent third-floor auditorium inside the school or in the amphitheater just below the school. And home economics classes taught the practical skills of daily living. Such classroom and extracurricular activities kept young students in St. Francisville involved with their friends and neighbors, making memories and friendships that would last lifetimes. (Collection of Bennett family.)

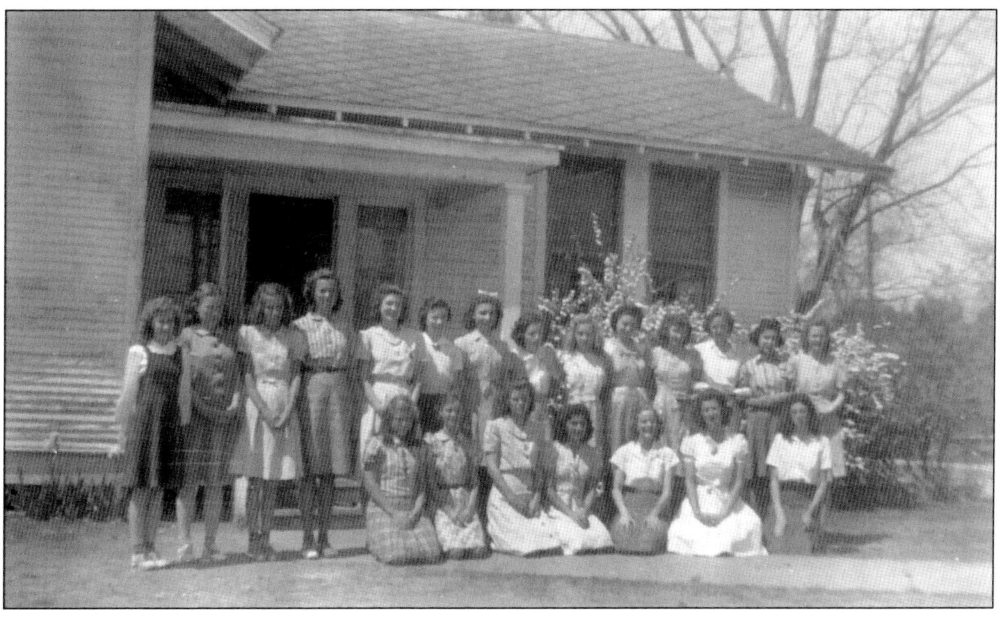

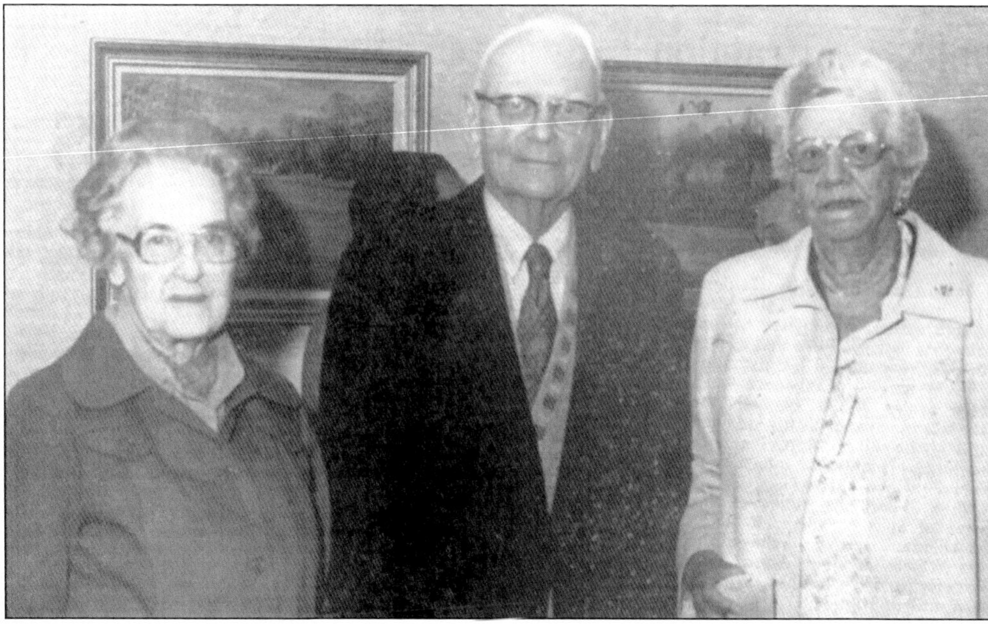

It was in 1947 that Davis Folkes, called the dean of the Louisiana Legislature for his many years of dedicated service, persuaded the state to purchase Oakley Plantation. White-haired and the quintessential Southern gentleman, Folkes, from Fairview Plantation, poses here with his wife, Alice Pipes (left), and longtime schoolteacher Margaret "Miss Mott" Plettinger. (Collection of Bank of St. Francisville Calendar.)

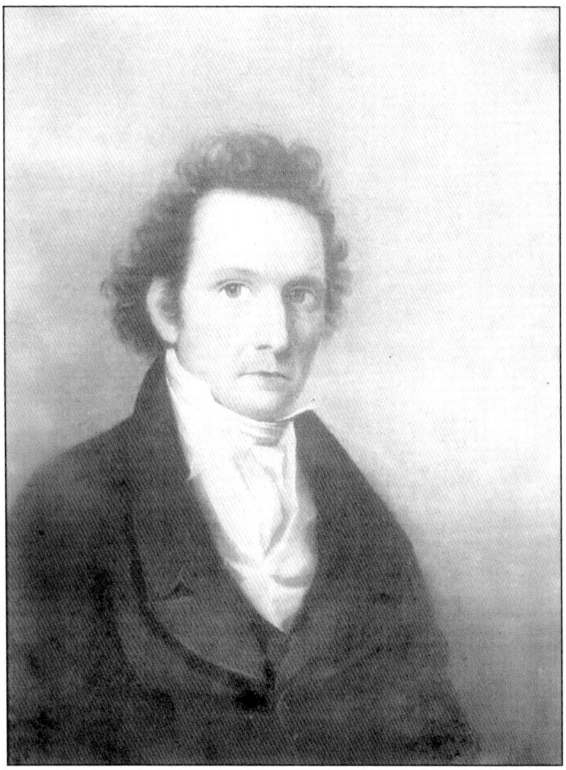

Its association with artist-naturalist John James Audubon gave Oakley Plantation its historic significance. In 1821, he tutored the young daughter of the family there and painted dozens of his bird studies. Audubon returned to the parish over the next few years to visit his wife, Lucy, who remained in the area. He is shown here in 1827 at Beech Woods. (Collection of Louisiana Office of State Parks.)

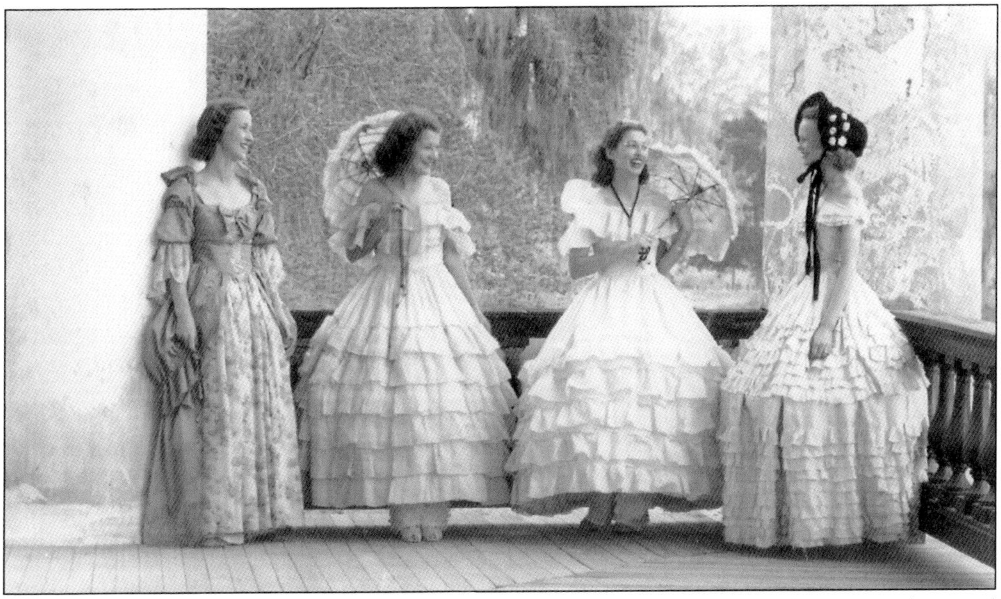

Frank and Naomi Percy purchased the 1830 Greenwood Plantation in the early 1900s and opened it for tours and as sets for movies, such as *Drango*, starring the dashing Jeff Chandler. Dressed in re-created antebellum costumes, from left to right, belles May De Laureal, Lillian Spillman, Rose Butler, and Polly Blevins greeted guests to the plantation. Plantations like Greenwood, Afton Villa, and Rosedown were opened periodically, at least until Greenwood (now rebuilt) and Afton Villa burned down in the 1960s. (WFHS.)

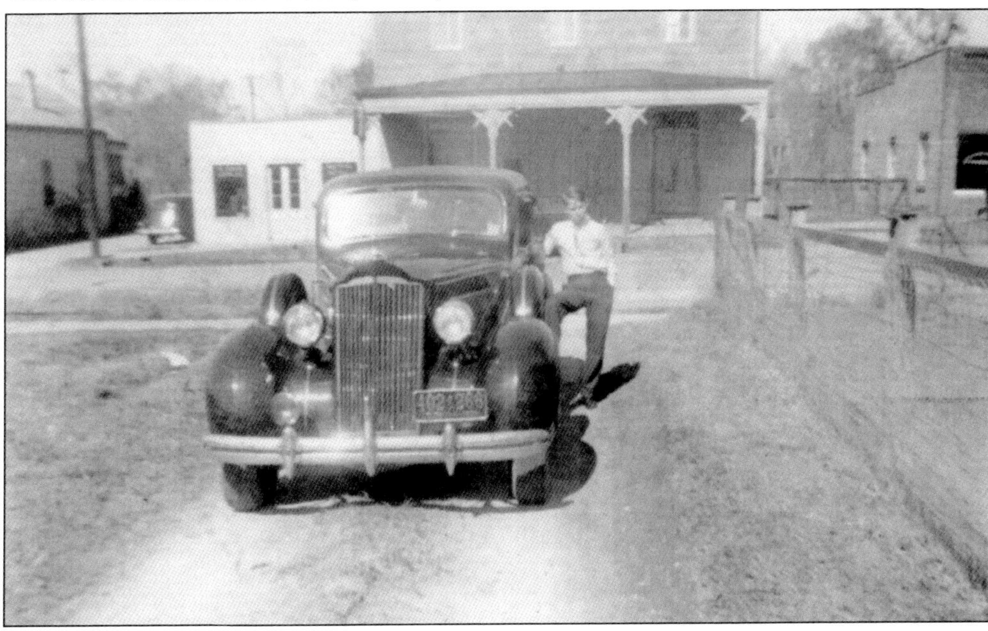

The 1880s hardware store of Charles Weydert, seen here in the background, was purchased by the West Feliciana Historical Society to house headquarters and a museum in the first coordinated effort to combine tourism and historic preservation. The society has restored a number of significant structures throughout St. Francisville and maintains its museum and tourist information center in the beautifully repurposed structure today. (Collection of Helen Kendrick Williams.)

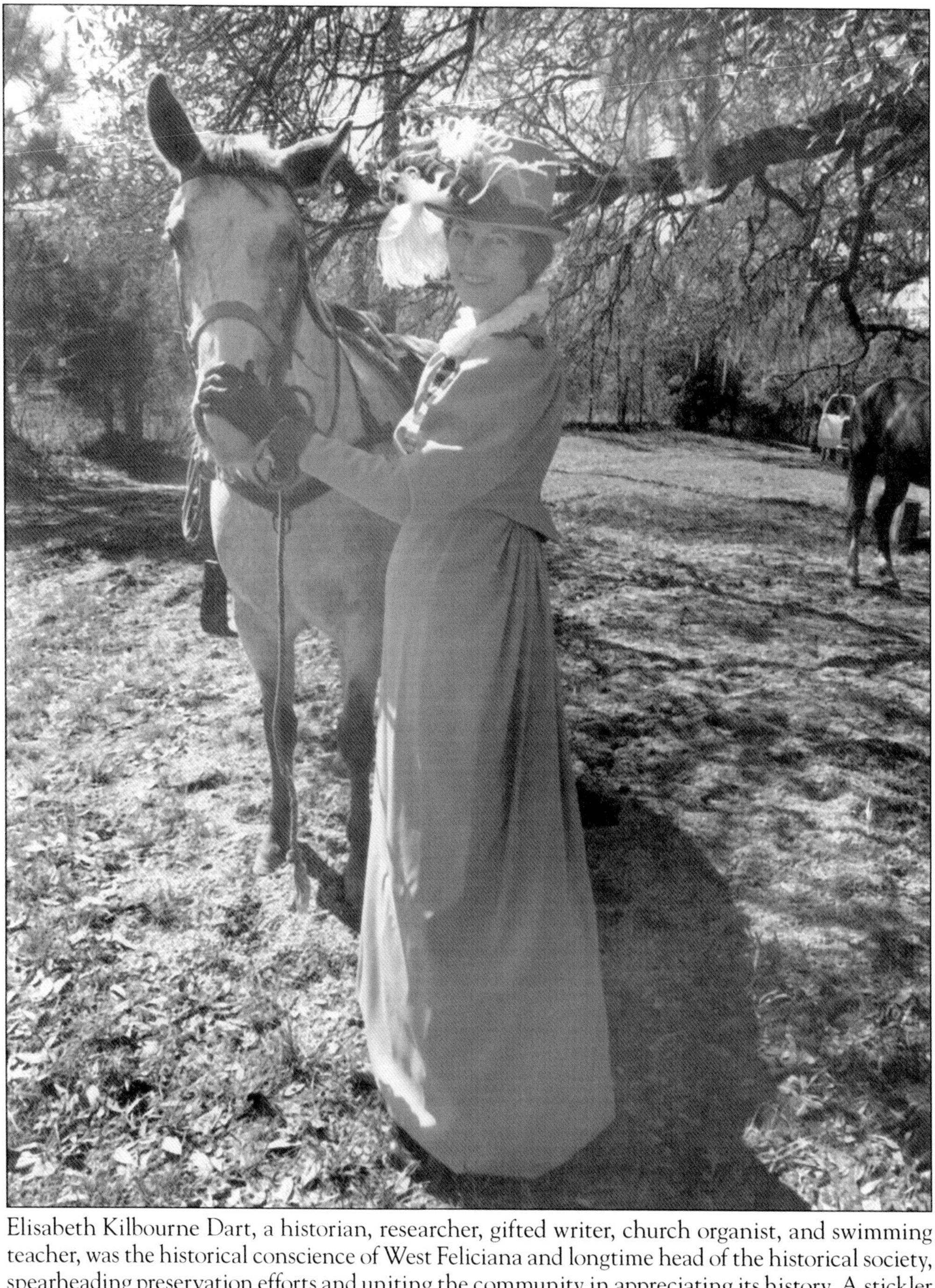

Elisabeth Kilbourne Dart, a historian, researcher, gifted writer, church organist, and swimming teacher, was the historical conscience of West Feliciana and longtime head of the historical society, spearheading preservation efforts and uniting the community in appreciating its history. A stickler for accuracy, she had an 1820s riding habit recreated in exact detail so she could ride her horse (sidesaddle, no less) at Audubon Pilgrimages. When the popular pilgrimage was started in 1972 at the suggestion of Lucille Leake, Dart was determined that the historical tours and activities would have as much to say to local residents as to visitors, fostering an increased awareness of local history and an awakened sense of place. (WFHS.)

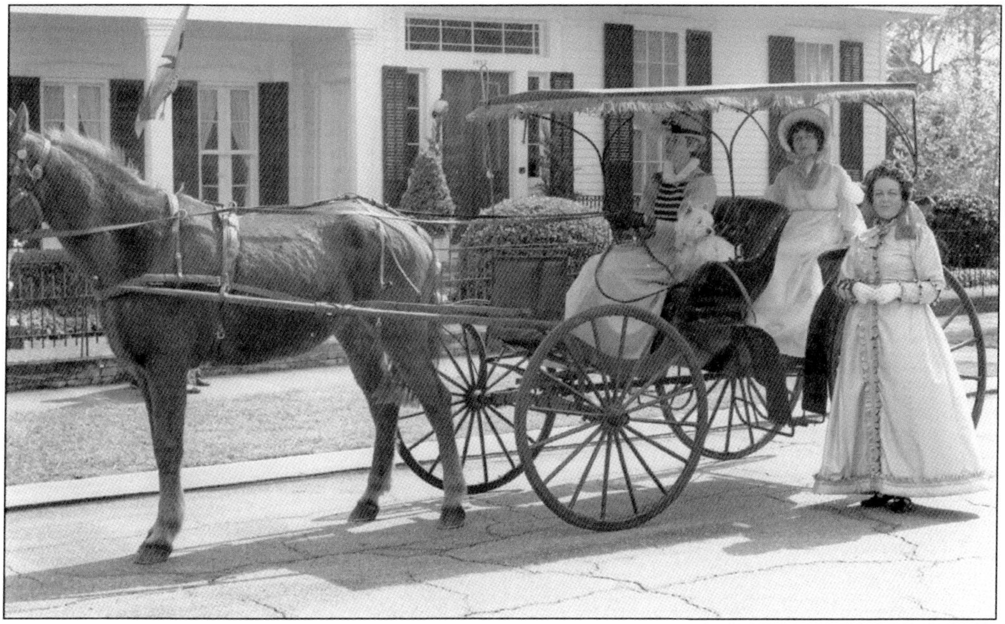

The Royal Street townhouse called Virginia was begun in 1817 as a one-room store. Its owner in 1859, attorney Lorenzo Brewer, was among the casualties when the steamboat *Princess* exploded on the way to the supreme court opening in New Orleans. Costumed Libby Dart, her faithful dog beside her, drives a one-horse surrey during the Audubon Pilgrimage. In the back seat is Ann Bennett. Vida Babers stands at right. (WFHS.)

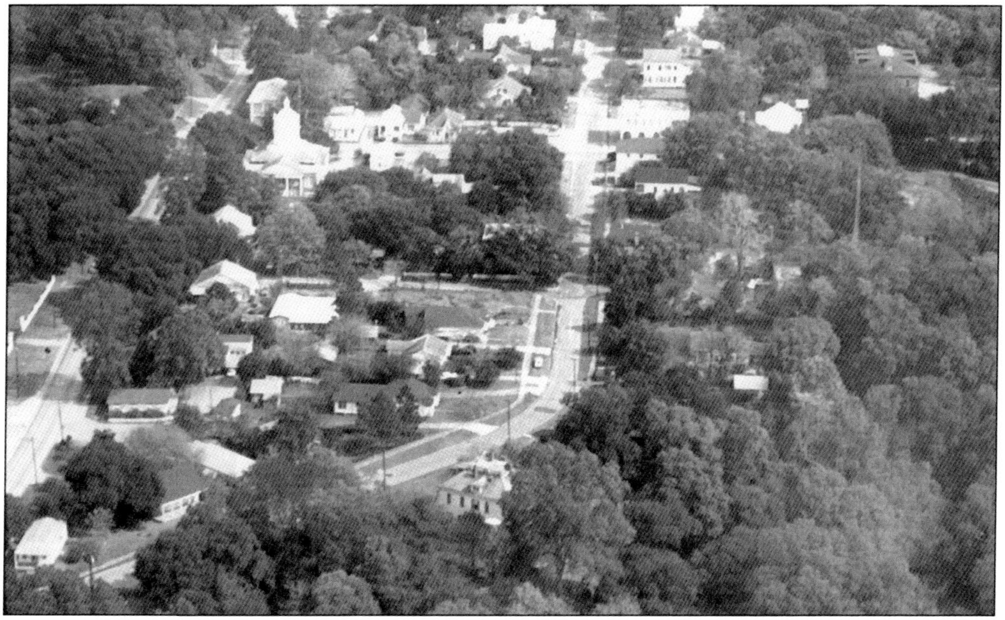

This aerial photograph shows why St. Francisville is called "the town two miles long and two yards wide." There are only two main streets, Ferdinand (left) and Royal (center), both named in tribute to the Spanish crown. The land falls off steeply behind the historic townhouses on Royal Street. For downtown activities and tours during the spring pilgrimages, the conveniently limited layout is ideal. (WFHS.)

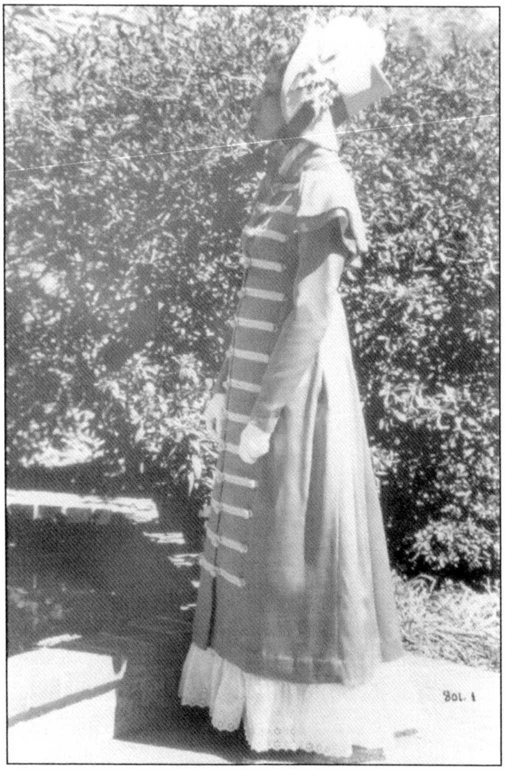

JoAnn Lawrason, a beloved art and history teacher, served as the first costume chairman for Audubon Pilgrimage. Commemorating John James Audubon's stay in 1821, the award-winning costumes authentically replicate the dress of that period, down to the last exquisite detail. Woe be unto the hostess who tried to get away with wearing comfortable tennis shoes instead of the appropriate flat slippers under the long skirts when Miss Lawrason was in charge. (WFHS.)

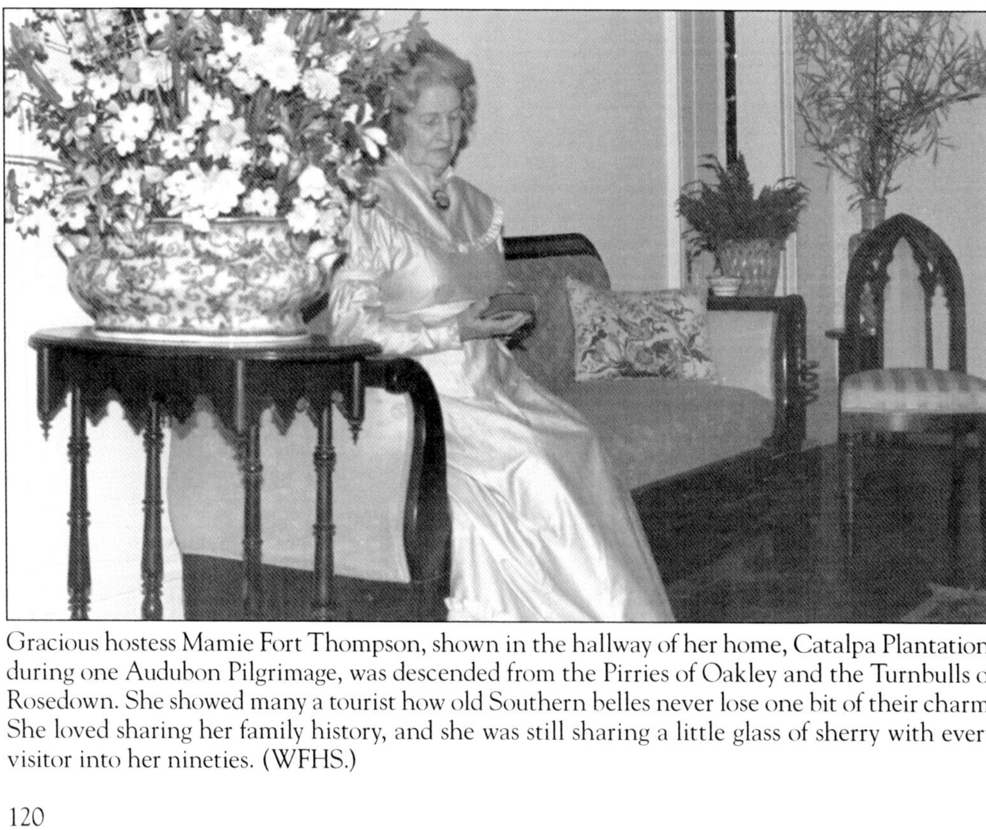

Gracious hostess Mamie Fort Thompson, shown in the hallway of her home, Catalpa Plantation, during one Audubon Pilgrimage, was descended from the Pirries of Oakley and the Turnbulls of Rosedown. She showed many a tourist how old Southern belles never lose one bit of their charm. She loved sharing her family history, and she was still sharing a little glass of sherry with every visitor into her nineties. (WFHS.)

Even the children get involved during the spring pilgrimage, and they have a good time doing it. Here, young Liza Leak (left), Sarah Smart (center), and Anne Cassity clamber in their costumes over the split-rail fencing at the Rural Homestead. There are in-town Maypole dances and playlets showing John James Audubon tutoring plantation children. (WFHS.)

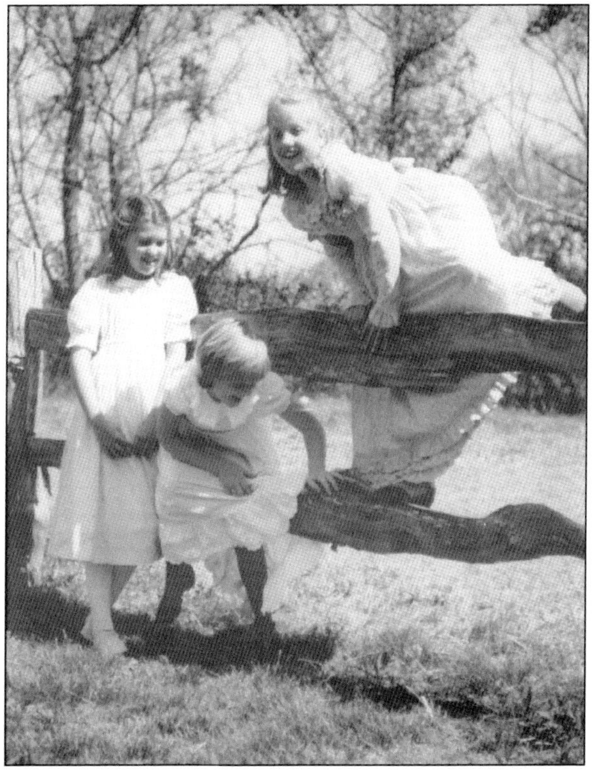

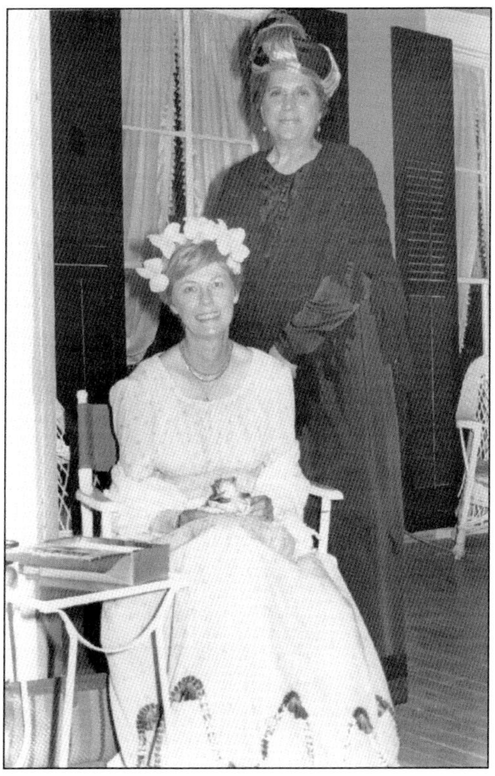

Evening dress of the 1820s, seen here on Libby Dart (left) and Dot Percy at Audubon Pilgrimage, was far more elaborate and daring than daytime costume. Necklines were lower and décolletage more daring, fabrics were fancier, and beading and other elaborate trim decorated the long gowns. Staid daytime bonnets gave way to silk turbans and elegant headdresses with ostrich feathers and fancy decoration. (WFHS.)

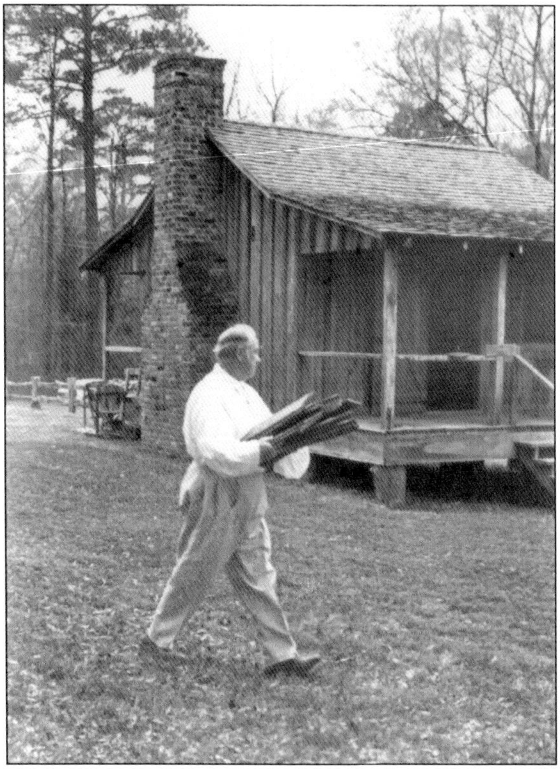

One of the most popular elements of the Audubon Pilgrimage is the Rural Homestead, begun in the early 1970s at the suggestion of Ed Daniel (pictured) to provide a balance to the presentation of plantation life. The homestead creates a rustic farm scene where the early skills of the pioneers can be demonstrated. Now the second, third, and fourth generations of Daniel's descendants continue his efforts. (WFHS.)

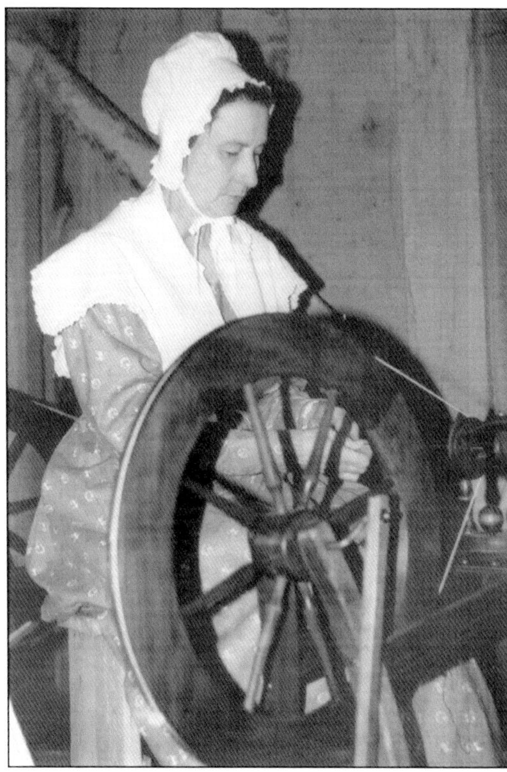

Evelyn Wilcox demonstrates the use of a spinning wheel to turn natural fibers into thread or yarn at the Rural Homestead during Audubon Pilgrimage. Other old-time skills on display include making cypress shingles, grinding cornmeal in a 19th-century gristmill for corn bread baked in a woodstove in the kitchen, plowing with a mule, horse-drawn wagon rides for children, livestock, and lively period music. The setting and demonstrations combine to produce a whole lot of fun. (WFHS.)

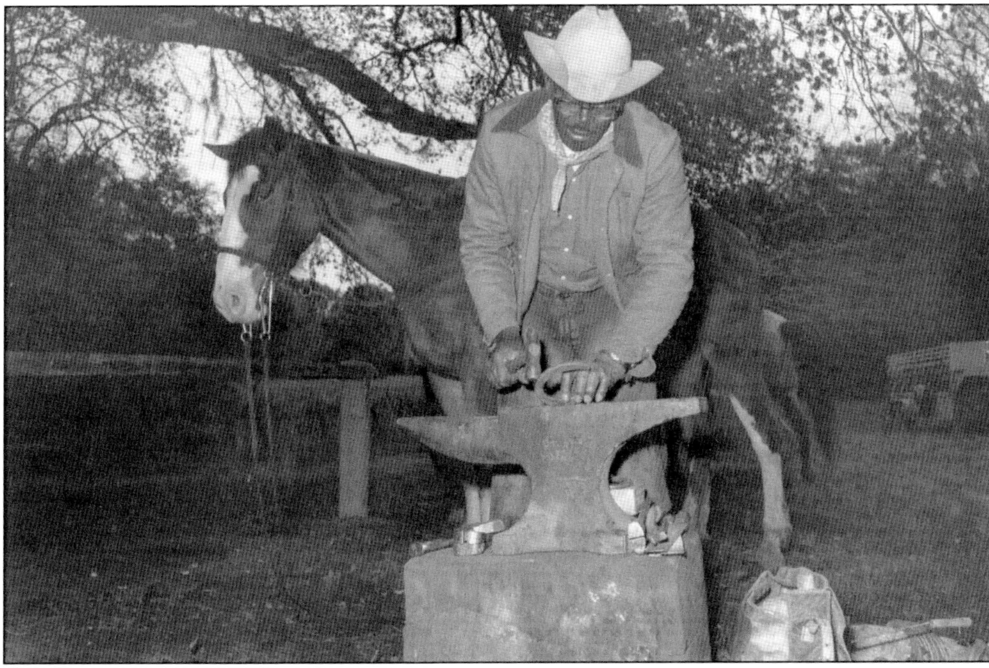

The Rural Homestead during Audubon Pilgrimage includes a blacksmith shop, where simple iron tools are forged. Here, Oliver "Preacher" McNabb beats a horseshoe on an old anvil in preparation for shoeing the horse behind him. In addition, there are demonstrations of other chores of daily life on early farmsteads. (WFHS.)

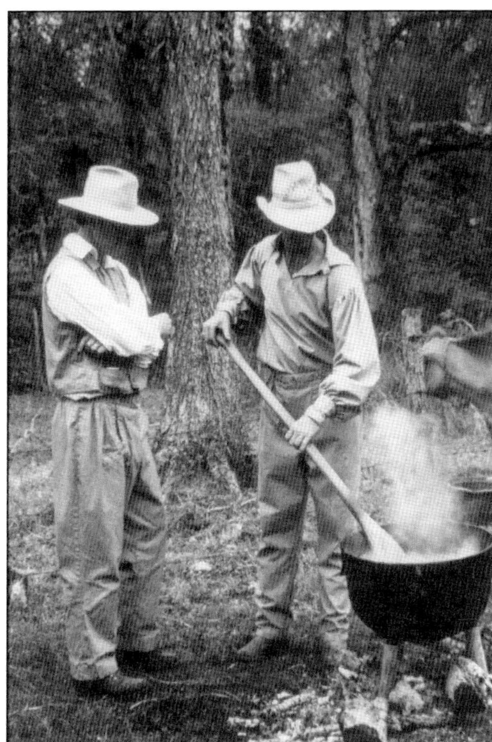

Baggy britches fastened by buttons and homespun open-collar shirts were worn by working men and boys on the rural farmsteads. The era is recreated here at Audubon Pilgrimage. Irv Daniel (left) and a friend stir cracklings boiling in an old iron pot over an open fire. Irv's father, Ed Daniel, was the inspiration for the Rural Homestead. (WFHS.)

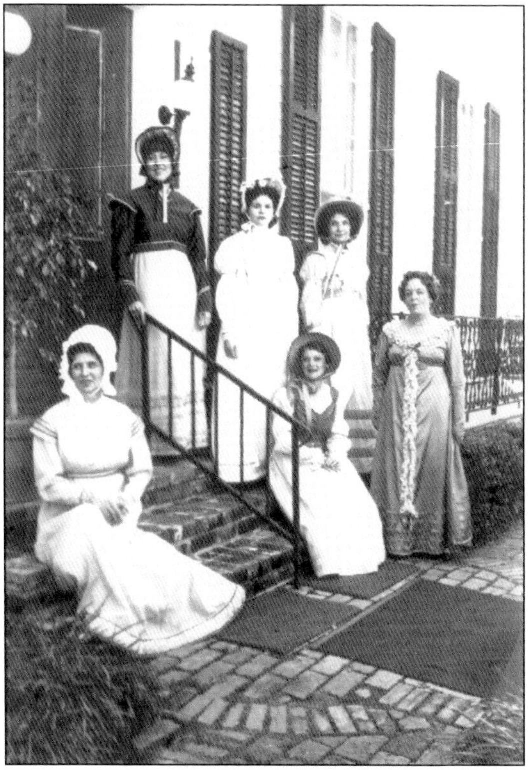

Attired in award-winning costumes replicating 1820s originals, Audubon Pilgrimage hostesses pose on the brick steps of a historic townhouse, Virginia, on Royal Street. These hostesses will conduct visitors on tours through the 1817 home. The women are, from left to right, (seated) Jerry Babers and Betty Sessions; (standing) Joan Cook, Arlene Hughes, Dot Temple, and Vida Babers. (WFHS.)

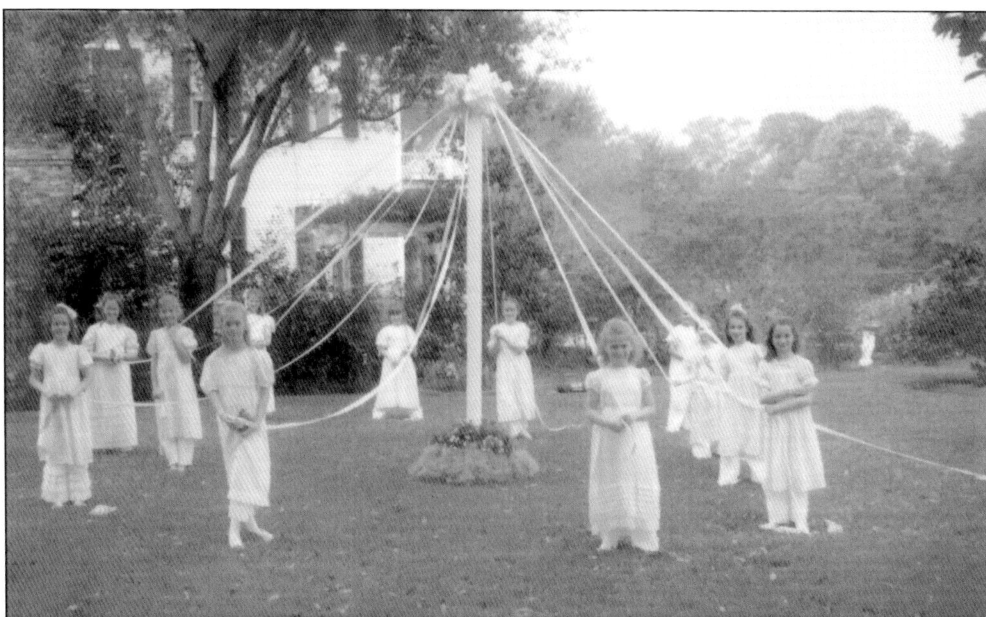

For nearly half a century, it has been a rite of passage for all the little girls of the area to participate in Audubon Pilgrimage activities. Arrayed in pantaloons and Empire-waisted long dresses, these lovely lasses dance the Maypole, weaving in and out with their streamers in an intricate dance celebrating the arrival of spring. (WFHS.)

Beautiful Temple Sinai, perched on a hill overlooking the river, was constructed in 1902 as a house of worship for the Jewish community of St. Francisville and Bayou Sara. In the 1920s, it served as a Presbyterian church. It has recently been restored by the Freyhan Foundation as a nondenominational community center, and it serves as a popular setting for plays and exhibits during the Audubon Pilgrimage each spring. (WFHS.)

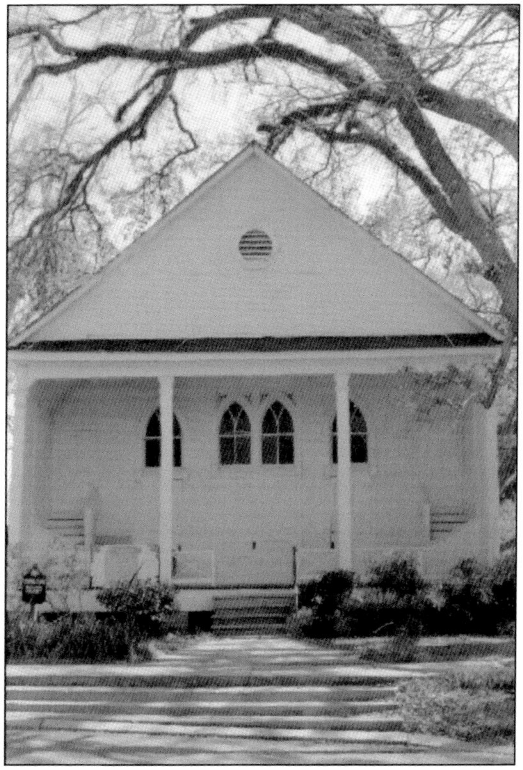

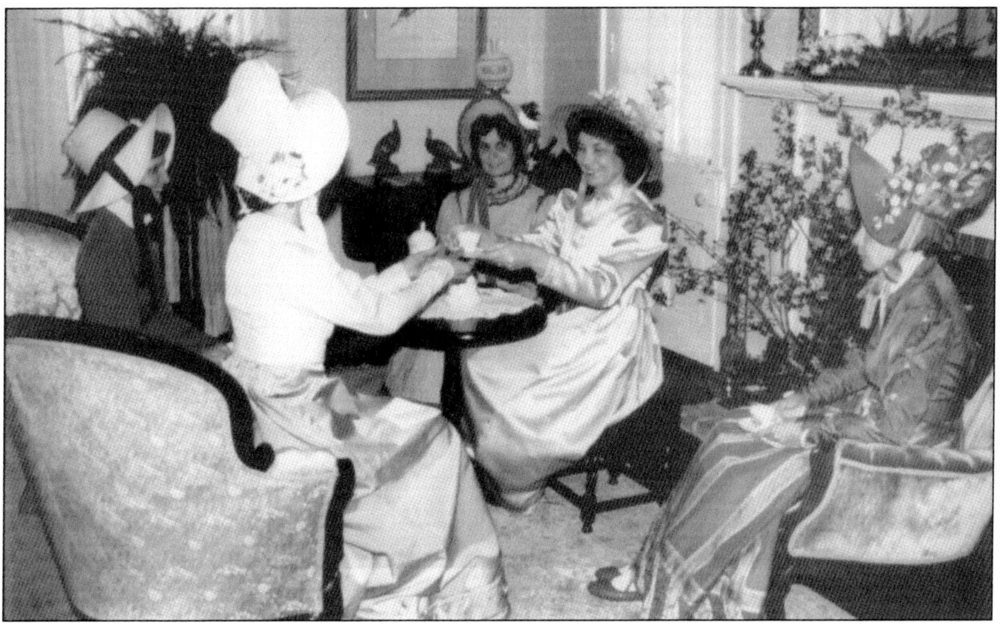

Elegant entertainments, with evening soirees and wine receptions, plus daytime teas (pictured), have marked the Audubon Pilgrimage schedules over the years. Here, JoAnn Lawrason (right), Dot Temple (second from right), and Shirley Reed (center) serve two other hostesses clad in the elaborate manner of the 1820s, when John James Audubon himself walked the thoroughfares of downtown St. Francisville. (WFHS.)

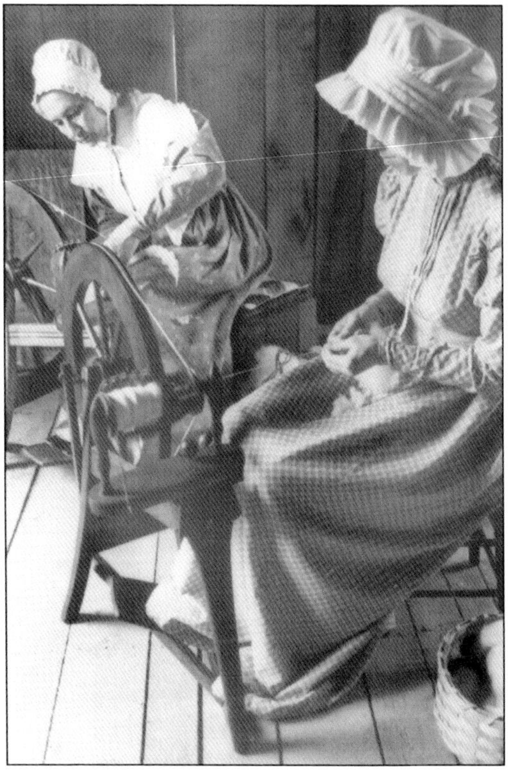

Cotton was the main 19th-century cash crop on the area's plantations and small farms. Cotton and wool, spun into thread or yarn with spinning wheels, were used by seamstresses or woven into fabric on looms in the days of self-sufficiency. In that era, fine needlework skills were highly valued, and nearly everything had to be made at home. Here, Evelyn Wilcox (left) demonstrates at the Rural Homestead. (WFHS.)

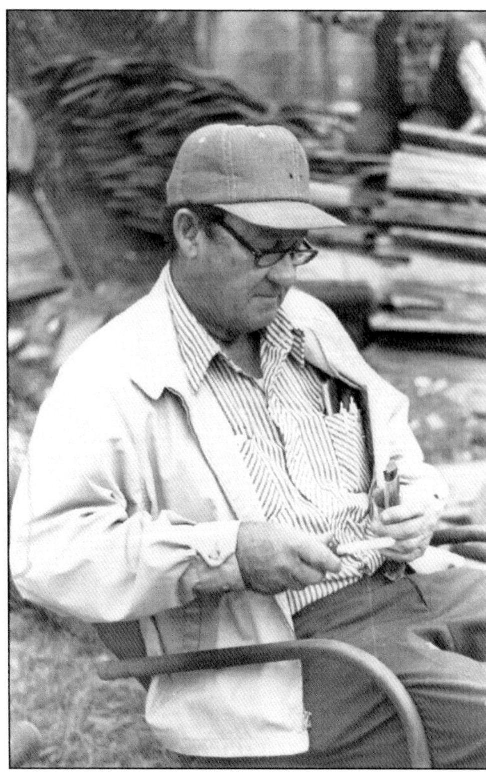

Carter Percy of Ellerslie Plantation whittles a whistle from a narrow chunk of wood at the Rural Homestead of the Audubon Pilgrimage. Such simple entertainments and pleasures as wooden whistles and peashooters kept boys amused in the days before televisions and electronic gadgetry. The homestead's working 19th-century copper whiskey still shows what kept the older menfolk entertained. (WFHS.)

Betty Sue Kendrick, later Mrs. Russell Daniel, is shown at right, cutting up with Madeline Lazarus in 1948. Kendrick was the longtime ticket chairperson for Audubon Pilgrimage, an annual event that involved the entire community in one way or another. Her mother was, for years, the director of the West Feliciana Historical Society museum, a job now held by her sister, Helen Williams. (Collection of Russell Daniel.)

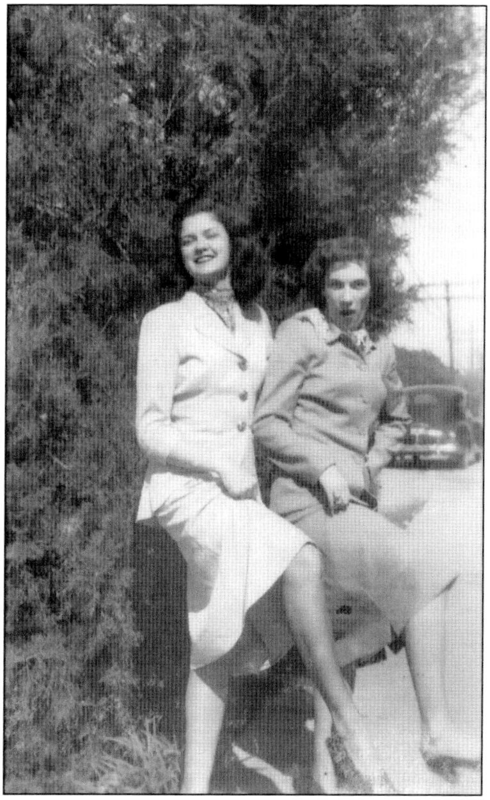

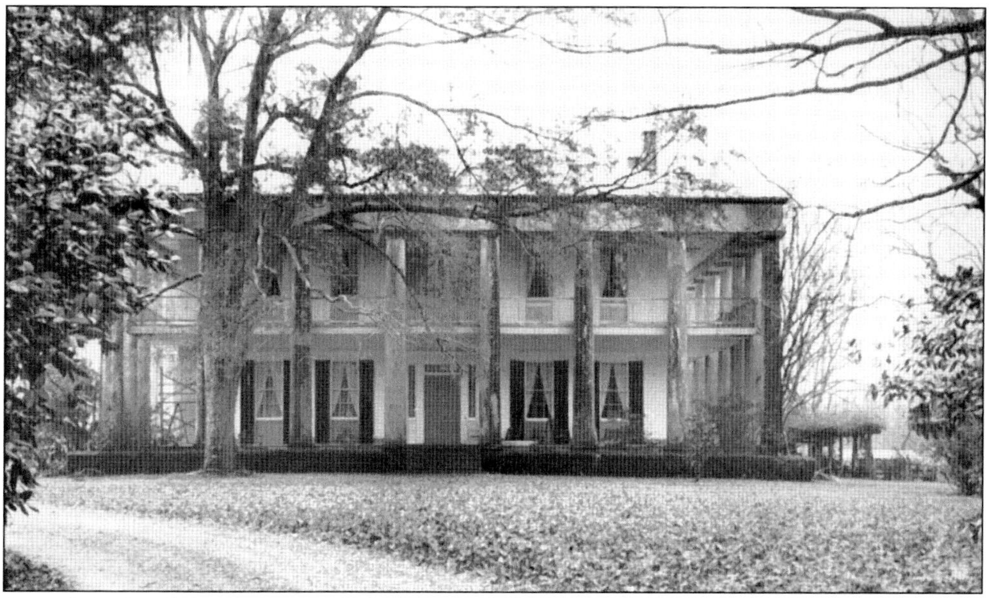

One of the South's most beautiful plantations, Ellerslie overlooks Little Bayou Sara from a high bluff. The Greek Revival structure was designed by noted architect James Hammon Coulter in the 1830s. Retaining a haunting beauty and character, it was long the home of the Ed Percy family, including remarkable Elena. Sporting a black eye patch, Elena reportedly drove a herd of cattle to Louisiana State University during the Depression to pay her tuition. (WFHS.)

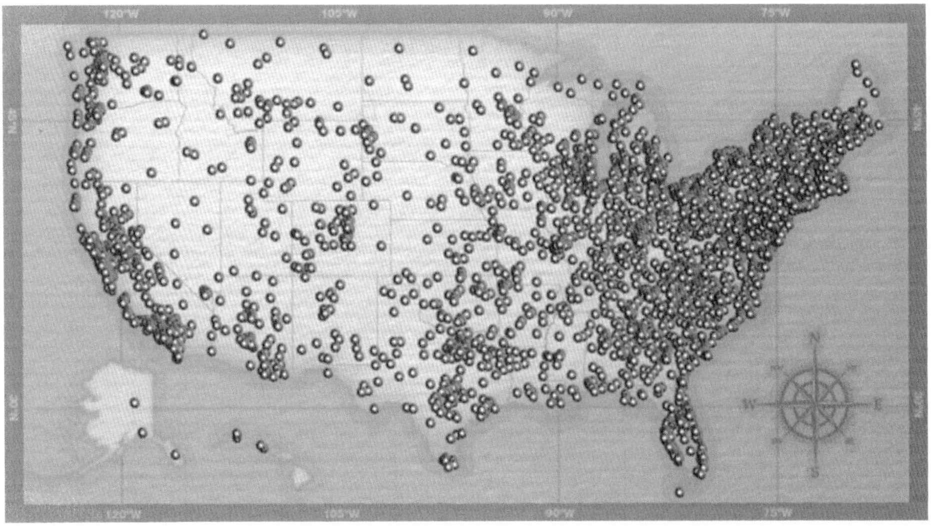

Consistent with our mission to preserve history on a local level, this book was printed in South Carolina on American-made paper and manufactured entirely in the United States. Products carrying the accredited Forest Stewardship Council (FSC) label are printed on 100 percent FSC-certified paper.

MADE IN THE USA